CHEROKEE DANCE

Ceremonial Dances & Dance Regalia

Written and Illustrated
by Donald Sizemore

Cherokee Publications, Cherokee, NC   28719
Copyrighted © 1999 by Donald Sizemore

First Edition
Printed in the United States of America

ISBN - 0-935741-21-6

Text & Illustrations by Donald Sizemore

First Printing - 1999 - 5,000

CONTENTS

PREFACE... 7

DEDICATION 8

ACKNOWLEDGMENTS.. 9

MUSICAL INSTRUMENTS USED IN DANCES DEDICATION 10
    Pottery Drums 10
    Water Drums 12
    Log War Drum 15
    The Tom-Tom Drum 18
    Drumsticks 22
    Tom-Tom Drum Beater 24
    Gourd Rattles 25
    Green Corn Dance Rattles 26
    Painted Gourd Rattles 28
    Medicine Rattle 29
    Wooden Rattle 31
    Rawhide Rattle 31
    Rawhide Gourd Shaped Rattle 33
    Turtle-Shell Hand Rattle 34
    Turtle-Shell Leg Rattles 36

DANCE STEPS 40
    Stomp Step 40
    Double Stomp 40
    Trot Step 40

FESTIVAL COSTUMES OF THE GREAT HIGH PRIEST OR UKU 41
    Coat Costume of the Great High Priest or Uku 45
    The Costume of the Great High Priest or Uku (worn with His Long Sleeved Shirt) 46
    How To Make the White Peace Time Chief's Hat 48

FESTIVAL COSTUME OF THE GREAT WAR CHIEF 54

COSTUME OF A PRIEST'S WIFE 55

WRAP-AROUND SKIRT AND JACKET 57
    Tassels for the Jacket 60

JACKET AND WRAP-AROUND SKIRT OUTFIT 62
    Jacket or Top 63
    Tassel for the Jacket 65
    Wrap-Around Skirt 66
    Making the Tie-Strings for Wrap-Around Skirt 67
    Decorations for the Skirt 68

OUTFIT FOR A VERY YOUNG MALE DANCER 69
    How To Make the Decorated Patchwork Strip 71

WOMEN GATHERING WOOD DANCE 74

THE FRIENDSHIP DANCE COSTUME 75
    How To Do the Friendship Dance 77

THE COMMON DANCE COSTUME 79
    How To Do the Common Dance 80

THE BURIAL DANCE 82

THE COAT DANCE 85

COSTUME OF THE ROUND DANCE 86
    How To Do the Round Dance 87

THE GREEN CORN DANCE COSTUME 88
    How To Do the Green Corn Dances 94

THE CORN DANCE COSTUME 97
    How To Do the Corn Dance 98

COSTUME FOR THE BEGINNING DANCE 101
    How To Do the Beginning Dance 102

THE EAGLE DANCE COSTUME 103
    Wands For the Eagle Dance 106
    How To Make Eagle Wings 108
    Feathers in the Hair as Part of the Eagle Dance Costume 113
        How To Make a Feather Ornament For a Man's Hair 114
    The Lead Eagle Dancer's Breechclout 116
    The Common Eagle Dancer's Breechclout 119
    An Eagle Dance Breechclout 124
    Bells Used in the Eagle Dance 127
        How To Make Garters With Bells 128
        Body Paint for the Eagle Dance 130
        Wooden Masks for the Eagle Dance 135
    How To Do the Eagle Dance 137

COSTUME FOR THE PEACE-PIPE DANCE 139
    The White Swansdown Head Ornament 140
    How To Make a White Swan Wing Fan 144
    How To Do the Peace-Pipe Dance 148

THE PIGEON DANCE COSTUME 153
    How To Do the Pigeon Dance 156

THE QUAIL DANCE COSTUME 157
    How To Do the Quail Dance 159

THE CHICKEN DANCE COSTUME 160
    How To Do the Chicken Dance 161

THE BOOGER DANCE COSTUME 162
    How To Do the Booger Dance 170

THE BEAR DANCE COSTUME 174
    How To Make a Bear Robe 178
    How To Do the Bear Dance 179

THE BUFFALO DANCE COSTUME 182
    How To Do the Buffalo Dance 186

THE HORSE DANCE COSTUME 188
    Painted Feather for Horse Dance Costume 193
    Horse-Tail Belt 194
    How To Do the Horse Dance 198

THE BEAVER DANCE COSTUME 200
    Robe for Beaver Dance 201
    Making an Imitation Beaver 203
    How To Do the Beaver Dance 206
    Beaver Dance Song 210

THE RACCOON DANCE COSTUME 211
    How To Do the Raccoon Dance 213

THE GROUNDHOG DANCE COSTUME 214
    How To Do the Groundhog Dance 216

THE ANT DANCE COSTUME 211
    How To Do the Ant Dance 219

THE WAR DANCE COSTUME 220
    How To Do the War Dance 223
    The Ordination Outfit of New Great War Chief 227
    Costume of the Great War Chief's Counselors 228
    Costume of a Warrior's Wife 229

THE SCALP DANCE COSTUME 231
    How To Make a Scalp Pole 236
    Costumes of the Four Scouts Attending Scalp Dance 241
        Costume of the Raven Scout 242
        Costume of the Owl Scout 243
        Costumes of the Wolf and Fox Scouts 244
    How To Do the Scalp Dance 245

THE SNAKE DANCE COSTUME 248
    How To Do the Snake Dance 250

THE BALL PLAYER'S COSTUME 254
    How To Make Dance Breechclouts 258
    How To Make a Metal Gorget 262
    Feather Ornaments Worn In the Hair 265
    How To Make The Ball Player's Feather Ornament 266
    How To Make a Ball Player's Hair Feather With Red Deer Hair String 269
    The Feathered Tails For Ball Players 271
    How To Make a Feathered Tail 274
    How To Make a Ball Player's Beaded Belt 278
    How To Make Deer-Tail Belt For Ball Player 280
    Ball Sticks For the Ball Dance 283
    How To Do the Ball Dance 287

THE UKAH DANCE COSTUME 290
    How To Do the Uku Dance 298

SUGGESTIONS FOR FURTHER STUDY 303

ABOUT THE AUTHOR 304

SOURCES 304

PREFACE

The thrill an audience experiences while watching any Native American dance is due in part to the beautiful regalia the dancers wear. What is worn by a dancer helps to relate the story behind the dance. The dance movements and sounds of the drum and rattle also help to relate the story.

At one time, the Cherokee dances were done in elaborate dress. After 1790 pressure from their white neighbors caused them to adopt the ways of the white man in order to survive as a people.

Tribal dances were still performed to some extent, but were now done in clothing adapted from the European explorers and settlers. Such a change took away the beauty of the dances and the unique look of the special regalia used for each.

The missionaries during those years taught that the dances and old ways of dress were pagan and wrong to do. Cherokee converts to Christianity were pressed to look down upon the old ways. In reality, the Euro-Americans condoned their own styles of dancing and dress, while on the other hand, condemned that of the Cherokee. However, the book brought by the missionaries as the authoritative guide for living, the Bible, says "Praise Him in the Dance".

The survival of Cherokee dances for future generations to appreciate and enjoy depends in part upon the revival of authentic and traditional Cherokee dance regalia. When I first watched the Eagle Dance and Green Corn Dance at the outdoor drama, "Unto These Hills", my interest in the Cherokee dances and colorful costumes soared. To my amazement, other Cherokee dances were not done in traditional dance costumes.

It was then I began to study the writings of the past about Cherokee dances and to dig for clues to what was worn by dancers of those glory years. Some descriptions of dance costumes were mentioned by those writers, but costumes for most of the dances were not mentioned at all. The vague information from the 18th and 19th centuries can help to reconstruct and conjecture a dance costume.

It is not my purpose to claim to know all about the old dance costumes or even the dances, but to write a book for people to refer to when needing an idea for a costume for a Cherokee dance. My other book, *Cherokee Clothing* will also be helpful in making costumes for dances.

Costumes in this book are versions, renditions and basic costumes of what may have been worn during a Cherokee dance. It is my hope that this book will inspire the interest of the Cherokee as well as other people to begin making and wearing dance costumes when these traditional dances are performed.

I hope this book will encourage you to dress appropriately for the dances in the Cherokee tradition.

This book is
Dedicated
to the
Loving Memory
of the
author's parents:

Camie
and
Nora
Sizemore

ACKNOWLEDGEMENTS

To show my appreciation of those who helped in various ways to present this book to you, they are listed as follows:

First, I wish to thank the Great Man Above, who has always been with me and blessed me with wisdom and knowledge in all my endeavors to share Cherokee culture.

May this book honor my late father, Camie Sizemore, through whom I received my Cherokee ancestry. Also, I wish to honor my late mother, Nora Baker Sizemore, who always encouraged me in whatever I set my mind to do.

I wish to thank my wife Mable who has been so helpful and understanding as I worked on this book. Her love I can never doubt. She and I were meant to be together.

Many thanks to Ed Sharpe and his great staff at Cherokee Publications who did such a great job on my earlier book, *Cherokee Clothing*. He and the staff are wonderful people to whom I owe a lot of gratitude.

Appreciation goes to Chief Oliver Collins and members of the Talligee Cherokee of West Portsmouth, Ohio for illustrating the *"Friendship Dance"* especially for me. Seeing dancers in tribal attire, doing Cherokee dances, is what this book is all about.

Ron Day of the Pineville Public Library has been very helpful with some of the research material for this book. He has been a real friend.

Thanks goes also to Kathy Ferris and Robert Messer for their help in taking some of the photos of the models at the danceground.

Many thanks go to the individuals who helped in modeling outfits and illustrating some of the dances for this book. They are: Sonny (Eagle Eye) Miller, Roger and Chastity Ramey, Carol Sizemore, Ellen Webb, Jimmey Gwinner, Everett and Pamela Johnson Sizemore, Lisa Howard, Carolynn Mills, Mable Sizemore, Terry Collins, Robert Sizemore, Fred Helton, Nora Sizemore, Myrtle Hausenflooke and the Mafnas family: Edward, Frankie, Elizabeth, Maggie, Toney, Caleb and Natasha.

Again, as in my first book, I wish to give a lot of credit to places in Cherokee, North Carolina, which have inspired me so very much in loving the old Cherokee culture: Oconaluftee Indian Village, Museum of the Cherokee Indian, Cherokee Cyclorama Wax Museum and the outdoor drama, "Unto These Hills".

Also, I wish to thank the Cherokee people for the culture they have handed down to other generations to share and to enjoy.

Donald Sizemore
Pineville, Kentucky

MUSICAL INSTRUMENTS USED IN DANCES

Music played a very important role in Cherokee life. From birth till death, days and nights were governed with dancing. Musical instruments are the life force behind the dances.

The drum, gourd rattle and tortoise shell leg rattles are the main items used during the dances. Before any dance costume described in this book can be put to use in a Cherokee dance, the instruments of music will have to be made. Let us now consider some of these instruments and how they were made:

POTTERY DRUMS:

carrying strap

pottery jar or bowl

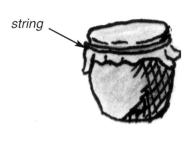

string

bells on string

The walls of the war drum can be stained or painted red with designs in black.

Everyone searches for an easy way to make drums for dances and ceremonies. This was true of the Cherokee.

Some of the Cherokee made their drums from pottery jars, as shown. A rawhide skin was stretched over the top and tied in place with a leather thong. Some of these drums had carrying straps fastened to handles on the pottery jar.

One such drum mentioned by John Howard Payne was made of a pottery jar, having a raccoon skin. It had a leather string with small bells around the rim of the drum. This was a kind of war drum, because it was used during the war dances.

Another stone or pottery drum was shaped like a turtle shell. Before Williamson's army invaded Cherokee towns in 1776, this drum hung in the council house in the village of Keowee. It was often loaned to other nearby towns to use in their ceremonies. This drum disappeared from history during the invasion.

The skin stretched over the drum may have been deerskin, since this was such a large drum. A leather string would have held the skin in place. The strap for hanging the drum would have been attached to the rim when not in use.

The pottery drum above is made of a large clay flower pot. The designs are painted on the sides. Deerskin covers the top of the drum. Leather or rawhide string is used to lace the skin to the drum. A strip of fur is glued around the rim of the drum. For those who do not make pottery, a clay pot such as the one above (from Mexico) is a good alternative.

WATER DRUMS

Hickory hoop

Hickory drum stick

15"

wooden plug

carved buffalo symbol

Water drum made of a nail keg. The groundhog skin for the head is held with a hoop made of hickory

The drum above is made of a portion of a buckeye log

A drum often used in Cherokee dance is called the water drum. Traditional Cherokee make the shell of the drum from a section of a buckeye tree. Less traditional people began using gunpowder and nail kegs as a substitute for the log drum.

To make a drum from a buckeye tree you will need to obtain a section of buckeye log no less than 8 $^1/_2$" in diameter and no less than 11 " long. The section of tree used for the drum, should allow the drum to be about 8 $^1/_2$" - 9" wide. The drum section is usually 11" - 13" long. The bark will have to be peeled away with a large knife. The sides of the drum should be smoothed either by sanding or scraping. Cherokee drums vary in size. Wooden drum logs should be allowed to season.

Next comes the more difficult stage of drum making. The log section will have to be hollowed out, leaving a 2" bottom on the inside. This process is accomplished using tools such as a gouge, wood chisel, crooked knife, mallet and, if needed, a drill. When the hollowing out of the drum shell begins, make sure the walls of the drum stay about $^1/_2$ - $^3/_4$" thick.

Most people use the gouge and mallet to hollow the section of log for the shell, but I have used a large drill bit to bore a series of holes into one end of it, as in the sketch below. Then a wood chisel and maul or mallet can be used to splinter away the wood until it is hollowed out. Choose your own method.

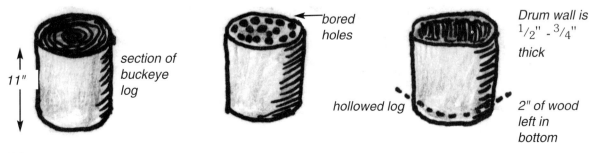

11"

section of buckeye log

bored holes

hollowed log

Drum wall is $^1/_2$" - $^3/_4$" thick

2" of wood left in bottom

Two -Inch Gouge

Wood Chisel

Mallet or Maul

Above are some of the tools used in hollowing out a drum shell.

The drum head is made of groundhog skin, but deerskin or other kinds of rawhide can be used. Deer hunters are good sources for rawhide. A leather craft store, such as Tandy Leather Craft is another good source for rawhide.

Once you have the rawhide ready, place the drum on the piece of dry rawhide, and mark around the drumshell onto the rawhide with a pencil . When drawing the circle on the rawhide make it about 2" larger in diameter than the shell. Use scissors to cut out the inscribed circle of rawhide for your drum head. Before placing the drumhead onto the top of the drum shell, soak the rawhide in water until it is soft. When ready to place on drum, remove the rawhide from the water, ringing out excess water.

To hold the rawhide in place on the top part of drum shell push a thin $1/8$ " thick wooden hickory hoop onto the drum. Let the drumhead dry in the sun or shade until it is stiff again. The hoop is $3/4$ " - 1" wide and round enough to go around the drum top with the rawhide underneath. The ends of the hoop when put together overlap about 6" - 7". See sketches below.

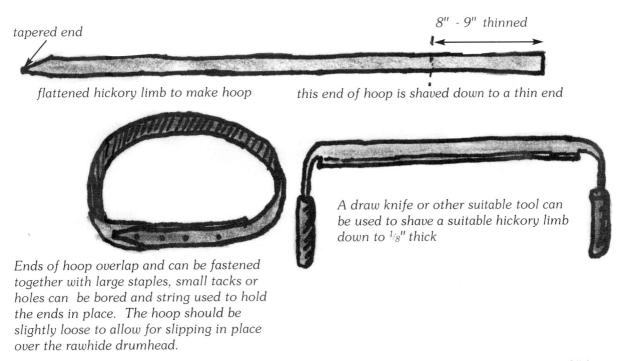

tapered end

8" - 9" thinned

flattened hickory limb to make hoop

this end of hoop is shaved down to a thin end

A draw knife or other suitable tool can be used to shave a suitable hickory limb down to $1/8$" thick

Ends of hoop overlap and can be fastened together with large staples, small tacks or holes can be bored and string used to hold the ends in place. The hoop should be slightly loose to allow for slipping in place over the rawhide drumhead.

Bore a hole into the side of the drum a few inches from the bottom. Use a 2" long wooden or cork plug to plug the hole. Using this hole, put water inside the drum. Varying the level of water changes the hollow sounds produced when the drum is beaten.

13

Around 1835, a man named J.P. Evans observed the Cherokee using a wooden nail or gun powder keg for a drum. It was covered on top with a piece of rawhide. This incident shows a drift away from the traditional way of making a drum from buckeye wood.

In the 1930's, people in the Big Cove town of the Eastern Cherokee were observed by Speck and Broom using a water drum with two buffalo carved on the side. This was an example of how some of the Cherokee people still practiced the old arts.

Wooden Wine
Cooler Bucket

To make a water drum that resembled the nail keg style drum, I used a reproduction of a wooden wine cooler or ice bucket. It looked like an old time wooden water bucket except for the plastic liner on the inside. This bucket was 7 inches high, $8^1/_2$ inches across the bottom, and $7^1/_2$ inches across the top.

I removed the handle, the red plastic liner, the wood lid and top hoop. Staples held the hoops and other parts in place. I then removed the staples from the unneeded parts. Once the wooden bucket was made to look like a nail keg, I bored a hole a few inches from the bottom for the wooden plug. Some people prefer to remove the top of the drum to add the water to the desired level.

For the head of the drum I used untanned deerskin (see sketch below). After the drum head had been softened with water, I used one of the removed wooden hoops to hold the drum head in place. Then the drumhead was allowed to dry on the drum until it was ready.

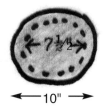

← 10" →

Cut the drumhead
bigger than the top
of the drum.

The walls of the drumshell can be stained with red clay, sumac, or pokeberry dye. A commercial stain or paint can be substituted.

When engraving the drum walls, it's helpful to mark the design in pencil and then use a wood carving knife.

LOG WAR DRUM

The drum shown above is made from a hollow poplar log. A bow saw was used to cut off a section of the log 8" high and 13" across. In making this drum, a wood chisel and hammer were used for finishing the inside. The walls of the drum are $^1/_2$" - $^3/_4$" thick. Deerskin in the form of rawhide covers the top and bottom and it is laced with rawhide string. Brass tacks decorate the rims. The designs were outlined onto the drum with pencil, and enamel paint used in coloring the designs.

The drum above was made by the author. The sketch can be referred to when making this drum. The same designs may be used or those of your own choice.

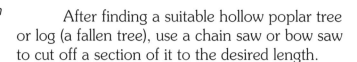
hollow all the way through

$\frac{1}{2}$" thick

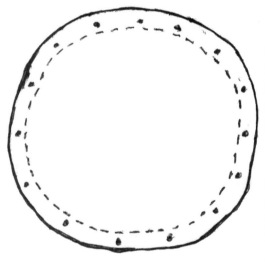

poplar drum shell

After finding a suitable hollow poplar tree or log (a fallen tree), use a chain saw or bow saw to cut off a section of it to the desired length.

Use a wood chisel and mallet to remove the unwanted wood on the inside. Refer to the methods used in making the shell for the water drum on a previous page. The wall of the drum should be $\frac{1}{2}$" thick.

After the drum shell has been made and sanded, paint the outside of the shell with red paint, then draw on the designs and paint them. Refer to the sketch on previous page.

deerskin rawhide

center drumheads as shown

Place the drum shell on top of the dried deerskin rawhide. Mark around the drum shell with a pencil. Once this disk has been marked on the rawhide, add an extra inch or more to the size of it, as in sketch at left. Make a rawhide disk for the top and bottom of the drum shell.

Use a nail or punch to make holes 4" apart and $\frac{1}{2}$" back from the edge of the rawhide disks, also shown in the sketch at left. These holes are for the lacing process. Next cut a rawhide string $\frac{1}{4}$" wide and long enough to lace the drum heads to the drum shell.

Soak the two rawhide disks and string in water until soft. Center the drum shell on disks and lace the rawhide disks on as in sketch. You may have to use a large needle on the lacing string. Rawhide shrinks quickly, so work fast.

Brass upholstery tacks are used for decoration. A few of these tacks can help in lacing the drumheads if put in place in advance of lacing.

TOP DESIGN ON DRUM

The Spotted Eagle design shown in the illustration to the left was used throughout the Southeast, as seen in museum collections. The eagle was a fierce bird of prey. It's claws were sharp for grasping its victim. The eyes of the eagle were very keen in spotting it's prey. An attack from an eagle was quick and accurate. It is no wonder the eagle was so honored among the Cherokee.

To put the above design on top of the drum, first sketch it in pencil on the assembled drum. Use enamel paints to color in the parts. A few hours later, when the design has dried, give the whole top of the drumhead a thorough coat of clear varnish. The varnish keeps the rawhide from becoming soft again, due to moisture.

Circle combinations stand for completeness, wholeness, the world, cosmos and the spirit. The island earth is represented in the center design.

BOTTOM DESIGN ON DRUM

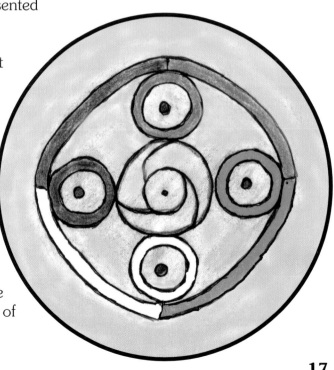

The blue north circle, the red east circle, the white south circle and the black west circle are for the four directions in which mankind exists. Life is a circle: birth, puberty, adulthood, and old age or death. The four colors of the outer ring are the paths we take in life. When a person completes his circle or cycle in this life, he then treads upon the path of the eternal.

These designs are painted on the bottom of the drum as described for top of drum above.

THE TOM-TOM DRUM

The drum shown above is the tom-tom type. It is sketched from a photograph, by the author, of a drum seen in the Edds Indian museum in 1979. Mr. Edds told the author he had purchased the drum from a Cherokee man about 10 years prior. He said it was over a hundred years old. Mr. Edds lived near Rose Hill, Virginia and is now deceased.

A drum of this type may have been borrowed or adopted from other tribes by the Cherokee. The drums on previous pages are the more typical types of drums used by the Cherokee.

This particular drum has a rawhide head on each side and is sown together at the center of the drum shell. The inside is made of a $3^{1}/_{2}$" - 4" wide wooden hoop. The drum is 14" - 16" across. 3 or 4 turkey feathers are attached to a leather string on each side of the drum, as shown above. The other side of the drum has a red dot in the center and a blue circle around the inside edge instead of a red circle.

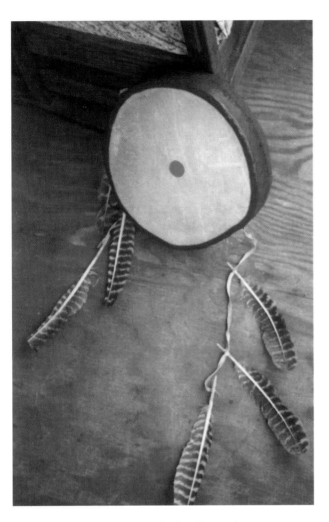

The photograph at left shows a replica of the tom-tom drum of Mr. Edds, which is mentioned on the preceding page.

When making this drum, a wooden hoop is needed. A hoop can be made from a sawed off section of an old wooden cheese box. Another way to make the hoop is to cut off a section of a hollow poplar log, $3 \frac{1}{2}$" - 4" by 14" - 16". Refer to the photo and sketches. The hoop will have to be chiseled out as mentioned with the other drum types. The wall of the hoop is about $\frac{1}{2}$" thick.

Rawhide is needed to make the top and bottom head of the drum. I used deerskin.

A tom-tom made by the author

Shell cut from a cheese box

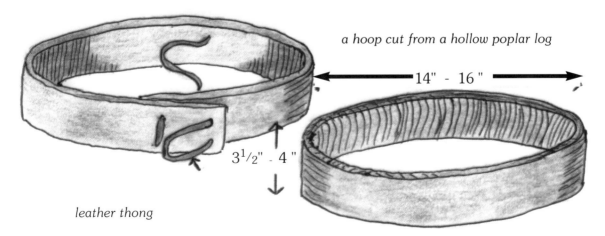

a hoop cut from a hollow poplar log

14" - 16"

$3\frac{1}{2}$" - 4"

leather thong

When the drumshell is ready, lay it on top on a large piece of dried rawhide, as shown in the sketch below.

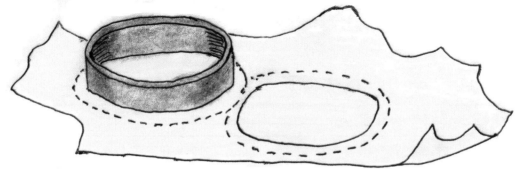

Mark around the hoop in pencil, then allow extra space so the rawhide disk will come up halfway on the side of the hoop when the two disks are stitched together. Mark out the second disk the same way. Allow the two marked out disks to touch, as in sketch above.

Next, use scissors to cut the disks out, except for the portion where the disks touch. Soak the disks in water until soft. Then place the wooden hoop or drumshell in position on the wet rawhide disk, similar to above. Flap the other disk over the top of hoop and quickly begin stitching where the two disks circles meet, using strong twine or sinew. It may help if small needle holes are punched in a series around the edge of the disks. Use a large sewing needle for the twine. Use the overcast or whip-stitch method.

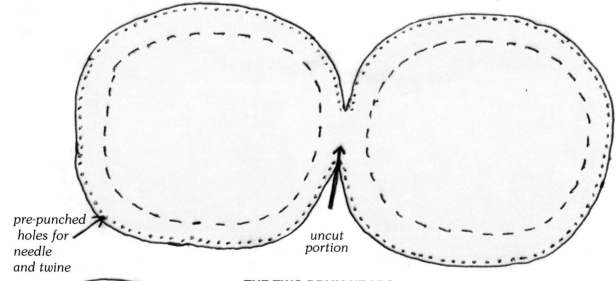

pre-punched holes for needle and twine

uncut portion

THE TWO DRUM HEADS

You may wish to do as much stitching as you can, then slip the hoop inside. When making this drum, I had to work fast because the rawhide started shrinking. I had to resoak the drum in progress several times to continue the stitching.

stitch middle of rawhide

20

When the rawhide disks have been stitched in place, allow the drum to completely dry. Next use blue and red enamel to paint the drum as shown on the preceding pages. Let the paint dry and then give the whole drum a coat of clear varnish. When the varnish has dried, you are ready to make the feather attachments as described below.

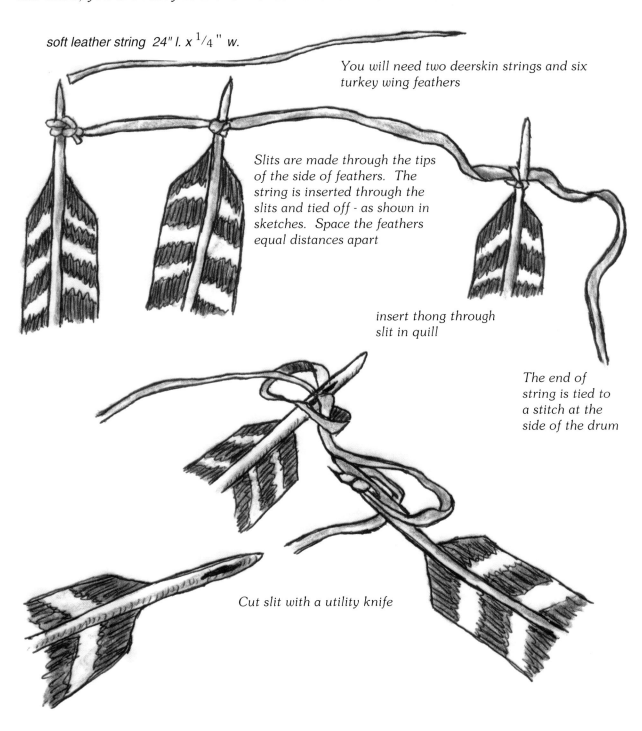

soft leather string 24" l. x $^{1}/_{4}$" w.

You will need two deerskin strings and six turkey wing feathers

Slits are made through the tips of the side of feathers. The string is inserted through the slits and tied off - as shown in sketches. Space the feathers equal distances apart

insert thong through slit in quill

The end of string is tied to a stitch at the side of the drum

Cut slit with a utility knife

The drum should now be ready to use. This drum may be used for Cherokee dances when other drums are difficult to obtain.

DRUMSTICKS

The Cherokee and other Native American tribes of the southeast used the drumstick to beat out rhythms on their drums. Beating a drum with the palm of the hand as often seen on television was not a practice in Cherokee culture.

The Cherokee usually make drumsticks of hickory or walnut. If these traditional woods are not available, then use the type of wood most available. Long drumsticks were 11" - 15" long, and the shorter styles were 7" - 10".

To make one of these drumsticks, select a suitable tree limb and cut off a section with a handsaw. A pocket knife is used to strip it of bark. You may wish to let it season out. Otherwise begin whittling the drumstick to it's proper form.

A common drumstick to use, when beating one of the water drums on preceding pages, is shown in the sketch below.

$1/2$" - $5/8$"

knob

1"

red painted stripes

The drumstick shown below is one made by the author for the Log War Drum on a prior page in this book. The black and red stripes are symbols of war.

To make the above war drumstick, whittle a tree limb or stick to the above shape. The bark must be removed. It is $1/2$" thick and 17" long. One end is made larger.

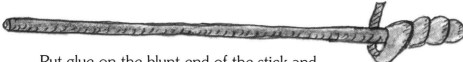

Put glue on the blunt end of the stick and wrap it with thick cloth, soft leather or wet rawhide.

When the wrapping is finished it should look like the sketch above.

Cut two pieces of soft leather as shown in sketch at right. Sew the two pieces together leaving an opening for the stick and wrapping. Put a little glue on the wrapping, then put the blunt end of drumstick into the two pieces of leather.

Finish stitching the cover over the padded end of drumstick.

The handle should be painted as shown above. All other parts are also painted, similar to the sketches on the preceding page. A piece of red cloth is sewed to the hand-hold on the drum stick. Use a little glue to hold red cloth in place.

Soft leather strings are tied on the handle for decoration. The drumstick should now be finished and ready to use.

TOM-TOM DRUM BEATER

The drum beater shown below is similar to one which was in Mr. Edds collection, near Rose Hill, Virginia. He had obtained it from an old Cherokee man, several years before 1979. It goes with the Tom-Tom Drum on a prior page.

To make the drumstick, I selected a hickory limb $\frac{1}{2}$" wide and 20 $\frac{1}{2}$" long. The bark was removed and the end of it, for a space of 8" - 9", was flattened and tapered as shown in the sketch below. Use a pocket knife to taper the end.

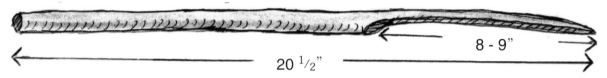

Bend the tapered end to form a loop. Use a piece of wire to twist around the splice and hold the loop in place, as seen in the sketch below.

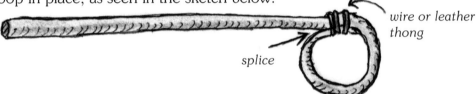

Next, use a pocket knife to whittle the handhold, as shown in the sketch below. The handhold is wrapped with a dark brown leather string. Use a little glue under the string

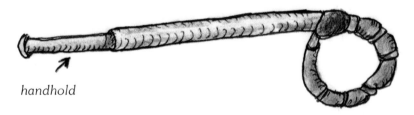

Wrap cloth around the loop to serve as padding. Twine is then spiraled around the padding to hold it in place.

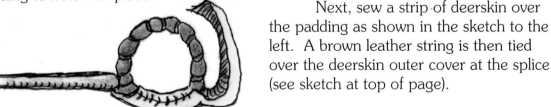

Next, sew a strip of deerskin over the padding as shown in the sketch to the left. A brown leather string is then tied over the deerskin outer cover at the splice (see sketch at top of page).

This type of drum beater may have been adopted from other tribes.

24

GOURD RATTLES

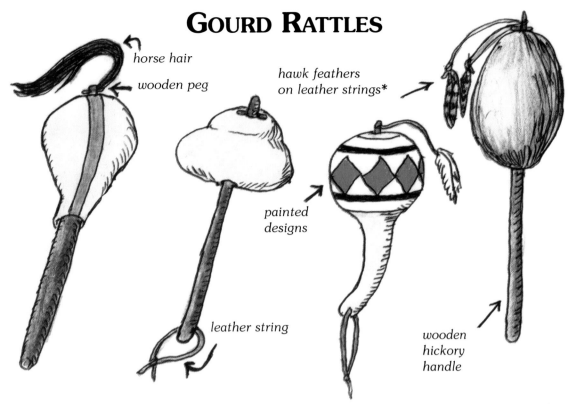

horse hair

wooden peg

hawk feathers
on leather strings*

painted
designs

leather string

wooden
hickory
handle

The hand rattle was found in several forms among the Cherokee. Above is shown various types of gourd rattles used as musical instruments during dances. They used other rattles such as the wooden rattle, rawhide rattle, terrapin-shell rattle and in recent years, the tin can rattle. Let's first discuss the gourd rattle and how it is made.

The gourd vine has been grown among the Cherokee for generations. Each vine usually produces several gourds, which can be harvested in the late fall.

The gourd should be dried until it becomes very hard. The handle is removed or a hole cut at the top of the gourd. Hot water can be used on the inside of the gourd to remove the pulp and seeds. The handle can be cut off or a hole made with a saw or knife. In the past, I have used a spoon or narrow knife to scrape the inside.

The gourd had many uses in addition to rattles. It was used for bowls, various food containers, water bottles, dippers, and storage vessels to hold thistle down for darts. For dance, the gourd was used as a rattle to make music.

For dance music, the leader usually held the rattle high above his head, shaking it quickly as it was lowered toward the ground. This rapid motion of the rattle signaled the beginning and ending of a dance. It was also shaken rapidly when a verse changed in a song, or to signal a dancer to reverse direction.

*NOTE: Hawk feathers as well as many other bird feathers are from protected species and it is illegal to own and/or use them. Be sure to check the laws of your state. Use substitute feathers where appropriate.

GREEN CORN DANCE GOURD RATTLES

The two gourd rattles shown in the photograph above are replicas patterned after a pair used in the Green Corn Dance in Cherokee, North Carolina.

To make these rattles, first select hickory limbs or other suitable wood for the handles of the gourds.

Cut and clean the gourd as mentioned on previous page. A hole must be cut out at the top of the gourd.

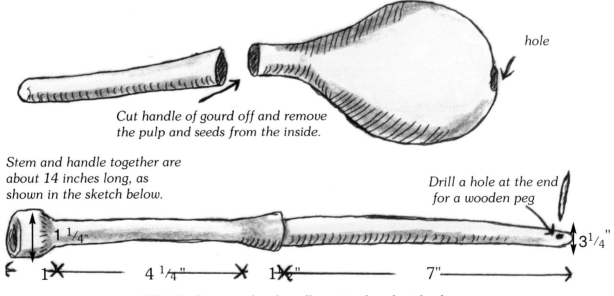

hole

Cut handle of gourd off and remove the pulp and seeds from the inside.

Stem and handle together are about 14 inches long, as shown in the sketch below.

Drill a hole at the end for a wooden peg

$1\frac{1}{4}$"

$3\frac{1}{4}$"

1" $4\frac{1}{4}$" $1\frac{1}{2}$"   7"

Whittle the wooden handle as in the sketch above.

Next put a few bean-size pebbles inside the gourd part. Also, a little glue should be put inside the rim of the neck opening of the gourd. Push the portion of the handle with the drilled hole in it through the gourd part. When the gourd part is on the wooden handle, put a $1\frac{1}{4}$" wooden peg through the hole. Put a little glue around the protruding handle at the top of the gourd.

You are now ready to paint the designs on the gourd using green and brown enamel paint. It is helpful to sand off the gourd or scrape it clean on the outside with a knife before starting to paint.

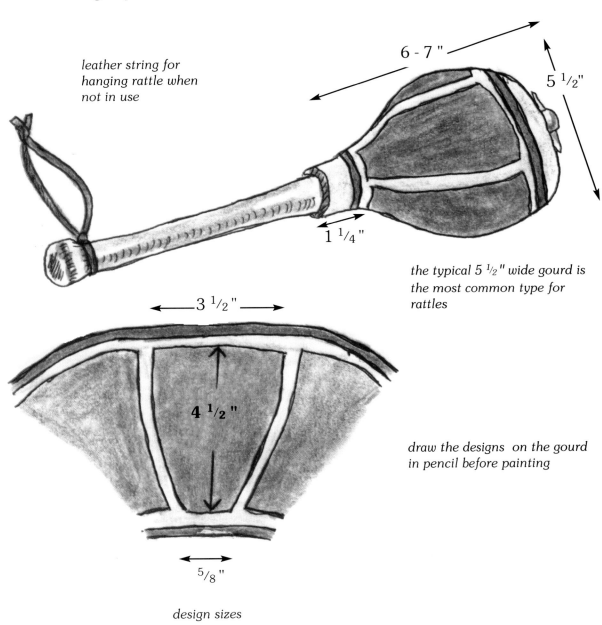

leather string for hanging rattle when not in use

6 - 7 "

5 $\frac{1}{2}$"

1 $\frac{1}{4}$ "

the typical 5 $\frac{1}{2}$" wide gourd is the most common type for rattles

3 $\frac{1}{2}$ "

4 $\frac{1}{2}$ "

5/8 "

draw the designs on the gourd in pencil before painting

design sizes

PAINTED GOURD RATTLE

The rattle below is similar to one seen at the Oconaluftee Indian Village in Cherokee, North Carolina.

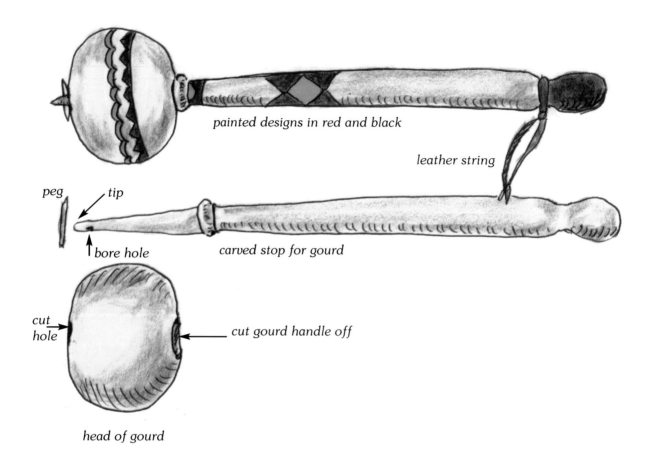

painted designs in red and black

leather string

peg   tip

bore hole   carved stop for gourd

cut hole   cut gourd handle off

head of gourd

To make the rattle pictured above, carve the wooden handle of hickory or some other type wood, using the sketch as a guide. Use a drill to bore a small hole near the tip of the handle and make a wooden peg to insert through the hole. Notice in the sketch above, there is a carved wooden stop for the gourd to rest against. The entire handle is about 15" long.

Next cut a small gourd to the shape above by sawing off the handle of the gourd. Put small pebbles the size of bean seeds inside the gourd part. Then insert the stem of the handle through gourd. Lock in place using the wooden peg through the hole, as shown above.

28

MEDICINE RATTLE

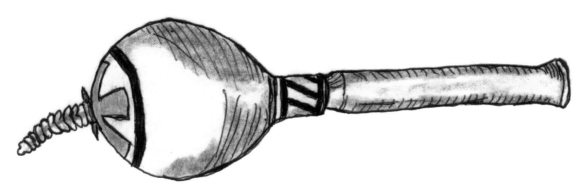

The sketch above depicts a type of rattle used by Medicine Men. It is based on an example in the book, *Cherokee Dance and Drama*, by Speck and Broom. To make the above rattle requires a rattlesnake rattle, a gourd, and a carved handle from a hickory or sourwood limb. Blue and black enamel paint is used to make the designs. A wooden peg holds the gourd onto the handle. To me, this a a very sacred gourd rattle.

The handle of the gourd should be cut off, as shown in the sketch to the left. A hole is cut at the top. Use hot water inside the gourd to soften the pulp and seeds, then use a knife to scrape out the inside of the gourd. The outside should be sanded or scraped.

Select a nice hickory or sourwood limb for the handle. Remove the bark and cut it to the dimensions shown below.

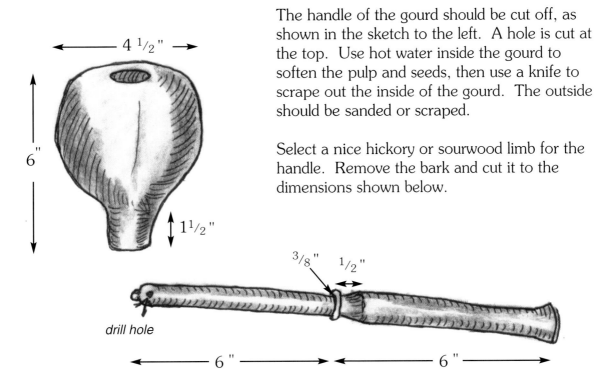

Use a small drill bit to bore a hole at the top portion of the handle for the wooden peg.

Put a few small bean size pebbles inside the gourd. Then slip the gourd in place on the upper portion of the handle. Put a little glue in the hole as shown. Push the wooden peg in place.

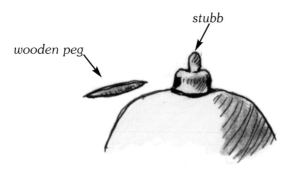

wooden peg

stubb

Next, put glue on the stub and place the rattler from the rattlesnake in place. You may also tie it on with thread to make it more secure.

Draw the designs with a pencil on the gourd and paint them blue and black, as shown in the sketch below. You may wish to give the head of the rattle a coat of clear varnish. This will protect the designs.

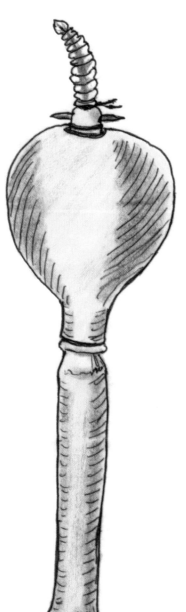

circle of life

The four seasons and four directions design

WOODEN RATTLE

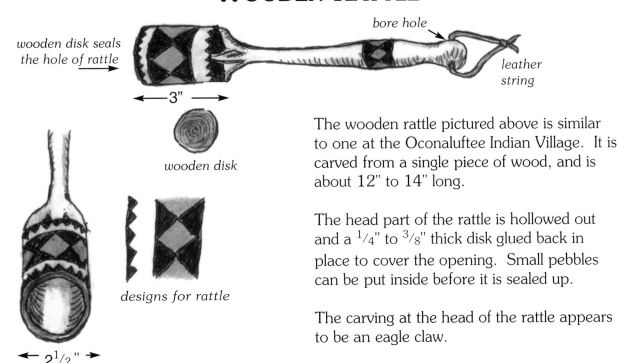

wooden disk seals the hole of rattle

bore hole

leather string

← 3" →

wooden disk

designs for rattle

← 2½" →

The wooden rattle pictured above is similar to one at the Oconaluftee Indian Village. It is carved from a single piece of wood, and is about 12" to 14" long.

The head part of the rattle is hollowed out and a $^{1}/_{4}$" to $^{3}/_{8}$" thick disk glued back in place to cover the opening. Small pebbles can be put inside before it is sealed up.

The carving at the head of the rattle appears to be an eagle claw.

The designs may be painted in black and red using flat or enamel paint.

RAWHIDE RATTLE

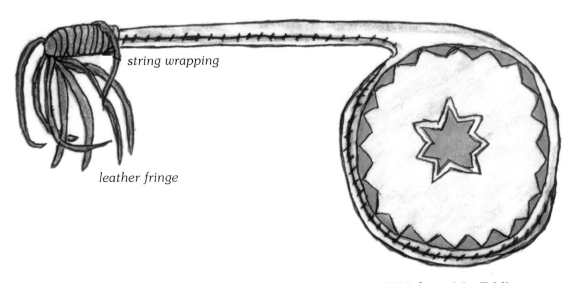

string wrapping

leather fringe

The rawhide rattle in this sketch is like one I photographed in 1979 from Mr. Edd's collection near Rose Hill, Virginia. It had belonged to a very old Cherokee man. Inside, the rattle is made of a hickory hoop and has small pebbles. The outside is of rawhide and has the painted seven pointed star design.

To make the rawhide rattle on the preceding page, use a hickory limb about $^3/_4$ " wide and 29" long.

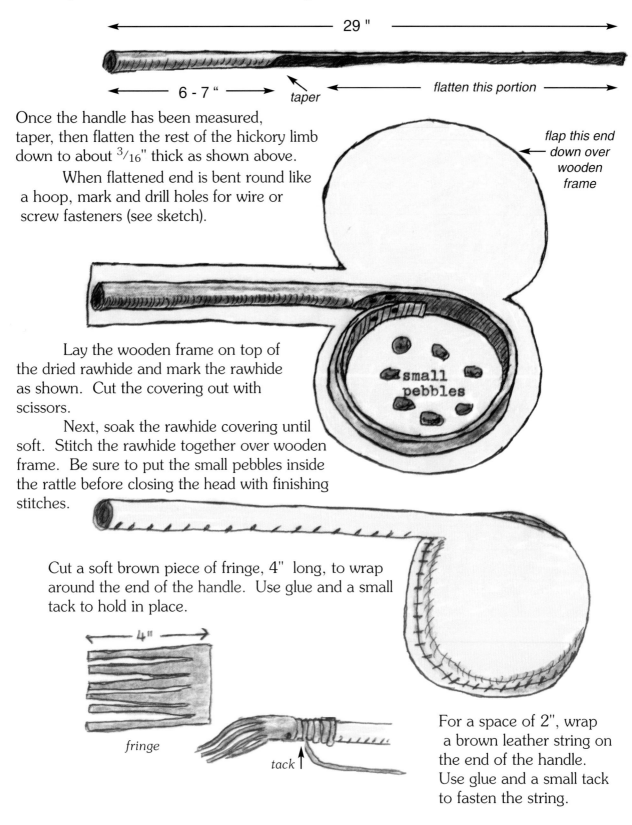

29 "

6 - 7 "

taper

flatten this portion

Once the handle has been measured, taper, then flatten the rest of the hickory limb down to about $^3/_{16}$" thick as shown above.

When flattened end is bent round like a hoop, mark and drill holes for wire or screw fasteners (see sketch).

flap this end down over wooden frame

Lay the wooden frame on top of the dried rawhide and mark the rawhide as shown. Cut the covering out with scissors.

Next, soak the rawhide covering until soft. Stitch the rawhide together over wooden frame. Be sure to put the small pebbles inside the rattle before closing the head with finishing stitches.

small pebbles

Cut a soft brown piece of fringe, 4" long, to wrap around the end of the handle. Use glue and a small tack to hold in place.

4"

fringe

tack

For a space of 2", wrap a brown leather string on the end of the handle. Use glue and a small tack to fasten the string.

32

RAWHIDE GOURD SHAPED RATTLE

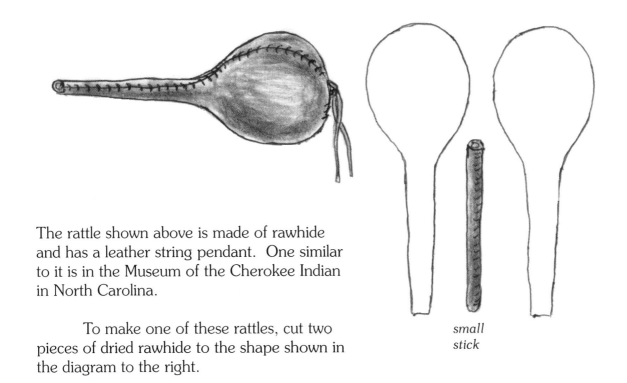

small stick

The rattle shown above is made of rawhide and has a leather string pendant. One similar to it is in the Museum of the Cherokee Indian in North Carolina.

To make one of these rattles, cut two pieces of dried rawhide to the shape shown in the diagram to the right.

Soak the two pieces of rawhide in water until they are very soft. Sew the two parts together around the head portion of the rawhide pieces. When this is done, pack sand and seven small pebbles inside of this bulb shaped part, to create the rounded form.

Next, put a stick between the handle parts, as shown above. Stitch up the sides of the rawhide handle. The stick will help to make the handle of the gourd more firm. Let the rawhide gourd-shaped rattle dry in the sun until it becomes very hard.

The hardest part is to remove the sand. This can be done by forcing the seam slightly apart at the top of the gourd. Use a punch or nail to do this. Another way is to make a small hole at the top at the seam and then tap the gourd against something while it is held upside down. The sand will begin to come out. This process will have to be done repeatedly until all the sand is out. Only the pebbles will remain inside to make sound. The leather string pendant is attached to a stitch at the top of the gourd.

TURTLE-SHELL HAND RATTLE

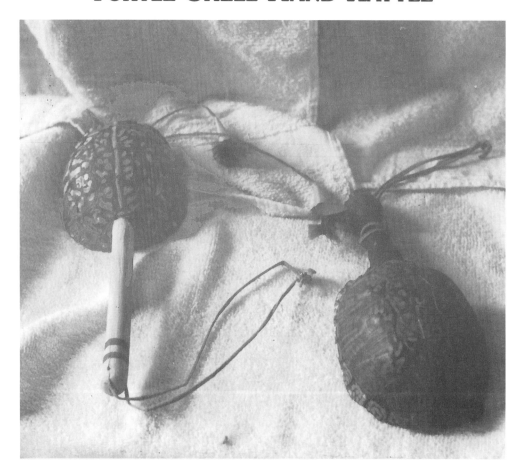

The turtle-shell hand rattle, as it is commonly called, is actually made from the shell of the land turtle. Above are two examples made by the author. These rattles were considered very sacred in the old days and were used by the medicine men.

While on the subject of rattles, it is worth mentioning how such rattles were made. The tortoise was caught and killed. Then, as much of the turtle was removed from the shell as possible. The shell was then placed near an ant hill and the ants finished cleaning the shell.

Since I do not prefer to kill a tortoise, I often find the shells in the forest when I'm out walking. The bottom of the shell is usually missing, but to remedy this, a piece of cardboard is cut and bent to fit the opening. Glue the cardboard bottom in place and use enamel paint to make it match the rest of the shell. I use the colors yellow, brown and black to touch-up the shell.

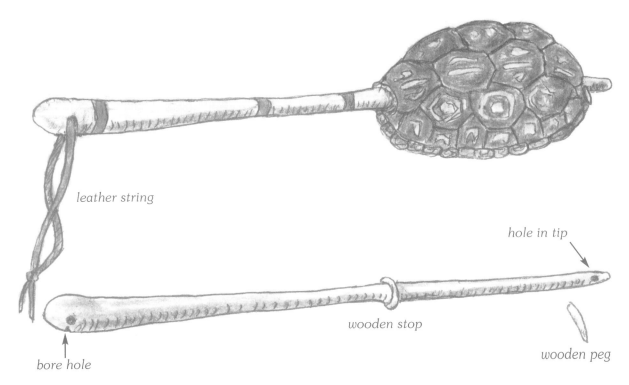

leather string

hole in tip

wooden stop

bore hole

wooden peg

Carve a wooden handle for the shell as shown above.

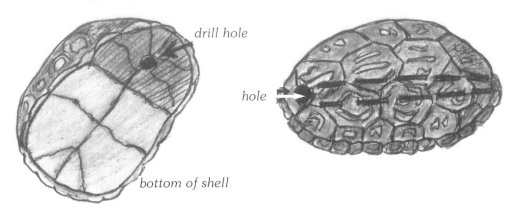

drill hole

hole

bottom of shell

drill holes through shell for the handle

After the shell is ready to use, carve out a handle to the desired length. Next, drill holes in the shell. Place small pebbles inside the shell, then push the handle through the holes as shown above. Put a wooden peg through the hole in the tip of the handle. The peg holds the shell in place. If the shell slips or turns on the handle, put a little glue around the handle where it goes through the shell. The handle can be painted with stripes.

TURTLE SHELL LEG RATTLES

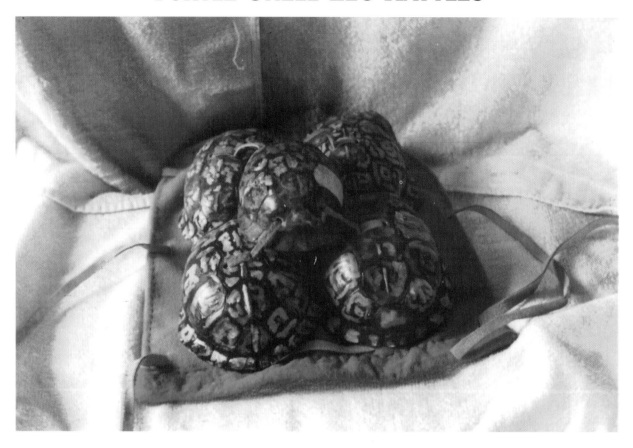

In many of the Cherokee dances, a leader led the dance. Behind him, in the dance circle, followed a woman wearing tortoise shells on a piece of leather, fastened below her right knee. In the old days, this woman was one of the "beloved women". The other dancers followed after her in the dance line. Turtle shell leg rattles of this type were made up of several shells with small stones inside of each shell. See the photograph above. More shells are added to make the sound louder.

The proper way to wear leg rattles is on the calf of the leg, to the side and somewhat back. One method to use in making sound with the leg rattles is to shuffle the leg twice, then hit the ground hard with the heel of the foot. Another way is to shuffle the leg twice, then hit the toes of the foot on the ground on the first beat of the drum. Next shuffle the leg twice, striking the ground with the the heel of the foot, on the second beat of the drum. Keep beat with the drum. There are certain times during a song, when the woman wearing the leg rattles makes her noise. At other times she is silent.

The following pages show how leg rattles are made.

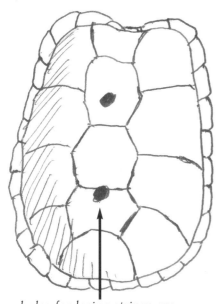

holes for lacing strings are drilled in shells, as shown above

After the square of leather is ready for use, prepare the desired number of tortoise shells as described on previous pages. Using an electric drill, bore two holes in each shell all the way through the top and bottom. Don't forget to add the small pebbles inside while the bottom of the shell is being put into place.

Cut two $1/2$" wide leather strings for the top and bottom. The strings should be long enough to lace across the piece of leather and to wrap around the leg once or twice as the strings are tied below the knee and above the ankle.

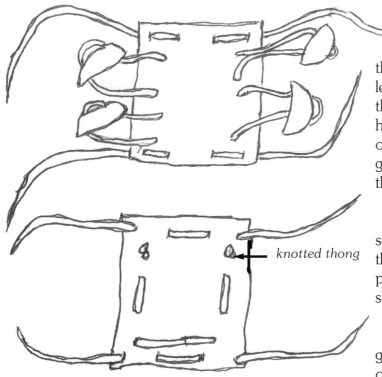

knotted thong

The shells are laced onto the square of leather, as shown at left. If you have trouble getting the leather thongs through the holes, fasten a needle and twine onto the end of the leather thong, guide the needle through pulling the thong behind it.

Some Cherokees today sew a piece of foam rubber on the back of leg rattles as a padding to keep them from sliding down to the ankle.

When dancing, it may be a good idea to have extra women on standby with leg rattles, because using leg rattles is tiresome.

37

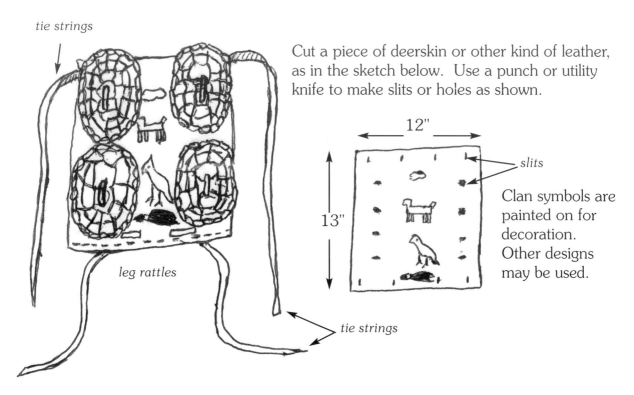

tie strings

Cut a piece of deerskin or other kind of leather, as in the sketch below. Use a punch or utility knife to make slits or holes as shown.

leg rattles

12"

13"

slits

Clan symbols are painted on for decoration. Other designs may be used.

tie strings

38

how to wear tortoise shell leg rattles

(models: Maggie Mafnas & her sister Elizabeth)

demonstrating the use of leg rattles

(model: author's wife, Mable)

DANCE STEPS

Cherokee dancing would not be complete without dance steps. J.P. Evans reported, "If all other native tribes dance like the Cherokees, some writers have greatly misrepresented them. There is no variety in the movement of their feet, stamping with one or both feet at a time in rapid succession and when stationary, jumping up and alighting on both feet in the same quick manner, constitute their only steps in dancing". (See Vol. VI of the John Howard Payne papers, The Newberry Library, Chicago, Illinois.)

As you study Cherokee dancing, you will find there are several dance steps that were used. I will briefly describe some of these steps.

Stomp Step: This step is the most common. Starting with the right foot, the foot is kept flat as it is raised and then stomped down to the ground, dropping the weight of the body down with it. Then the same step is performed with the left foot, letting the weight of the body drop to the left . These simple dance steps are alternated over and over as the dance continues in beat with the drum.

Double Stomp: Starting in rhythm with the drum, both feet are kept side by side, jumping forward to land flat and together. Next, jumping forward another step, both feet hit flat again with the right foot slightly ahead of the left foot. On the next jump, the feet land together again, side by side. And then, finally, the feet land with the left foot slightly ahead of the right. The process of the double stomp step is repeated over and over throughout the dance to the beat of the drum.

Trot Step: This a type of running dance step, in which short or long paces can be used. With the ankle stiff and the foot flat, the right foot trots, landing flat to the ground. The same step is then done with the left foot. This process is repeated over and over to the beat of the drum.

J.P. Evans also described the dance steps of the Booger Dance. He witnessed dancers in a stooped over position, gliding around the fire. Their feet were moving so fast, it resembled a top spinning. The dance consisted of a trembling or rapid vibration of the muscles, and at the same time, a regular and brisk movement forward, requiring the utmost exertion of muscular power. (See sketches of *Cherokee Character, Customs and Manners, Payne Papers* Vol. 4, pp. 1-39.)

To explain it in a simpler way: as the entire body trembles and shakes from head to toe, the knees move quickly in all directions to the beat of the drum. Some dancers keep one knee stiff. Other steps that are easier to perform may be incorporated in the Booger Dance. As one can deduce from trying the Booger Dance steps, the movements resemble the feebleness of old age.

There are more dance steps of the Cherokee that may be researched from other sources.

FESTIVAL COSTUME OF THE GREAT HIGH PRIEST OR UKU

Long ago the Great High Chief or Uku performed his duties in the national council house. There were town chiefs in the other villages of the nation.

While in the council house, the Uku or PeaceTime Chief wore white garments. White is the symbol for peace, sacredness and holiness. White clothes were also worn during the annual festivals. The Uku had certain clothes he wore for governmental purposes, while at other occasions his costume varied.

Let's first consider his festival costume. As can be seen in the sketch of the Uku Duty Costume, he wore a headdress made of white swan feathers. The headband on this hat was made of folded or doubled swanskin with the feathers in tact. The upper part of this conical hat was covered with the white hair of tanned deer-tail skin. Enough strips of this white fur were sewn together to form the upper part of the hat. The grain of the hair flowed upward on the hat. On top of the hat were attached upright curved white feathers. These curved feathers hung down all around, as seen in the sketch. The lining for the inside of the hat was probably made of otter skin.

Earrings and shell bead necklaces, as well as tattoos were also worn by the Uku. Around his neck hung a large shell gorget type necklace. This white shell disk had two holes bored near the center. An otter leather string was inserted through these holes. Then on each leather string was a single bead, similar to a thick button or tubular bead. These type beads were made of male deer horn. Medicine men also wore this type necklace.

With this outfit, the Uku wore a sleeveless, white deer skin shirt which extended down to his waist. It was sewn across the shoulders and up the sides.

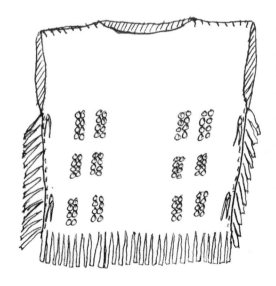

The sleeveless shirt at the left is an example of the Uku's shirt, which I made. White crow beads and fringe may be used for ornamental purposes. This is only a reconstructed version, since no real example exists to my knowledge.

When a shirt was worn by the Uku, as he was performing his duties during the warm months, this type was very suitable.

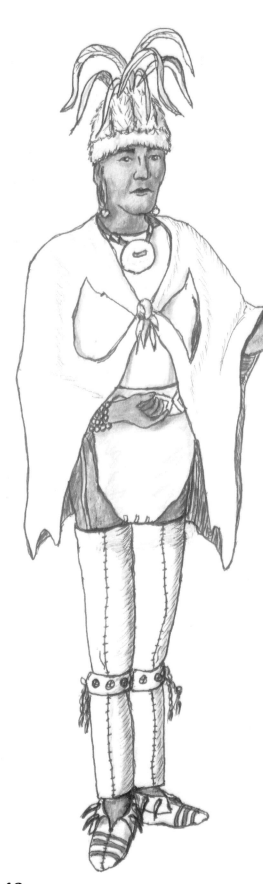

swan feather headdress

earrings

conch shell neckless

white deerskin mantle or a long cape of white feathers

bracelets

sleeveless white shirt

wide white, finger-woven belt

apron-type breechclout

center-seam leggings could be worn with this costume

garters with bells

white center-seam moccasins with red stripes and turkey gobbler spurs

The Uku wore a wide finger-woven belt around his waist. This belt was made of plant fiber threads and in later years with yarn from the white traders. Such a belt is worn tied at the side. A white strip of leather is also suitable for the Uku's belt. It might be decorated with designs.

Also, an apron-type breechclout was worn by the Uku. It tied at the sides of the waist with the wide woven belt covering up the ties. The front and back flaps of the aprons were tied together at the crotch with leather strings. This made it more form fitting. Refer to the sketch of the Uku's duty costume. It is my opinion that, whether these breechclouts were standard items worn by all men, or by just the leaders, the style quickly faded in history. Some engravings on shell gorgets of the southeast showing men in dance costume seem to reflect this type of breechclout. This would take the costume back to the mound building era of the southeast.

As late as 1830-40, Catlin, an artist who traveled among the Southeastern Indians, as well as with tribes to the west, such as the Osage for example, depicted some Indian leaders wearing a breechclout tied at the crotch. However, in historic times, many Cherokee wore the breechclout the common way, like other Native Americans, without tying the flaps together at the crotch area.

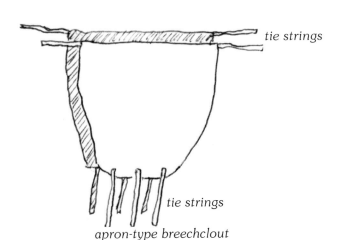

tie strings

tie strings

apron-type breechclout

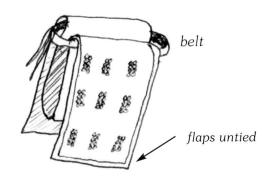

belt

flaps untied

regular or common style breechclout

The Uku also wore a deerskin draped around his shoulders, in mantle fashion, when he was on duty in the national council house. The legs of this white deerskin were tied in a knot around the chest area, as seen in the prior sketch of the Uku. Garters of the woven type, or of white deerskin were sometimes worn below the knees by the Uku. In historic times, bells were added to the garters.

On the feet of the Uku, white deerskin moccasins were worn. Red stripes were painted, using blood root to produce the color, above the toe section of each moccasin. Red, the color of vermillion, was the war color and was not used on sacred peace time items.

These kind of moccasins were probably the center-seam style. Turkey gobbler spurs were also attached to the moccasins, perhaps at the cuffs. Bells were later added, instead of the spurs, as the culture changed.

James Adair, in his "History of the American Indian", gives his account of this costume on pages 87-89, for further study.

NOTE: *Sometimes the Uku or Great High Priest of the national capitol wore a long cape covered with white feathers. The chiefs of individual Cherokee towns outside of the capitol sometimes wore mantles made of the tail-feathers or the breast-feathers of the wild turkey This type of mantle had white feathers on the upper part of the shoulder area.*

Pictured on the following pages are some other costumes worn by the Uku or Great High Priest as he performed his various duties.

In one of the sketches, a long sleeved shirt was added to the costume. When the weather became cooler in Cherokee, this shirt was probably worn as well as leggings.

It would be reasonable to assume that the long sleeved coat of the Uku was added as part of his costume for warmth when the weather became even colder.

The following drawings of the Uku garments are from my own conjecture in trying to recreate such costumes from the descriptions given by writers of the period, such as James Adair and John Howard Payne.

Coat Costume Of The Great High Priest

Swan feather headdress

Shell gorget necklace with an otter-skin neck thong

Woven ornaments on both shoulders of coat

Bells sewn to cuffs

The coat was made of white deerskin

Long white fringe and tassels hung down to the knees. These were attached to trim rolls of white deerskin

The coat reached nearly to the feet

White center-seam leggings were worn

Bells were sewn to the bottom cuff

White moccasins with red stripes on the toes and turkey spurs attached to the upper section

Costume Of The Great High Priest Or Uku Worn With His Long Sleeve Shirt

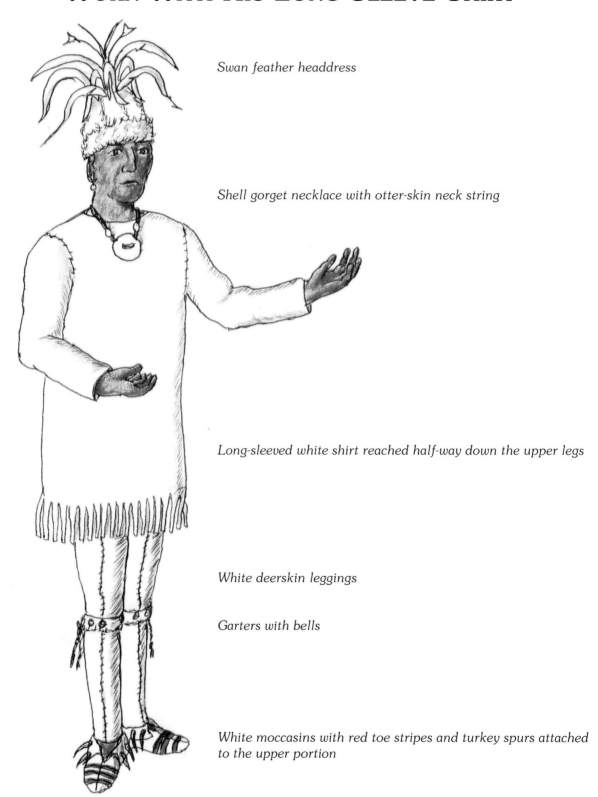

Swan feather headdress

Shell gorget necklace with otter-skin neck string

Long-sleeved white shirt reached half-way down the upper legs

White deerskin leggings

Garters with bells

White moccasins with red toe stripes and turkey spurs attached to the upper portion

The white long-sleeved shirt, breechclout and leggings shown above are made of white blanket cloth. This is the attire of a Peace Chief.

(Model: author's brother, Robert)

How to Make the
White Peace Time Chief's Hat

Peace Chief's Hat

In the old days, when the Peace Chief was in office performing his duties of the council house, he wore a hat made of white swan feathers. The inside of the hat was made of otter skin for a base. White upright swan feathers curved down all around at the top of the hat. The white fur of deer tails were sewn together in pieces or strips and attached to the hat, covering all of the outside of the otter-skin base or lining. A headband attached to the bottom edge of the hat was made of a doubled skin of the swan. The headband was white with fine soft fluffy feathers. Small bells were attached to the bottom of the headband at the back of the hat.

In the photograph above, a version of this hat is pictured. I made this hat based on an example from the Oconaluftee Indian Village in North Carolina. I had no instructions on how to make the hat, so I used my own methods and substitute materials.

The base of the hat, instead of using otter-skin, can be made one of three ways. One method is to cut the brim from a brown felt hat, which can be easily obtained at a used clothing store. See illustration below.

48

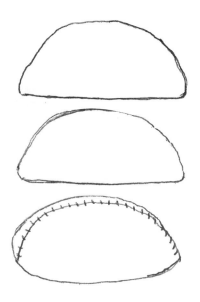

The second method, I sometimes use to make a hat or the base, is to measure from the center of the forehead to the center of the back of the head. This gets the length of the hat parts. Then measure from the tip of the upper part of the ear to the center of the top of the head. This measurement will give you the height of the hat. Once you obtain those measurements, cut soft or semi-stiff leather in a rounded or conical shape as in the sketch to the left. The two parts of the hat are then sewn together, as shown in the sketch. The seam running down the center of the hat is the front and back of the hat base. Allow $1/4$ of an inch extra for the seams. This method described can be used to make other styles of hat bases.

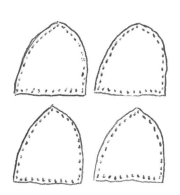

The next method is one that I used to make the hat base. It is more difficult to do. Cut four pieces of split cowhide in the shape shown in the sketch to the left. Use a baseball cap as a model to go by, making a paper pattern.

Lay your pattern on the leather, marking out the form on the leather. Use scissors or utility knife to do the cutting. Holes should be punched around the pieces of leather as in the sketch.

Next, stitch the parts together, using strong thread or twine. See sketch at the left. It is up to you which method to use in making the hat base.

Next, select proper feathers for the hat. Since white curved swan or heron feathers will be difficult to obtain, substitute feathers will have to be used. White rooster tail feathers can make a good substitute.

When I made this hat, not having the proper feathers, I had to use 12" - 14" white turkey wing feathers, purchased from the Tandy Leather Company. Eight left bend and eight right bend feathers are needed. Trim each feather with scissors, as shown in the sketches below.

The next step is to glue short curved white feathers onto the tip of each trimmed feather. Such short curved feathers can be taken from a feather duster made of rooster tail-feathers. See the sketches below.

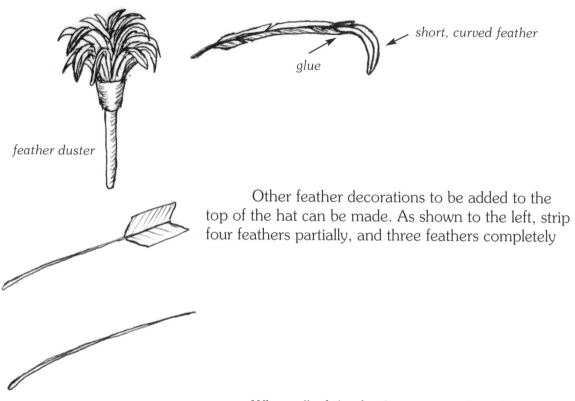

short, curved feather

glue

feather duster

Other feather decorations to be added to the top of the hat can be made. As shown to the left, strip four feathers partially, and three feathers completely

When all of the feathers are ready to be attached, choose one of the following methods:

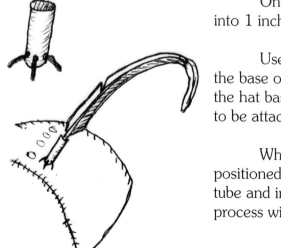

One method is to use river cane by cutting it into 1 inch tubes. A hack-saw is best used for this.

Use a very small drill bit to bore four holes near the base of each tube. Then sew a cane tube onto the hat base at each spot where an upright feather is to be attached.

When enough of the cane tubes have been positioned on the hat base, put tack glue inside of the tube and insert the feather. Then, continue this process with the remainder of the feathers

wood piece for feathers

A second method one might use to attach feathers to a hat base is to bore a series of holes into a piece of $1/2$" wood. Holes are also drilled for attaching the piece of wood to the proper place on the hat using twine. At least three pieces of wood will have to be made. One piece goes on each side and the other on the top of the hat. Glue is put in each hole with a feather inserted. See the sketch below.

A third method of attaching the upright feathers is used on the headdress in the photograph on page 48 is described as follows:

After the feathers have been prepared, use a large needle to punch two sets of holes near the ends of the quills of each feather. These holes are used to lace the feathers onto the hat base.

holes in quill point

Next, mark out in pencil where each feather is to go on the hat. Then use a no. 30 or 40 nail to punch holes at the spots for feather positions on the hat base. Use a block of wood on the inside of the hat, as the holes are punched with the nail and hammer.

Once the holes are made, insert a feather into each hole, remembering to put left bend feathers on the left side of hat and right bend feathers on the right side of hat. Refer to the prior photograph as a guide for mounting the feathers on the top of the hat and sides.

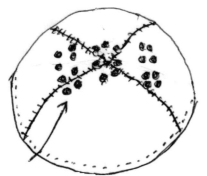

*Holes made in hat base for
upright feather positions*

Use strong twine and a large needle to go through the holes in each quill on top of the hat base, anchoring the twine on the ends of the rows of the upright feathers. Then go underneath the hat base with a needle and twine, passing the needle through the holes in the quills underneath the hat base, as shown.

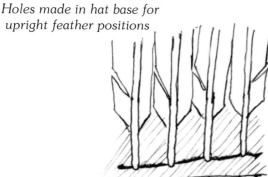

The sketch to the left shows how needle and twine are used to lace the feathers to the hat base.

Twine goes through holes in the feathers both above and below the base

Once all feathers have been attached by one of the methods, white fur is sewn all over the hat base and between the feathers. In the old days, the white fur of tanned deer tails were sewn on the hat. Enough of these deer tails were sewn together to cover the hat. The grain of the fur pointed upward on the hat. In modern times, white rabbit fur or some other kind of fur is usually used. Perhaps a fur coat could be utilized.

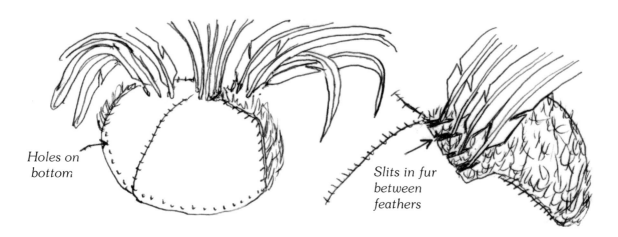

*Holes on
bottom*

*Slits in fur
between
feathers*

Sew one section of fur on the hat base at a time, until it is completed all the way around the hat. Then cut slits in the upper part of each section of fur. Push the fur into place between the feathers at the top of the hat. Then in that area between the feathers, using thread and needle, tack the slits together in a neat way. Glue may also be used to attach the fur.

52

In the old days a band was made of a strip of folded swan skin with the soft white feathers showing. This band was sewn around the bottom portion of the hat. A strip of soft rabbit fur can serve the same purpose.

To make an imitation band of feathers to go around the hat, cut a strip of white cloth 5 or 6 inches wide and long enough to go around the hat. Fold this piece of cloth in half lengthwise, as in sketch below.

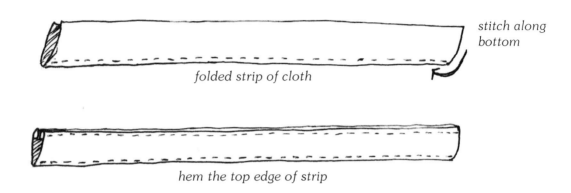

stitch along bottom

folded strip of cloth

hem the top edge of strip

Sew along the bottom edge of folded strip, then turn the upper edges under to hem as shown above. Next glue or sew white fluffs, such as turkey fluffs, in overlapping rows on the band of cloth from one end to the other as shown below.

over-lap fluffs on band

Start stitching the band onto the back side of the hat. It can be attached to the holes at the bottom edge of hat base and to the fur, using white thread.

A few small bells can be sewed to the bottom edge of the hat band at the back of the hat.

This is only a version of the peace chief's hat as it is portrayed in North Carolina. One version of this hat has the curved white swan feathers hanging down all around the top of the hat. The hat above shows the feathers only on the right and left of the hat. Arrange the feathers either way.

FESTIVAL COSTUME OF THE GREAT WAR CHIEF

During the Ripe Corn Ceremony, the Great War Chief wore a costume similar to the one shown here. He was carried around on a platform equipped with a seat for him.

He wore a red hat as his identifying symbol. Upon his visit to the Cherokees, Sir Alexander Cummings obtained such a hat or crown made of red dyed opossum fur.

The chief wore a white robe-like shirt which would have been quite long. The sleeves of the shirt were probably made of otter skin or otter skin arm bands were worn over sleeves made of white deerskin.

He also wore white leggings, garters and moccasins.

Costume of a Priest's Wife

This costume was worn to ceremonies such as the Festival of the First New Moon of Spring. It was also a proper dress to wear at other special peace time events, including the dances.

Such a dress was made of white deerskin, but can be made of white blanket material.

This was a gown-like dress which reached down to the knees. For cooler weather, longer sleeves were added. Underneath this gown-like dress, a petticoat or wrap-around skirt was worn reaching down to the middle of the lower leg.

These dresses can be beautifully decorated with beads or quillwork. Feathers were also sewn or woven to the dresses to add beauty.

A row of small bells were attached at knee level on the petticoat or skirt.

Wives of the priest also wore short ornamented feathered capes.

The short boots they wore reached half-way up the lower leg.

They wore their hair up higher than ordinary women. Also, a leather headband with 3-inch horns attached was worn to show their status.

The white ceremonial dress above is made of white blanket cloth.

(modeled by the author's mother, Nora)

WRAP-AROUND SKIRT AND JACKET

Outfit typically worn to dances
(Maggie Mafnas, model)

The jacket and wrap-around skirt shown above is made of tan imitation leather cloth. Designs for this outfit are made of blue velvet and red flannel patchwork, with white crow beads sewn down the center of each design. The tassels are made of leather strings with large brown wooden beads and pink and brown crow beads.

This is a suitable outfit for any woman or young girl to wear and participate in a Cherokee dance or ceremony.

In the instructions given on the following page, the measurements are designed to fit a girl ten years and older. It should be noted, you may have to alter the outfit, which you make according to the size needed. A simple way to attain a custom size is to use a loose fitting blouse and skirt as patterns.

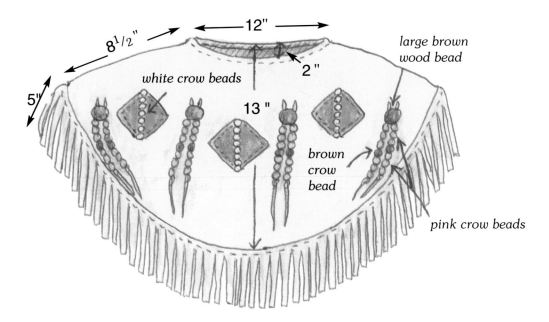

Cut the front and back of the jacket using the same dimensions as shown. The back of the collar is slightly curved, but the front of the collar has a 2 inch drop. Turn the front and back pieces of the jacket inside out and sew across the shoulders. Next, hem the collar as shown, and then turn the jacket right-side out.

A 6 inch wide strip of cloth is cut long enough to be sewn all around the bottom of the jacket. Remember to hem the top edge of this strip of cloth as it is sewn in place. When all of the decorations are finished, cut this strip into fringe.

Use blue velvet to form the left half of the diamond design and red flannel cloth to form the right side of the design. Refer to the sketch at the top of the page again.

a. 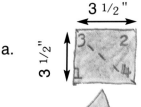 Cut squares of blue and red cloth to the dimensions shown in sketch (a).

b.  Fold a blue square of cloth from corner 2 to corner 1 as in sketch (b).

c.  Fold corner 3 to corner 4 as in sketches (c) and (d).

d.  Position the triangle of blue cloth at the desired position on the front of the jacket, sewing it into place. Next fold one of the red squares of cloth in the same manner.

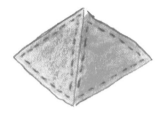

a.

After the red triangle has been sewn into place as shown, a diamond design has been formed using the patchwork method. Complete the remainder of diamond designs the same way.

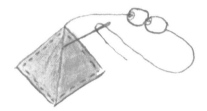

b.

You will now need an embroidery hoop to stretch the areas of the diamond designs in order to sew on white crow beads. This method keeps everything even.

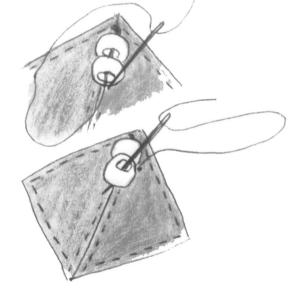

c.

String on two white crow beads, attaching them as shown.

Go down into the cloth with the needle and back up at the edge of the seam, between the two beads, as demonstrated.

d.

Pull the slack out of the thread, as shown in sketch (d), and string on two more white beads, repeating steps (b) - (c). Repeat this process from one end of the middle seam to the other.

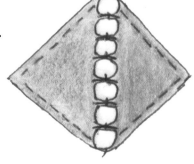

e.

Sketch (e) demonstrates how the beading on each diamond should look when finished.

TASSELS FOR THE JACKET

Cut four leather strings 14 " and $^1/_4$ " wide. These strings will be used to make the tassels.

Use a utility knife or scissors to make pairs of slots for the strings to be laced through. You can mark the positions of the strings on the jacket with a pencil by using the previous sketch of the jacket as a guide.

The large wooden bead is $^5/_8$ " of an inch in diameter. Wooden beads of this nature can be purchased at a craft store. Pink crow beads can be bought at a Walmart or Tandy Leather store.

Always tie a knot at the end of a strand of beads on a tassel!

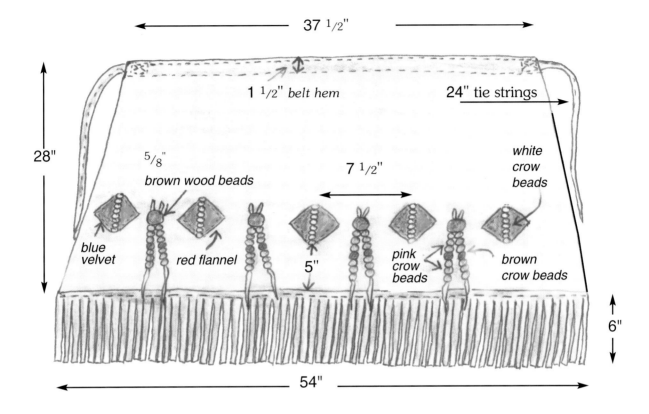

The wrap-around skirt shown above is also made of tan imitation leather cloth, as is the previous jacket.

Belt tie strings for this skirt are 24 inches long by $1^1/2$" wide. The leather strings for the beaded tassels are cut 15 inches long by $1/4$" wide. Diamond designs are the same size for this skirt as the last - $3^1/2$" by $3^1/2$" square.

The designs and tassels are evenly spaced as shown. Further details in making this skirt will be described in the instructions for the following skirts in this book.

JACKET AND WRAP AROUND SKIRT OUTFIT

proper dance wear
(model: Elizabeth Mafnas)

The jacket pictured is also made of tan imitation leather cloth. This type of cloth may be purchased at Walmart or other department stores during the fall season. The diamond designs consist of red cloth and white crow beads, and the two tassels are made of leather strings with plastic cones and crow beads.

To make the jacket, cut two pieces of cloth to the dimensions given on the following page. One piece is cut for the front, and one for the back.

Next, turn the pieces inside out and sew them across the shoulders. Then hem around the neckline. You're now ready to sew a 6" wide strip of cloth around th bottom edge, hemming it to the round bottom part of the jacket. This strip of cloth serves as the fringed part, and should be all the way around.

JACKET

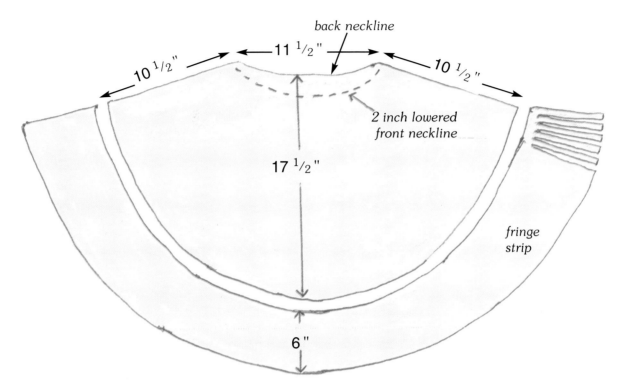

back neckline

11 ¹/₂"

10 ¹/₂"

10 ¹/₂"

2 inch lowered front neckline

17 ¹/₂"

fringe strip

6"

Completely assembled jacket is pictured below

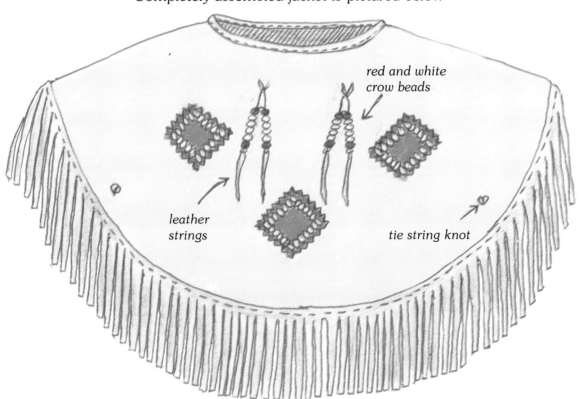

red and white crow beads

leather strings

tie string knot

When the jacket is finished, as shown on the prior page, you may wish to embellish it with a few decorations. Instructions for the diamond designs and tassels are as follows.

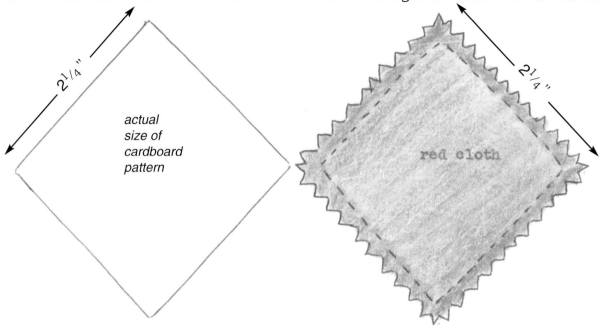

To form the designs as illustrated earlier, cut a piece of cardboard from a cereal box to the dimensions shown above. Use a special pair of scissors that will cut the cloth as illustrated. Thick cloth such as red flannel may be used. Use a pencil when tracing the design to the cloth and cut to the outside, making the cloth a little larger than the pattern.

When an ample number of red cloth diamonds have been cut, lay them out on the jacket to the desired spacing using stick pins to hold them in place. Then stitch the red diamonds in place as shown. The designs are usually worn on the front of the jacket only.

The white crow beads are sewn on the red cloth diamonds as shown.

String on enough beads to extend from one edge to the next. Then sew the ends of the bead strand to the cloth. Back stitch between each bead to hold them in place.

TASSEL FOR THE JACKET

Slots for the strings can be made with a utility knife or scissors

3/4"   3/4"

cut ends off with hacksaw

bone or plastic hair-pipe

To make the two tassels for the jacket, cut two leather strings 16" long by 1/4" wide. Then cut two sets of slots at the points on the jacket where the tassels will hang. Insert a leather string through a pair of the slots, lacing it into place. The tassels are centered 7 " above the lower diamond design on the jacket.

The white cone-like beads can be made by sawing off the ends of a bone or plastic hair-pipe bead. Insert both ends of the leather string through the cone bead. String on a red crow bead, four white crow beads and another red crow bead to one of the strings, as shown. To hold the beads in place, tie a knot, as shown. Use the same method to make the other matching beaded string. The other paired tassel is made the same way.

If you have trouble getting the two ends of the leather string to go through the cone bead, use a needle and thread, as shown in the sketch above. The strings can be pulled through easier this way. Then remove the thread and string on the red and white beads to the single strings.

The front and back of the jacket is stitched or tied at the armpits with leather strings. This is done so the jacket will stay in place when it is worn.

WRAP AROUND SKIRT

The skirt below is made of tan imitation leather cloth. It matches the jacket described on the preceding pages. This outfit, with the jacket, would be proper to wear by a woman in a dance such as the Horse Dance, or other social dances of the Cherokee. A necklace, moccasins and turtle-shell leg rattles are all that would be needed to make this costume a complete dance ceremonial outfit.

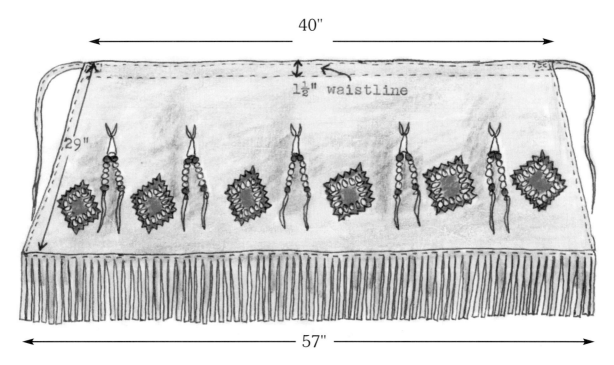

When using the above measurements, add extra cloth to the measurements given due to the hemming process. Add about 2 - 2 ¹/₂" of extra cloth at the top measurements of the skirt for the waist-line hem.

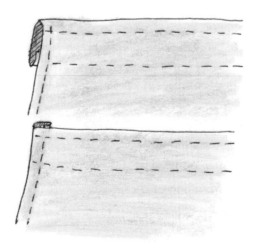

As you sew the waist-line, fold the cloth backward and then hem the waist-line on the back side of the skirt as shown.

The sides of the skirt are folded back and also hemmed on the backside.

MAKING THE TIE STRINGS
FOR THE WRAP-AROUND-SKIRT

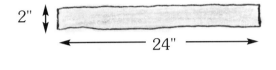

2" ↕

← 24" →

The tie strings for the skirt are made of a strip of cloth 24" long by 2" wide. Fold the strip of cloth in the middle, with the edges turned in, as shown at left. Sew along near the seam from one end of the tie string to the other.

Taper the tie string at one end by folding it into the desired shape and sewing it.

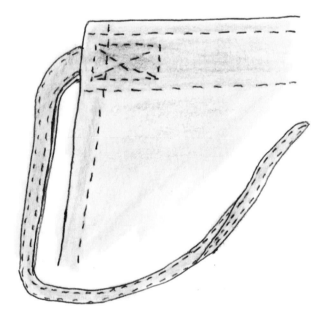

When the tie string is finished, sew it to the back side of the waist-line as shown. Make another string and sew it on the other end of the waist-line of the skirt

The bottom fringe of the skirt is made of a 6" wide strip of cloth and long enough to be sewn the length of the bottom of the skirt. Since this type of fringe is made of cloth instead of leather, the top edge of the cloth will have to be turned back and under as it is sewn in place. See the sketch below.

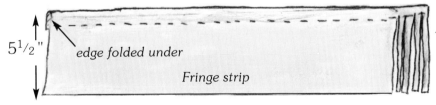

$5\frac{1}{2}$"

edge folded under

Fringe strip

Fringe should be cut when the skirt is finished.

This type of skirt should be made long enough to over-lap at the ends when it is worn. The measurements given for this skirt should fit females from age 16 to adult.

67

DECORATIONS FOR THE SKIRT

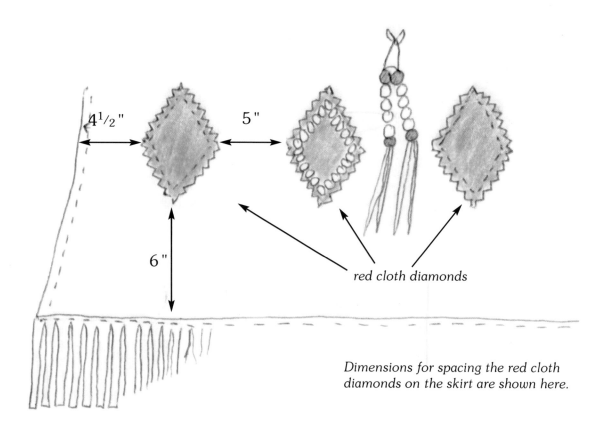

Dimensions for spacing the red cloth diamonds on the skirt are shown here.

The patches, beadwork and tassels are formed the same way as previously instructed for the jacket.

After the skirt is ready to be worn, if the length is too long, a quick adjustment can be made. Just fold the waist-line as many times as needed at the waist hem, or belt, to shorten the dress as it is tied in place.

This dress was designed to be worn by the female dancer during the Horse Dance. But of course, it can be worn at other occasions too.

OUTFIT FOR A
VERY YOUNG MALE DANCER

*This outfit can be enlarged up to adult sizes. It is
very suitable for a dance costume*

(model: Frankie Mafnas)

The above outfit should fit a young boy 10 years or older. This costume is made of tan imitation leather cloth. Designs are done in patchwork using cloth in such colors as white, dark blue and yellow. There are many kinds of decorations, such as seed bead edging, tassels, cones, etc. which could be added to the shirt and leggings.

The leggings are the side-seam style which were sometimes worn by the Cherokee in the late historic period from the 1830s - 40s.

The easiest way to get the desired size of the shirt and leggings is to fold the material double, and then lay a long sleeve shirt or trousers on top as a guide. Mark around the edges of the shirt or trousers with a pencil allowing $1/2$" extra for the seams to be sewn together.

69

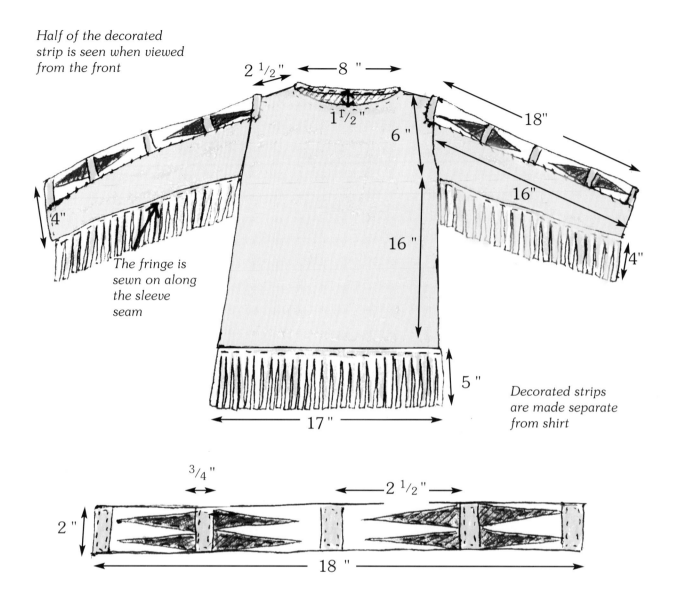

Half of the decorated strip is seen when viewed from the front

2 1/2" ← 8" →

1 1/2"

6"

18"

16"

16"

4"

4"

The fringe is sewn on along the sleeve seam

16"

5"

Decorated strips are made separate from shirt

17"

3/4"

2 1/2"

2"

18"

The decorated strips are sewn to the center of the tops of the sleeves using an overcast stitch. As you can see above, the fringe is sewn to the bottom of the sleeve seam from the cuff to the armpit.

Use a loose fitting long sleeve shirt as a pattern if desired. Once all of the pieces of the shirt are cut, turn the front and back to the shirt inside out, and then sew across the shoulders and down the sides. The sleeves are sewn on next. Hem the neck and sleeve cuffs. Fringe strips, cut to the dimensions shown above are then sewn on, but cut only after decorated strips have been sewn on.

Always allow 1/4" to 1/2" extra to all measurements of these outfits for the hemming process and areas where the parts are to be sewn together.

70

How to Make the
Decorated Patchwork Strip

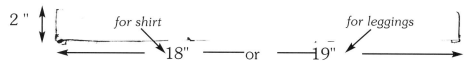

2" | for shirt | for leggings

← 18" — or — 19" →

Cut a strip of white blanket cloth 19" long by 3" wide for the shirt. Fold the top and bottom edges under to hem. Then fold the ends to hem. Make another strip for the other sleeve. Cut strips for the leggings 20" long by 3" to hem.

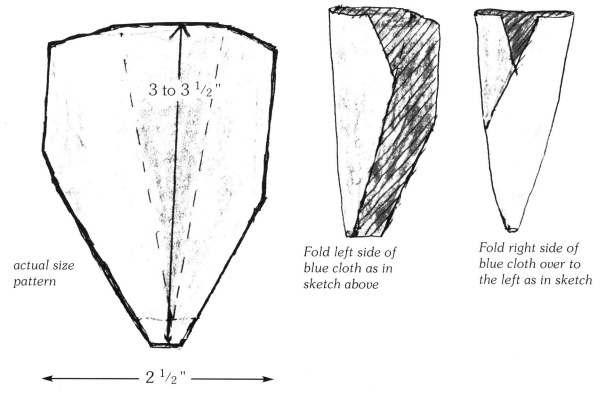

3 to 3 1/2"

actual size
pattern

← 2 1/2" →

Fold left side of
blue cloth as in
sketch above

Fold right side of
blue cloth over to
the left as in sketch

Hold the cloth firmly in place, using stick pins to hold the shape. Position the blue cloth design on the white strip of cloth and sew into place with needle and thread, or a sewing machine.

Now make the other blue cloth designs, positioning and sewing them to the white strips in the same manner, until all designs have been sewn for the shirt, leggings and belt. Next, make the yellow stripe designs, as shown below, sewing the stripes in place.

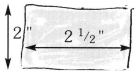

2" | 2 1/2"

Cut cloth to this size

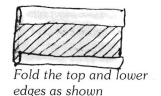

Fold the top and lower
edges as shown

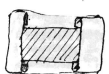

Fold the edges and then fold the
left and right ends as shown.

71

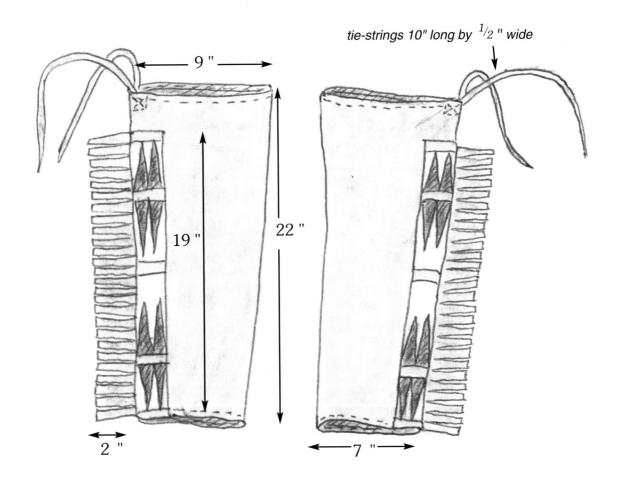

tie-strings 10" long by $^1/_2$ " wide

9 "

22 "

19 "

2 "

7 "

The leggings above match the shirt previously described. As seen, these side-seam leggings have fringes. One type of legging also worn by the Cherokee, had a seam up the front of the leggings and usually no fringe.

Decorated strips are also made separately and sewn onto the completed leggings. Any manner of decorations may be added to the leggings to give them a more fanciful style. Tassels of fur, beads and hair were all used to decorate. The leggings pictured above, worn with the matching shirt, were ideal for young boys and teenagers to wear to ceremonies and dances.

To get a proper length measurement for the leggings, measure a pair of trousers from the cuff to the crotch, or use the pants as a pattern.

Shown below is a narrow belt, $^3/_4$" wide and 2' long *(length sizes vary)*. It is made of soft tan leather, but it may be made of doubled imitation leather cloth. This belt is worn around the waist for the tie-strings of the leggings to be attached to. The breech-clout shown below is also worn over this belt.

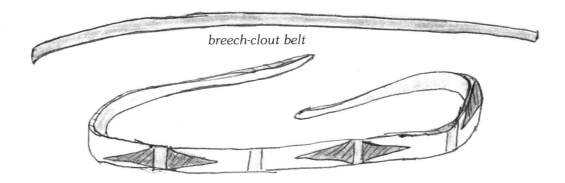

breech-clout belt

Also pictured above is a sash-like belt to be worn over the other belt which holds up the leggings and breech-clout. This decorated belt is primarily for style and aesthetic value. To make this belt, I used white doubled blanket cloth. It was hemmed along one edge and sewn along the other. The sash belt is 2 ' and 10 " long and 2 " wide. The designs are done in blue velvet and yellow patchwork.

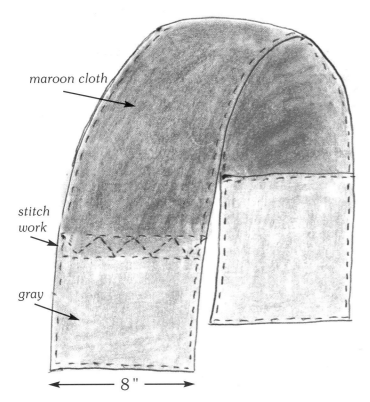

maroon cloth

stitch
work

gray

← 8 " →

The breech-clout shown here is made of the thick gray and maroon cloth. Cut to the dimensions shown. Allow extra cloth at the edges for the breech-clout to be hemmed.

It should be about 58" long.

WOMEN-GATHERING-WOOD DANCE

The "Gathering-Wood Dance" was a preliminary dance, done among the first of the evening dances. This dance was performed by women to symbolize their contribution of providing the wood for the dance fire and hearth. The Wood Dance was important because without fire wood there would be no dance fire for the night dances and no fire beneath the hearth where the women cooked. A lot of people would have been in the dark and very hungry had this task not been done by the women.

The dance could be given in any season and performed early in the evening, probably before the Friendship Dance. According to *Cherokee Dance and Drama*, by Speck and Broom, the "Gathering-Wood Dance" was done in the same manner as the "Round Dance". It may have also had a place in the night time dances during the Green Corn Dance Festival.

Some tribes have what they call the "Grass Dance", in which they go through the motions of tromping down the tall grass to provide a place for the people to dance. The "Women-Gathering-Wood Dance" served a purpose as well, as their dance provided wood for the fires.

Dresses such as these are suitable for the "Women Gathering Wood Dance".

(Models: Lisa Howard, Mable Sizemore and Carolynn Mills)

This was the only dance in which Cherokee women could take the lead. The women in this dance wore tortoise shell leg rattles. A male chanter is off to one side of the dance circle beating a drum. The women do not sing during this dance. The dance songs are now forgotten and lost to the past. It is known, however, that there were seven songs that were sung in a lively fashion.

In the dance, the women move counter-clockwise in a single-file circle. Primarily, they move back and forth, pretending to pick up and gather wood for the fire. See: *The Eastern Cherokees*, by Gilbert, page 266.

To see the costumes for this dance, refer to the other basic dresses in this book, or in my other book - *How To Make Cherokee Clothing*. Also published by Cherokee Publications.

74

THE FRIENDSHIP DANCE COSTUME

*Chief Oliver J. Collins of the Tallige Cherokee Nation of
West Portsmouth, Ohio is wearing a white ceremonial outfit*

The Friendship Dance is one of the well known dances of the Cherokee. I have seen this dance done several times, but I've always been disappointed to see that the dancers were not wearing traditional costumes. However, the last time I witnessed the dance, in Portsmouth, Ohio, the dancers were wearing Native American costumes. It was a beautiful sight.

In the old days, when the Friendship Dance was done, the dancers wore their white outfits. As noted in the book, *Travels of William Bartram*, page 225, Bartram writes of having seen the Friendship Dance performed in a council house. The young women who were a part of the dance were wearing "robes of chaste white deerskin", unlike their everyday clothing.

White is the color for peace, friendship and goodwill. It is no wonder that it is also the chosen color for the Friendship Dance costume.

75

Before the 1790's, the male dancers of the Friendship Dance would have worn their white deerskin shirts, leggings, breechclouts and moccasins. These costumes can be made of thin white blanket cloth, with or without fringe.

The outfit Chief Collins is wearing, on the preceding page, has colored stripes. This indicates that he is a leader. This type of outfit was worn by some leaders of the pre-removal period.

White outfits for the men can be decorated with beads and other decor to make them beautiful. There are other examples of men's outfits elsewhere in this book. Another good reference is my other book, "How to Make Cherokee Clothing".

white fringe dress

(model: author's sister, Ellen Webb)

White dresses and white Peace Chief's outfit

(models: Ellen, Nora, and Robert, author's sister, mother, and brother)

The outfits for the women of the Friendship Dance can be made of white deerskin or thin blanket cloth. A Clan Mother or Beloved Woman may wear a feathered hat or wear her hair in the wreathed hair style to show her status. Ordinary women wear their white dresses with their hair loose, coiled , or in the club style. Necklaces and bracelets can also be worn.

76

HOW TO DO THE FRIENDSHIP DANCE

This dance, as indicated by it's title, depicts friendship, peace and goodwill. It is usually performed for fun and entertainment at any time during the social dances.

People of all ages can find enjoyment in the Friendship Dance. It gives married couples a chance to express affection for their mate. Young courting couples can get more acquainted. Singles can socialize, and possibly find a mate. The dance overall is for fun and relaxation.

The leader of the dance is followed by a woman who wears tortoise-shell leg rattles. Everyone is grouped with their partners and forms a single-file circle, moving counter-clockwise. The steps alternate between an ordinary walk and the shuffling trot. After one or two complete rotations done in this manner, the dance will change as the second song starts. The leader will perform certain gestures as the rest of the dancers in the circle imitate his movements. Each gesture will last for a complete rotation before changing, and may follow a sequence as given below:

1. Couples face their partners and hold hands.

2. Couples dance side by side, creating two circles, with the male to the left of the female. They then hold hands with their partner by crossing their arms.

3. Couples face each other as they touch palms or hold hands.

4. As they continue to face each other, couples place their hands on their partner's shoulders.

5. Couples dance side by side again with their arms on each other's shoulders.

6. Facing each other, couples touch and stroke their partners under the chin.

   NOTE: *The following two gestures are optional and are often omitted from the dance, especially if strangers are present. They are reserved for married couples, and in some cases, responsible boy and girl relationships. These gestures are sometimes a part of the Booger dance as well. It is to be noted that they were never considered vulgar, as in dances of other cultures.*

7. If circumstances are suitable and the dance partners are not relatives, males may touch the females on the breast.

8. Given favorable conditions, as stated above, partners may touch each other's clothes at the crotch area.

As the dance draws to a close, the dancers all hold hands as they move around in the circle. The circle may then start to zig-zag imitating a crawling snake, and then it may suddenly change directions, moving backwards. These movements create a lot of confusion among the dancers and causing a lot of laughter and good feelings as the dancers leave the dance grounds.

For more details on this dance, see *Cherokee Dance and Drama* by Speck and Broom, pgs. 65-67. Music for the dance can be found on the cassette, "Where the Ravens Roost", a recording of traditional Cherokee songs by Walker Calhoun.

The Friendship Dance is usually performed in a single file line, however, an alternate formation may be created with the women forming an inner circle as their male partners form another circle to the outside of them.

In order to fully appreciate and understand the Friendship Dance, one should see it performed live. There are many alterations and changes from one group to another that exemplify the broad range of Native American style. While viewing the Friendship Dance of the Tallige Cherokees, I noticed that they used the two circles with the women on the inside and the men surrounding them. They moved around slowly, tapping or stomping the right foot twice, and then the left foot once. This step was repeated throughout the dance.

To signal the dancers to change movements, the drummer would slowly tap the drum three times, with a pause between each tap. As the dance continued, he would pick up the tempo again using a pattern consisting of two quick beats followed by one regular beat. This pattern continued throughout the dance interrupted only by the slow signal-change beats.

THE COMMON DANCE COSTUME

Common dance outfits

(modeled by Pam Johnson Sizemore and Everett Sizemore)

    The only type of costume necessary for this dance would be one's finest Cherokee clothing. One may dress similar to the styles shown above, or in a personally made outfit.

HOW TO DO THE COMMON DANCE

The Common Dance is so named because it is the dance that is performed most often. This dance was witnessed by J.P. Evans in 1835. The dance is also mentioned in the *Howard Payne Papers* in Vol. VI. The Common Dance is done for fun and entertainment.

In the old days, the village chief was usually the one to set the time and place for the dance, which would begin after dark. It was custom for the people to whoop and yell as they came to and from this dance.

A certain beat was sounded on the drum to signal the dancers that the dance was beginning. The priest or leader would then enter the danceground and walk around the dance fire in a counter-clockwise circle. Upon circling one or two times, he would then urge a woman wearing turtle shell leg rattles to join in behind him. The other dancers would then join in behind, with the men going first.

As the leader would chant and stomp his feet to the quick time of the drum, the men would imitate him while the women joined in. There was usually an equal amount of men and women and the females would fall in behind their male partners.

Some people do the stomp step with one foot, while others use both feet.

As the leader dances around with the others following, he performs various movements which the dancers will attempt to mimic. He may clap his hands, raise his arms, turn, twist, or bow. As the dancers imitate him and try to stay in sequence, confusion often occurs, initiating laughter and fun.

As the dance comes to a close, the dancers all join hands. The leader will then lead them in a twisting and winding motion resembling a snake crawling. After this he may suddenly start moving backwards, creating more confusion. As the dancers burst out in laughter, the dance ends and they all leave the danceground whopping and yelling.

There are many stomp dance songs. Some leaders make up the songs as the dance progresses. Most of the songs have a fast tempo and range from high to low in pitch. As the leader chants, the dancers respond to his words with a refrain.

Several stomp dance songs appear in "Journal of Cherokee Studies" Vol. IV, No. 3, Summer 1979, pgs. 136-141.

The counter-clockwise movement of the Common Dance

Dancers trying to imitate the mannerisms of the dance leader in sequence

THE BURIAL DANCE

At one time, the Eastern Cherokees practiced the Burial Dance, but it is now a thing of the past. According to *Cherokee Dance and Drama* by Speck and Broom, pg. 11, "It alleviates the grief of the bereaved family and helps to turn their thoughts again toward the normal affairs of life".

In November of 1792, Chief Dragging Canoe was killed near Nashville, Tennessee. His body was taken to his village, and the people mourned for seven days and nights. This was the Cherokees' traditional mourning period for a chief in those days. Messengers were sent to all the villages to inform the people of his death.

Seven priests from Dragging Canoe's clan came and washed the body in sacred herb medicine, probably willow root tea. They wrapped the body in white handwoven cotton cloth and put his war mantle of thousands of red bird feathers on his body. His red headdress of woven bird feathers was placed on his head The coffin was made of a hollowed out cedar tree. The bottom and sides of it were lined with white and blood red handwoven cotton cloth. The men from his clan dug the grave and lined it with large flat stones.

Then Dragging Canoe was put inside the coffin with a bowl of salt upon his chest, and four large strands of gold cut beads around his neck. His gun and gold-handled hunting knife were placed by his side. The "Death Dance" (which must have been the same as the Burial Dance) and feast took place, after which everyone attending the funeral came by to touch and hold his hands. Next, seven warriors, one from each clan, put boards on the coffin and carried it to the side of a certain mountain for burial.

Dragging Canoe's two widows tore their clothing, throwing them aside, and cut their hair just below their ears. Their hair was then put in a basket and placed on the grave. Neither of the widows could remarry until their hair had re-grown to shoulder length. See *Tell Them They Lie* by Traveller Bird, pgs. 69-70.

At Dragging Canoe's funeral, the Burial Dance was done at the graveside. *Cherokee Dance and Drama*, pg. 11, states that the Burial Dance took place at the home of the deceased, and it lasted seven continuous nights after the death or funeral. Thomas E. Mails mentions in *The Cherokee People*, pg. 77, that the Burial Dance was a "solemn dance" done in the council house while the bereaved and friends of the family were there. However, it is my opinion that this was an additional and separate dance, perhaps the Friendship Dance that William Harlem Gilbert mentions in his book, *The Eastern Cherokees*, pg. 259, to help put the bereaved family in a better mood. This dance was done in the council house, but the Burial Dance would have polluted it.

The Burial Dance of the Cherokee is no longer performed and information is very sketchy concerning the dance. However, the Iroquois were relatives of the Cherokee and it it seems likely that their way of performing the dance was very similar to the Cherokee. Following is a description of this method, as given by Morgan, who wrote *League of the Iroquois*. More information may be found in *North American Indian Burial Customs* by Stephen Powers, pg. 78.

The Burial Dance could last for seven nights during the mourning period. Morgan states that women only, participated in the dance. Singers were close by, and as they sung, the dancers would join in on the chorus of the song. The songs were plaintive and mournful. They were sung as if one were crying, and usually had two syllables that were repeated over and over. The dance was usually requested by family members and would start near dusk or soon after. The spirit of the deceased was believed to linger somewhere in the shadows nearby, and would come to join in the dance. People wailed and shed tears of grief during this dance. They would sway their heads, bending, whirling and quivering their bodies. The only dance steps used were short steps that would slowly move up and down. The music would also be at a slow tempo.

In James Moody's *Myths of the Cherokees*, pg. 253, there is a legend entitled "Daughter of the Sun - the Origin of Death". In this story, the dance was done in a circle. When a lot of dancers are present, there may be an additional outer circle. In this legend, the bereaved mother cries, "My daughter, my daughter". She sheds many tears, keeping her face covered and her head down. Such motions were probably a part of the Burial Dance as well. All legends hold some truth toward reality.

In *The Payne Papers*, Vol. 4, pg. 97, it is mentioned that females wept exceedingly at the death of a loved one. It was a doleful lamentation in which they sang over and over, with only brief pauses, the name of the deceased one, for as long as they could hold their breath. The male relatives held back their grief and did not weep. These men put ashes on their heads and wrapped themselves in worn clothing.

After the burial and during the mourning period, the family and relatives who had come in contact with the deceased around the time of death were considered unclean. The house of the deceased had to be cleansed by sprinkling it with the willow root tea and burning cedar branches, which worked as an incense to freshen the house with the fragrance of the smoke. A lot of the furnishings and food were thrown away, while the remaining personal items of the deceased were taken to the grave to either be burned or left there. The family members then drank some of the willow root tea and washed themselves with it.

Next, the priest took the family members to the creek or river. There, they stood in the water and performed a ritual in which they would face east, turn and face west, and then immerse themselves. This procedure was repeated for a total of seven times. Their old clothing was destroyed or allowed to float downstream, and new clothes were put on as they came out of the river.

At this point, the friends and neighbors of the cleansed bereaved people gave a friendship dance in their honor at the council house. This is the dance that I believe Gilbert was referring to, as opposed to the Burial Dance, which had already been done. Gilbert reported in page 259 of his book, "the enjoyment of the Friendship Dances was so great, that whenever a family had suffered loss of a loved one, the neighbors gave a Friendship Dance to help them forget their sorrow. One of the features of the Friendship Dance was clapping the hands to show joy and happiness".

Further study of Cherokee death and burial rites can be found in *The Cherokee People*, by Thomas E. Mails, pgs. 76-77 and 133.

The dress of this dance and mourning period was quite simple. Some mourners blackened their faces. The men put ashes on their head and wrapped themselves in worn clothing, while the women wore torn clothing. The widow would cut her hair off just below the ears and would not comb it for the duration of the mourning period.

When the friendship Dance was done for the cleansed bereaved family, the family would wear new white deerskin clothing .

THE COAT DANCE

This dance was called ghasule'na in the Cherokee language. It is said that in the old days, men bought their brides with deerskin coats, as payment to the girl's parents. During this dance, the men go through the motions of putting a deerskin coat on their female dance partner. This act shows that he is claiming her as his own. Apparently, this dance was originally done between the bride and bridegroom as a wedding ritual. The "Coat Dance" seems to be the same dance referred to as the "Blanket Dance" in the book, *Tell Them They Lie*, by Traveller Bird, pg. 100.

According to Gilbert in *The Eastern Cherokees*, pg. 263, the gestures of putting a coat on the bride in the Coat Dance are similar to some of the gestures in the Friendship Dance. In the Friendship Dance, male dance partners put their hats on the heads of the female dance partners. At other times, the men will also put their arms on their partners shoulders or around their necks.

When Sequoyah married his new bride, Eli, he gave her a sacred white buffalo robe from the west. She in return, gave him a colored ear of corn to show her willingness to become his wife. On the seventh day, the Blanket Dance and feast was held.

Sequoyah wore the following outfit to his wedding:

1. A white deerskin shirt that reached down to his knees with a fringe along the sleeves and around the bottom. It was also decorated with turquoise and red stone beads across the back and down the front
2. A finger-woven belt made of red and black horse hair
3. White deerskin pants tied at the waist with a drawstring
4. Moccasins dyed brown with walnut smoke
   (see *Tell Them They Lie*, pgs. 99-100)

It is reasonable to assume that Sequoyah's bride was also dressed in a white deerskin dress and moccasins.

Around 1829-30, Sam Houston lived with Chief Jolly in Arkansas Territory. When he married his wife, Tianna, he wore the following outfit:

1. Hair in braids
2. An encirclement of eagle feathers on his head
3. A white deerskin shirt with beadwork on the chest
4. Yellow leggings
5. A blanket over his shoulders
6. Moccasins, of course

NOTE: (See *The Trail of Tears* by Gloria Jahoda, pgs. 51-52. Also *The Raven: A Biography of Sam Houston* by Marquis James, pg. 67) Little else is known about this dance. Most of it has been lost to the past.

COSTUME OF THE ROUND DANCE

The Round Dance required no lavish costumes. The costumes of both the men and women of this dance looked nice but did not have to be of the ceremonial type. Even during the 1930s Cherokee dancers wore their common clothes to most of these social dances. Earlier in Cherokee history they would have worn deerskin clothes at this dance.

Men preferred to wear their breechclouts during most of the dances in the old days. A shirt and leggings could be worn also, but it was the man's choice. He wanted to be as comfortable as possible considering possible weather changes. A man usually wore his eagle feather, or feathers of other types, attached to his scalp-lock.

Other items that he might wear were a necklace, earrings, armbands, sash and garters.

As shown above, the women of this dance can wear their beautiful deerskin dresses and moccasins. Other items would include vermillion at the hairline, earrings, necklaces and bracelets. The lead woman dancer wore terrapin shell leg rattles.

86

HOW TO DO THE ROUND DANCE

The Round Dance, sometimes called the Running Dance was a social dance in which both men and women took part. This dance usually was the last dance done before daylight at the end of a series of dances that lasted all night.

Music for the dance is provided by a drummer who also chants.

To start the dance, the lead woman dancer, wearing leg rattles, is followed by the other women to form a circle moving in a counter-clockwise direction. The women use slow dance steps as the chanter sings four songs or verses (see illustration on previous page).This is the first phase of the dance.

To begin the second phase, the drumbeat changes to a fast beat and the male dancers join the dance circle. The circle is then made of alternating male and female dancers (also previously shown). Soon thereafter, the circle starts making a winding serpent-like motion, resembling a snake crawling on the ground.

As the chant ends and the dance comes to a close, the dancers start shouting, bringing the dance to a final close as they all leave.

In the book, *The Eastern Cherokees*, by Gilbert, pg. 266, it is noted: "The Round Dance finishes off the various night time dances. It is a farewell dance and symbolizes how the people leaving the dances have to go around the mountains on their way home". Also see *Cherokee Dance and Drama*, pg. 68.

THE GREEN CORN DANCE COSTUME

In celebration of their corn crops, the Cherokee had what is called the Green Corn Ceremony. It was held in August of each year at the new moon. Another festival, called the Ripe Corn Ceremony, was held in September.

These festivals went through many changes after contact with the white people. The costumes worn during the dance part of the festival were soon abandoned, probably before the turn of the 19th century. I am primarily interested in these costumes, and the changing of them. In my opinion, if the dances are done without the costumes, the effect is lost and the dance is done in vain.

The festivals were very important, in that the people were forgiven for their sins and crimes of the past year by everyone. It was a time of renewal. Old fires were put out and new fires lit. Houses were cleaned and repainted. All kinds of repairs were done to the village. The holy square was swept and redone. Even the council house was re-adorned. Old pottery and other warn out items were discarded and replaced with new. This was a time of rejoicing, dancing and feasting. It was a time of great thanksgiving!

The older beloved women and men of the tribe usually did this dance, but in later years as white contact increased, the rules were relaxed and more people of lower status became dancers.

The beloved women of this dance wore white deerskin wrap-around skirts. Since it was the custom in the southeast, a top for these skirts were probably not worn, due to the warm weather. By 1803, Schwarze, a Moravian , witnessed female dancers in the Green Corn Dance wearing their best clothes. No doubt, these were complete dresses due to the contact with the white people. To do the dance in modern times, a full dress would be quite necessary.

The beloved women wore their hair up on the head in a top-knot, held in place with a bone comb and shell hair pins. Necklaces of white shell beads were also part of the costume, as well as earrings. Tortoise shell rattles were fastened to a piece of white deerskin and worn tied to the right lower leg below the knee. White moccasins or short boots were worn by these women. Also in the right hand of each woman, a green tree branch was carried, obtained from the arbor at the holy square grounds, which was put there for that purpose.

It should be noted, the costumes for the dance were always white, since this was a sacred and holy time of the year.

For more study on this topic, you may wish to study the writings of such men as Adair, Evans, Hicks, Hudson and Mails. All of these men wrote about the Cherokee and the dances. *Cherokee Dance and Drama* by Speck and Broom, is also a great source to study.

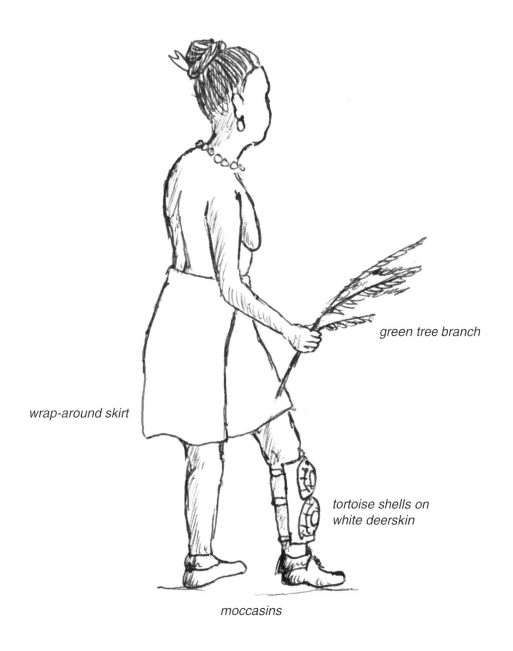

green tree branch

wrap-around skirt

tortoise shells on
white deerskin

moccasins

Pictured, is an early form of the costume worn by the lead woman dancer during the Green Corn Dance. Later, after contact with the white people, a complete dress was worn.

The male dancers, or beloved men, who did this dance before 1800, greased their hair with bear grease. They wore white heron or swan fluffs in a patch on the top or crown of their heads. White turkey fluffs can be used in our time as a substitute.

A headband made of the skin of the swan or heron was worn. This band was doubled and the fluffy feathers were left on both sides of the headband. In our time white rabbit fur can be used. Also a band of soft leather, or cloth with white fluffs glued or sewn around it, can be used.

A white sleeveless deerskin shirt was worn. This shirt reached only to the waist. In our time, if white leather is not available, white blanket cloth can be substituted. The men also wore a deerskin belt and breechclout, also easily substituted with white blanket cloth. Garters were also a part of the costume, which can be optional. White moccasins were also worn. The center-seam type would be the kind to make for this costume. One other item the men wore to show their status was a shell gorget necklace.

In their right hands, the men carried green tree branches from the arbor at the square grounds. In the left hand, they carried a cane wand. This dance wand had white swan or heron fluffs attached to the end of it. After the dance was greatly altered, after much contact with the white people, some of the men began carrying guns, pistols, and clubs. This was probably due to the part of the dance resembling a mock battle. Speck and Broom in their book, *Cherokee Dance and Drama,* mention dancers carrying guns. Before this period, the male dancers probably carried war clubs, spears, bows and arrows. And *even* before that, the dancers probably carried the dance wands to simulate weapons in some way.

It is my understanding at one time during peace-time rituals and ceremonies, weapons of war were not permitted on sacred ground or in the council house. It would be far better if men, even of today, carried cane wands of peace instead of guns as a symbol that all malice was forgiven of one's brother.

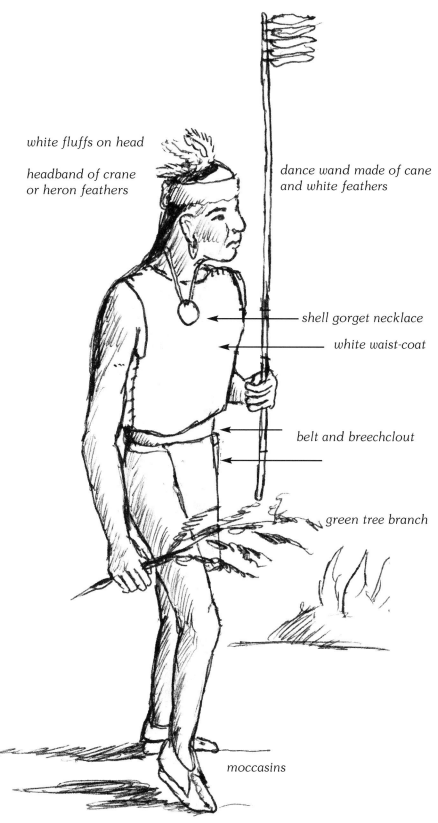

white fluffs on head

headband of crane
or heron feathers

dance wand made of cane
and white feathers

shell gorget necklace

white waist-coat

belt and breechclout

green tree branch

moccasins

This sketch depicts the dance costume of a
Beloved Man dancer of the Green Corn Dance.

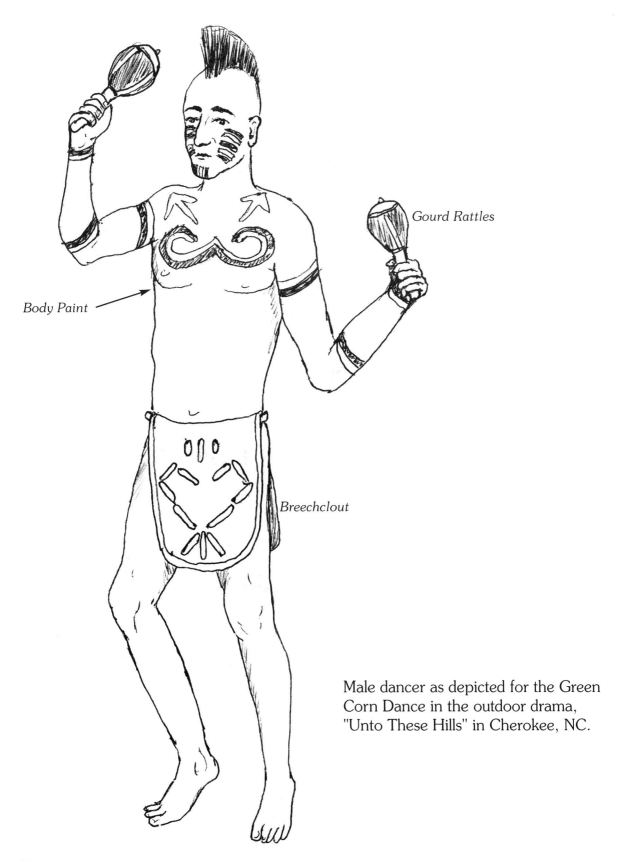

Gourd Rattles

Body Paint

Breechclout

Male dancer as depicted for the Green Corn Dance in the outdoor drama, "Unto These Hills" in Cherokee, NC.

small feathers in hair

bra

A bundle or
green tree
branch was
carried in her
hand

wrap-around skirt

A female dancer
of the Green Corn
Dance is depicted
in this sketch
wearing a wrap-
around skirt of white
deerskin. To adapt to
a modern audience, a leather
bra or top should be added. In
the old days, women did not
wear tops during the warm
months around the home and
at certain dances. In our time,
a full white deerskin dress can
be worn.

HOW TO DO THE GREEN CORN DANCES

At one time, the Cherokee celebrated "The New Green Corn Festival" in August and "The Ripe Green Corn Festival" in September. However, by 1835, the only remnants of these occasions became known as the Green Corn Dance. This was a time of thanksgiving for a good harvest. For greater details on these dances and the festivals connected with them, I recommend the writings of William H. Gilbert, *The Eastern Cherokees* and *The John Howard Payne Papers*, Vol.1, pgs. 79-88. Another good source on this subject is *Cherokee Dance and Drama* by Speck and Broom, pgs. 45-54.

By 1803, a man by the name of Schwarze witnessed the Green Corn Dance being done in August. The Green Corn Dances described by Speck and Broom closely correspond with what Schwarze witnessed. He stated that he saw five different dances being performed.

Gilbert describes the first of these dances starting in the morning with the men carrying and firing their guns. This dance was done off and on throughout the day. Some refer to this as the Gun Dance. Then he mentions three other dances taking place during the afternoon hours, still all part of the Green Corn Dance:

1. The Grandmother's Dance - done by the men only, imitating the preparation of corn meal as done by the women and grandmothers.
2. The Meal Dance - done by women only, imitating the preparation of corn meal.
3. The Trail-Making Dance - done by the men and women imitating the preparation of the trail for the next year.

These dances, which lasted all day, were considered by the Cherokee to be an important celebration of a good harvest.

After the dancing, the people had a feast. Many people of today have a traditional Thanksgiving meal, but seldom have a prayer of gratefulness to thank the Great Man Above. Perhaps the ancient Cherokee were truly children of God.

Now to look further into how these Green Corn Dances were performed.

The first dance is done in the morning, and then several times again throughout the day. It is usually done by 10 or more men. They had a separate dance ground that was a certain distance from the "square grounds", perhaps to one side of the council house. The male dancers carry their rifles and pistols as the leader or priest carries a gourd rattle in his right hand. Before the Cherokee obtained guns for this dance, it is claimed that charcoal was spat upon and then placed upon a white rock and struck with a club to produce a loud explosion imitating thunder.

94

To begin this morning dance, the leader with the gourd rattle and the other male dancers form a single file circle moving counter-clockwise. As the priest chants and gives certain signals in his song, he will then suddenly and rapidly shake his rattle. As he does this, the dancer behind him fires his gun. Then the next man fires his gun, as do all the other dancers in succession. The last man fires his gun twice. Shots are then fired each time the leader gives the signal with his song and rattle. These sounds symbolized thunder which meant rain for good crops.

In the next phase of the men's dance, the dancers form two single file rows side by side, resembling a platoon of soldiers. The priest, still at the head of the line, then leads them toward the square grounds. As they enter, they march all the way across the grounds, then the priest will give another signal with his song or rattle. He will say "Asi hu ya ka" which tells the dancers to quickly turn and go back across the square. In some cases, the dancers will march all around the square and then enter it crossing back and forth until they have trampled the entire square. "Asi hu ya ka" was probably said each time the dancers were to turn and cross the square again. Sometimes the leader might suddenly turn toward them and bow down to the earth. The dancers also bow with him. After trampling the square grounds, the dancers march back to their dance ground where they would rest and eat. The dance is repeated several times during the morning hours.

The next dance was the Meal Dance, also called the "Women's Dance". It is performed by women only, probably the Beloved Women. According to Gilbert, pg. 265, the Meal Dance portrayed the women preparing corn meal. This dance was done in the afternoon in the square grounds.

In the square, the women form a single file line standing side by side. The leader, wearing tortoise shell leg rattles, stood on the far left of the line. The women had a male chanter who stood a few feet away near the center of the square ground using a gourd rattle. The drummer sits on a stool at the center of the dance ground, under the arbor made of a pole with green branches fastened to the top.

To begin the Meal Dance, the drum beats slowly as the women slowly dance toward the chanter. As they near the chanter, they quickly turn around and return to their first position. The drummer switches to a fast rhythm for this retreating movement . This process of slowly dancing forward and quickly retreating may be repeated several times. Then the woman on the left of the line leads the others in a counter-clockwise circle for one complete rotation around the inside of the square grounds. The male chanter remains in the center of this circle. After this, the women return to their original side-by-side single file line and join hands

The Meal Dance may be repeated over and over as desired.

At some point as the women of the Meal Dance are moving in their circle, the men leave their dance ground and form a new dance as follows:

The men form two single file side by side rows. Their priest, using the gourd rattle, leads them in a shuffling trot dance step to the square where the women are. As they enter, the women are in the circular movement of the Meal Dance. The men then form a clockwise moving circle around the women and close in closer to them. Next, the men's circle joins the women's circle creating one large counter-clockwise moving dance circle. Partners have now been formed in a male to female alternating order. This symbolizes the fertility of the corn.

The chanter and drummer for the women now retire their services for a while and the men's priest, using his gourd rattle, leads the dance circle for the remainder of the dance. After this dance, the people feast on the ripe corn and other foods.

Before the sun goes down and the people have eaten their fill, another dance is performed:

As before, the men go to their dance ground and repeat their dance as the women repeat their Meal Dance at the square ground, this time using only the gourd rattle and the tortoise shell leg rattles. As the men join with the women again, this time they start a zig-zagging movement with the circle which is known as the Trail Dance, and is done to prepare the path for the next year. This dance is continued until the sun goes down, after which the night is filled with more feasting, social dances, animal dances, etc. The first of these dances is the Friendship Dance. The Corn Dance is also done before daylight, and finally, the Round Dance is done to finish the night of dances before the people go back to their homes. The only dances not done during this festive night are the Eagle, Booger and Bear dances.

The following is the Green Corn Dance Song, as it was handed down through generations to men like Will West Long and Walker Calhoun of North Carolina:

"Ti toh hi yah
Ti toh hi yah
Ti toh hi yah
Ti toh hi yah

Ha ni nay gi Ha ni nay gi
Ha ni nay gi Ha ni nay gi
Ha ni nay gi Ha ni nay gi
Ha ni nay gi Ha ni nay gi"

THE CORN DANCE COSTUME

It is believed at one time the Corn Dance was a part of a great celebration, perhaps the "First New Moon of Spring Festival".

Usually, the costumes of such sacred festivals were made of white deerskin to represent something holy and sacred. In the 1930's, when a lot of the Cherokee dances were being recorded, the Corn Dance was done right after the Friendship Dance during the night time dances. Back in old times, people who saw the Friendship Dance reported that the costumes were white deerskin. This suggests that the Corn Dance costumes were also white because the color stands for peace, friendship, holiness, purity, etc.

When making costumes for male and female dancers of the Corn Dance, use basic clothing structures as seen elsewhere in this book, or consult my other book, *How to Make Cherokee Clothing*.

If the weather is cool during the time of this dance, the men can wear white long sleeved deerskin hunting shirts, breechclouts, leggings and moccasins, plus their jewelry.

Women may wear their white deerskin dresses and moccasins with their jewelry. The lead female dancer also wears tortoise shell leg rattles.

Blanket cloth can be used as a substitute for deerskin when making the costumes.

Pictured is a white ceremonial dress made of blanket cloth.

HOW TO DO THE CORN DANCE

The Corn Dance expressed thankfulness for good crops that the Cherokee hoped for at the end of the growing season. It also mimicked the planting of the corn seed, according to Gilbert, pg. 263, in *The Eastern Cherokees*.

This dance was done in the early spring on the night before planting seeds. By the 1930's, the dance was done at any time, usually after midnight or toward the morning hours, just after the Friendship Dance. It became a part of the nighttime dances during the Green Corn Dance Festival in August.

At one time, the Great High Priest or Uku and his seven counselors decided on the time when all of the people were to plant their corn. This was decided at the National Capitol and was done so that the corn would be ready at the right time for the New Green Corn Festival in August and the Ripe Corn Festival in September.

The fields were prepared before the Corn Dance and the seeds planted after the dance. According to James Mooney in his book, *History, Myths and Sacred Formulas of the Cherokees*, pg. 435, splinters from a tree that was struck by lightning were, at one time, buried throughout the field. This in some way symbolized the Cherokee myth of the Thunder Boys. The boys killed their mother, known as "Agawela", or Corn Mother. She was also called "the old woman". They dragged her body twice around the corn field scattering her blood throughout the field causing corn to sprout from the ground. See Mooney, pg. 422, for the formula using the splinters.

Women usually planted the seeds and the men covered them with their hoes. At one time, seven seeds were planted in each hill.

Another good reference in study of the Corn Dance is the story of "Kanati and Selu - the origin of game and corn" found in *History, Myths and Sacred Formulas of the Cherokees, pgs. 242-249*. Following is a description of the Corn Dance:

A corn mortar is set up in the center of the danceground. A priest using a gourd rattle is at one side of the dance circle. The lead woman is wearing tortoise shell leg rattles.

A counter-clockwise circle is formed alternating men and women as partners doing the trot dance step. As the dancers go around, they pretend to be dipping and pouring corn or meal into a basket held by their left hand. Actual baskets can be used in this dance to make it more realistic. Gestures of this kind represented a plentiful crop.

As the song changes, the women separate from the circle and move to the inside forming their own circle around the corn mortar and facing outward toward the men. The women then dance sideways led by the woman with the tortoise shell leg rattles. The men also dance in this way facing in toward the women. Both circles continue around two or three complete rotations as the dancers resume the hand motions of dipping and pouring corn or meal into a basket.

Next, the men and women switch positions. The male dancers move to the inside to form a circle and the women form the outer circle facing them. They dance around two or three more times using the same gestures.

In the final phase of the dance, the men and women return to their original positions, forming one big circle. A more detailed account of this dance can be found in Speck and Broom's *Cherokee Dance and Drama*, pgs. 77-79.

The Corn Dance Song has been passed down through the generations as well. It goes as follows:
"Ho we ye lo ye Ye go wa lu ye Ho we lo ye Hey go way nu ye Ho we ne yah"
(chanted three times)
"Ho we ye lo ye Hey go way lo ye"
(chanted three times)

As the corn sprouted out in each hill of the rows, it was not thinned out. When they worked the corn fields for the first time, a short ritual followed. The priest or owner of the corn field went to each of the four corners of the field and he would weep and cry out loudly. Some believe that this ritual was done to cry for the death of "Agawala the Corn Mother". As the legend goes, her sons thought she was a witch. They saw her holding a basket at her stomach, and as she rubbed her belly, corn filled the basket. Before they killed her, she told them to drag her body around the field seven times. The sons disobeyed her and dragged her body only twice. For this reason, the Cherokee only hoed their corn twice. See Mooney's *History, Myths and Sacred Formulas of the Cherokees*, pg. 245.

After the corn was worked or hoed for the last time, the owner of the field would build a small hut or enclosure in the middle of the field. There he and the priest of the village sat, never raising their heads. The owner kept quiet while the priest smoked sacred tobacco in his pipe and shook a rattle. The priest then scattered grains of corn seeds and sung songs to the Corn Mother (or "Old Woman"). Sometimes the owner bought the songs and rituals from the town priest and performed the rituals himself. See Mooney again, pg. 423.

As the priest and the owner sat under the hut, if they heard the blades of corn making a rustling sound, they knew the Corn Mother was in the field bringing in the true corn. When the priest finished his songs, they raised their heads. But as they looked, the Corn Mother had already come and gone.

This ritual was done for four consecutive nights. No one was allowed to go into the field for the following seven nights after the ritual was done. The priest then went into the field to inspect his progress. If the rituals had been done well, he would find, as he observed the stalks of corn, young ears of corn blessed by the Corn Mother.

Also, in the old days, the owners of the fields would build a corn crib or storehouse in the middle of the field. Unlike the hut, the structure was built high upon poles to keep the animals out. It had a bark covered cone-shaped roof. This corn crib had only one door. See Mooney, pgs. 244 and 433.

The owner always kept a clean path from his house to the field of corn. This custom showed that he cared for the well-being of the corn, so it wouldn't feel neglected and wander off.

If one finds it difficult to understand the meanings of some dances, it is helpful to study the myths of the Cherokee as they relate to a particular dance.

Seven ears of corn from last years crop were always put carefully aside in order to attract the corn until the new crop was ripe and it was time for the harvesting of the crop later in the year. Then these seven ears were eaten with the new corn. See Mooney, pg. 423.

There is more interesting information in Gilbert's *The Eastern Cherokees* on page 327. In discussing the "First New Moon of Spring Festival", he states, "This was celebrated when the grass began to grow and had no special title. The present day Corn Dance called adan wisi, or 'they are going to plant' may be descended from this rite of March". Could the Corn Dance be "the sacred night dance that he mentions on pg. 329? It seems reasonable to believe that a great festival went along with the Corn Dance, the same as in the months of August and September with the New Green Corn and the Ripe Corn Festivals. Also see *Tribes That Slumber*, pgs. 176-180.

William Gilbert reported, on page 263 of *The Eastern Cherokees*, that "The men in the Corn Dance cup up their hands and pretend to pour grains of corn into the aprons of the female dancers."

Next, the women go through the motions of giving the corn to the male dancers. Both male and female dancers use various other arm movements between the sexes.

It is believed the "Yon ton wi sas" mentioned by James Mooney in *History, Myths and Sacred Formulas of the Cherokees*, pgs. 365-367, is the same as the Corn Dance.

Costume For The Beginning Dance

If this dance is done to start off a series of informal dances, such as social and fun dances of minor importance, then the men and women can wear their tan colored outfits.

When the Beginning Dance is connected to a series of religious or sacred dances, then white outfits should be worn. Appropriate times for these white outfits would be during the Green Corn Dances, festivals and other important occasions.

It should be noted that no set standard or elaborate costume is required for this dance.

woman's white outfit
(modeled by Ellen Webb)

tan-colored man's outfit
(modeled by Eddie Mafnas)

HOW TO DO THE BEGINNING DANCE

When there is to be a series of dances such as the social and fun dances, the Beginning Dance should be the first of these dances performed. It starts the festivities.

The purpose of the Beginning Dance is to help get the dance partners more acquainted with each other and to help the people feel at ease and show hospitality to one another. Or in other words, it "breaks the ice".

The drummer for this dance sits off to one side. The leader for the dance carries a gourd rattle and does the chanting. The woman who follows the leader or priest in the dance circle wears tortoise shell leg rattles. In the old days, this lead woman would have been one of the Clan Mothers or better known as a "Beloved Woman". Today, any talented woman who can do the dance is welcomed to do so.

In the first phase of the dance, a counter-clockwise circle is formed of alternating male and female dancers. The man with the gourd is followed by the woman with the leg rattles. Everyone faces forward in the circle and dances a complete round.

Then, the male dancers turn and face their partners and continue dancing backwards for one complete round. The men may stretch their arms toward the women and hold hands with them or place their hands on their partners shoulders. This part of the dance is useful for husbands and wives, boy and girl friends, or other friends to show affection and friendship for one another.

Next, the male dancers take the hands of the women and swing them around reversing positions. Now the women are facing the men and dancing backwards for one round.

Finally, the dancers return to their original positions and dance another round or repeat the whole dance again.

For more details on this dance, see *Cherokee Dance and Drama* by Speck and Broom, pg. 65, and *Cherokee Perspective* edited by Laurence French and Jim Hornbuckle, pg. 131.

THE EAGLE DANCE COSTUME

costume of the lead dancer of the Eagle Dance

(model: Roger Ramey)

The Eagle Dance is one of the most colorful of all the Cherokee dance costumes. Each time I see the dance performed in the outdoor drama, "Unto These Hills", in Cherokee, North Carolina, I am always amazed at the beauty of the costumes. The costume I will describe is largely based on what I have observed from the drama.

In studying prehistoric era engravings on shell gorgets of the Southeastern mound builders, possible images of the early Eagle Dance costumes are found. A good book on this subject is "Sun Circles and Human Hands" by Emma Lila Fundaburk and Mary Douglas Foreman.

copper ornaments on headdress

necklace of shell beads and large shell

shell arm and wrist bands

painted designs on body

shell bead belt

tail of feathers

cape made of feathers

leg and ankle bands of shell beads

In this sketch, I have depicted an eagle dancer as he may have looked during the Mound Builder era of the Southeast. A lot of the Cherokee culture seems to have been derived during this era.

The spotted eagle engravings on shell gorgets of prehistoric times show men dressed in costumes consisting of headdresses, feathers in the hair, painted designs on the face and body, necklaces, and bands of shell beads around the arms, wrists and legs. They wore sashes, belts, breech-clouts, tails of feathers, masks and capes or wings made of feathers.

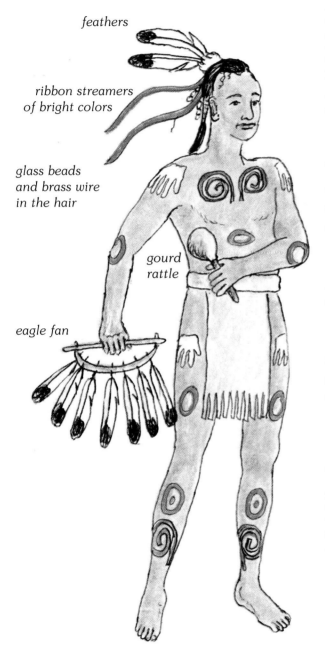

feathers

ribbon streamers
of bright colors

glass beads
and brass wire
in the hair

gourd
rattle

eagle fan

In historic times, many of the dance items of the Eagle Dance Costume were no longer used as in former times. Below is my sketch based on the description of Alexander Cummings upon his visit to the Cherokees in 1730.

The dancer's body was painted in various designs, such as red circles and blue curly cues. White handprints were also painted on the dancers body.

A breechclout and belt would have been worn.

Since the body of the dancer had all these designs, a shirt, leggings and moccasins were not feasible.

Wings as part of the dance costume were not mentioned by Alexander Cummings. It stands to reason that the Cherokee had already discontinued the use of many of their dance costume items by this time.

105

WANDS FOR THE EAGLE DANCE

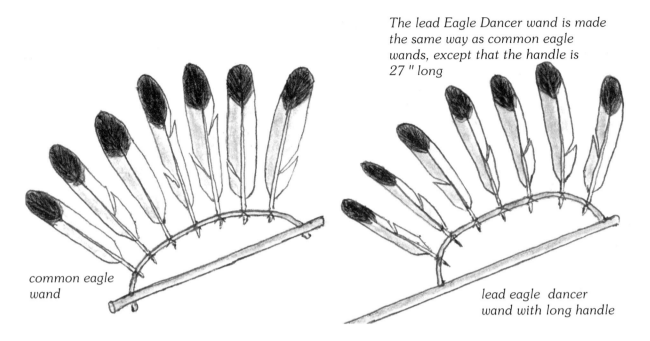

The lead Eagle Dancer wand is made the same way as common eagle wands, except that the handle is 27 " long

common eagle wand

lead eagle dancer wand with long handle

The thing that is most captivating about the Eagle Dance is the Eagle wand. Each male dancer carries a wand in his right hand and a gourd rattle in the left hand. The female dancers carry eagle wands in both hands. In the outdoor drama, "Unto These Hills", the male dancers are portrayed carrying wands in both hands which creates a more dramatic effect.

Imitation eagle feathers are used today since it is illegal to kill a bald eagle. These can be obtained from a Tandy Leather Craft Store. The left hand wand requires feathers that bend to the left and the right wand requires feathers that bend to the right.

It is said that the wands used to be made with five feathers per wand, but I prefer to use seven, since it is a sacred number to the Cherokee.

In making the fan, or wand, the proper handle and arch wood should be made from a Sourwood tree. Sourwood is sacred and is used to prevent contamination when handling eagle feathers. It also wards off offense of the eagle for using it's feathers, according to Cherokee belief. An alternative would be to make it from a thin piece of pliable wood.

The following method of making the wand is my own self-taught version. Other slightly varying methods are used to produce the same type of wand. The instructions given are for the common eagle dancer's wand and the lead eagle dancer's wand. The only difference being the length of the handle. Several sets of the wands are needed according to the number of dancers.

106

As shown below, the handle portion is 15" long and about $^5/_8$" thick. Two holes are drilled in the handle 2" from each end, using a $^1/_4$" drill bit. Scrape away all of the bark from the handle. Next, scrape the bark from a small limb from the Sourwood tree. The limb will need to be about 18" long and $^1/_4$" thick.

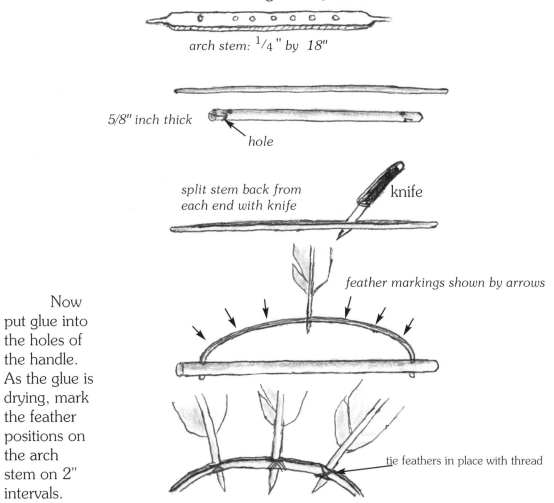

arch stem: $^1/_4$" by 18"

5/8" inch thick

hole

split stem back from each end with knife   knife

feather markings shown by arrows

Now put glue into the holes of the handle. As the glue is drying, mark the feather positions on the arch stem on 2" intervals.

tie feathers in place with thread

Use a knife to split the arch stem down the middle after it has been inserted into the holes of the handle as shown. The arch limb will have to be bent slightly, using great care not to break it.

Flatten the quill ends of each feather with your teeth. Insert the flattened quill tips of the feathers through the split of the arch stem at each of the markings as shown. The split may have to be slightly spread apart to get the feather through. Next, use strong thread or twine to make an X tying to hold each feather in position, then put a little bit of glue around the stems where they are inserted.

Another method of holding the feathers in place is to use an arch made of flattened piece of pliable wood as in the sketch at the top of the page. It is attached to the handle and holes are drilled for each feather.

HOW TO MAKE EAGLE WINGS

A back view of the eagle wings

One of the easiest type of wings to make for the lead dancer of the Eagle Dance is pictured. Throughout the history of the "Unto These Hills" drama, several different styles of wings have been used. Although the wings weren't always a vital part of the costume, the wand and gourd rattle have always been established items of the dance.

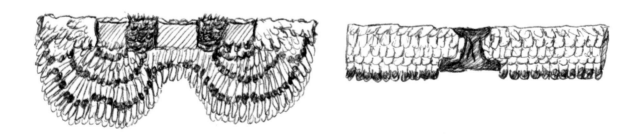

The two sketches above show a couple of more recent wing construction styles. Black and white feathers are used.

FRONT VIEW OF WINGS

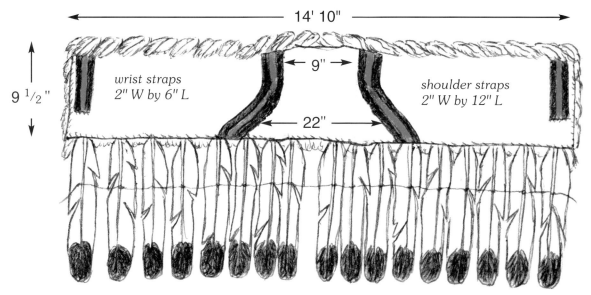

The wings shown above depict a set of eagle wings using doubled white blanket cloth for the base. White fluffs are sewn in rows on the backside of the wings. 12" imitation eagle feathers are attached along the bottom. The wrist and shoulder straps are made of black and red cloth.

To make the base for the wings, cut a long piece of white blanket cloth large enough to be doubled, using the above measurements. You can get the length by having someone to measure your size from wrist to wrist as you stretch out your arms.

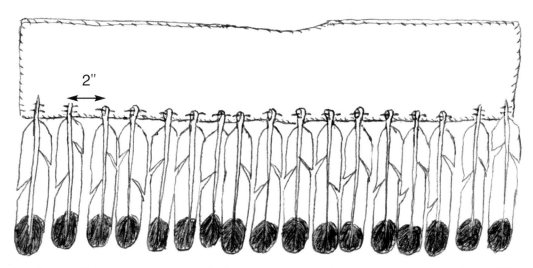

It will take 26 feathers to reach from one end of the wings to the other. These feathers are spaced 2" apart. Feathers of this type can be purchased. (see the "sources" page in the back of the book) Half of these eagle feathers should be left-bend, and the other half to the right.

109

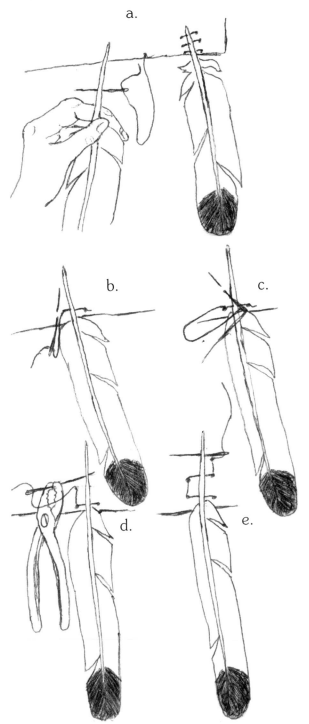

a.

b.

c.

d.

e.

First, attach thread to the material as shown. Use pliers to push the needle through the side of the feather (a).

Attach the thread on left side of quill to the cloth (b).

Go up about 1" on the left of the quill and attach the thread to the cloth. Then push the needle back through the quill. Attach the thread to cloth on the right side of the quill (c,d,e).

Now go up another 1" and attach the thread as shown. Push the needle through the quill to the left and attach the thread to the material (e).

Repeat the process to the next stationary feather. Once those two feathers are attached to the end of the wing, cross over to the opposite end of wing base and attach two more stationary feathers. (refer to the illustration on the prior page).

The other feathers which are attached along the bottom of the cloth base are looped on the ends. When the wings are finished, the looped end feathers will have movement as the lead dancer wears the wings during the dance.

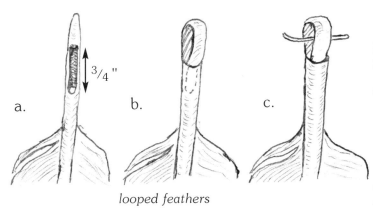

looped feathers

Use a single edge razor blade or a utility knife to cut out a $^3/_4$" gap on the back side of the quill (a).

Squirt a little glue up inside of the quill. Flatten the end of the quill, turning it backward into the quill opening (b).

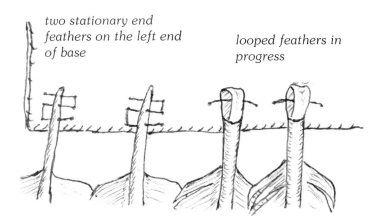

two stationary end feathers on the left end of base

looped feathers in progress

Let the glue dry for a few minutes per feather. Then lace or string each looped feather into position on the cloth base (c).

Near the middle half of the wing base, leave out a feather as a separation point of the left and right wing. Once all of these long imitation feathers of the eagle have been sewn in place, use a needle and thread, stitching each eagle feather together (see prior sketch of "front view of wings").

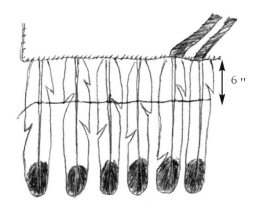

lacing extends 6 inches down the quill

The sketch below shows how feathers are laced together, much as the feathers of a warbonnet are done.

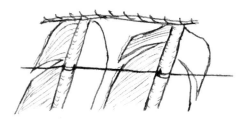

close-up of feather lacing

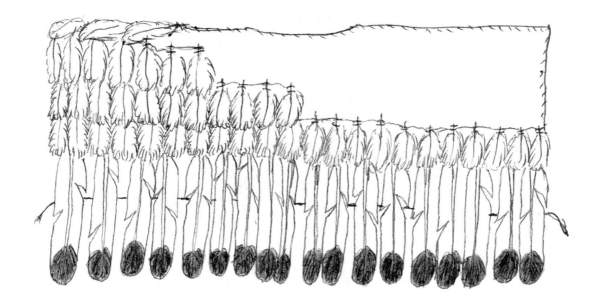

The sketch above shows how 5" to 6" white turkey fluffs can be sewn or glued on the backside of the wing base. Fluffs are attached in horizontal over-lapping rows, starting at the bottom of the wing base, to the top.

In sewing the fluffs onto the base, a needle and thread are inserted through the sides of the fluffs, attaching each fluff to the cloth.

*sewing a fluff
to the base*

The last row or two of fluffs at the top of the wing base will run crosswise to cover up the tips of the preceding row as shown.

White fluffs can be sewn or glued onto the front side of the wing base. The wings I have made have fluffs only on the back.

Again, there are other styles of wings which can be made with slightly varying shapes.

It will take two or three days of steady work to make the wings, according to the given instructions. One will require a lot of patience, as the thread will at times break or get entangled with the fluffs. Other minor problems may also occur, but steady persistence with the project will produce a beautiful set of wings for the lead eagle dancer of the Eagle Dance.

FEATHERS IN THE HAIR
AS PART OF THE EAGLE DANCE COSTUME

The first time I saw the Eagle Dance was at the "Unto These Hills" drama in North Carolina. The costumes were outstanding, but I noticed that they wore no feathers in their hair.

Both Sir Alexander Cummings in 1730, and J.P. Evans in 1835, observed Cherokee Eagle dancers wearing feathers in their hair. Also, during the 1830s, Catlin, a well known painter of the period, portrayed a group of Choctaw Eagle Dancers with feathers on their heads along with glass beads, ribbon streamers and brass wire.

It is my opinion, based on these observations along with others made during the 18th and 19th centuries in the Southeast, that the feathers, as decorations in the hair, were an accepted part of the Eagle Dance costume. Also, I do not think that the male dancers, who were also warriors, would have failed to wear their earned, honorable eagle feather, which was always worn with pride.

Therefore, from these early observations, we can deduce that feathers were worn in the scalplock during the Eagle Dance

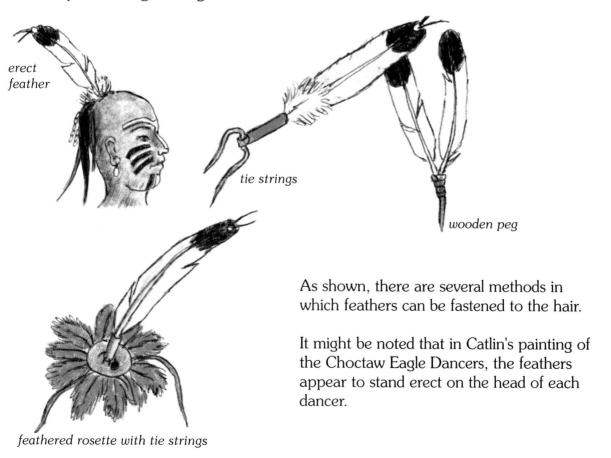

erect feather

tie strings

wooden peg

feathered rosette with tie strings

As shown, there are several methods in which feathers can be fastened to the hair.

It might be noted that in Catlin's painting of the Choctaw Eagle Dancers, the feathers appear to stand erect on the head of each dancer.

HOW TO MAKE A FEATHER ORNAMENT FOR A MAN'S HAIR

An eagle feather standing up on the male dancer's head seems to be the traditional way for an eagle dancer to wear his feather, assuming that the Catlin painting illustrates the typical tradition for most Southeastern tribes.

FEATHERED ROSETTE WITH EAGLE FEATHER

 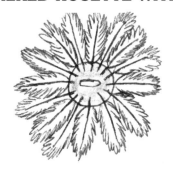

First, cut a cloth or leather disk the size shown and make two holes in the disk to insert a leather tie string through.

Then glue white fluffs or another desired color on to the disk to make a rosette, as shown.

Now glue another 2" disk on top of the feathered rosette. A sketch of the completed rosette is on the previous page.

Cut a piece of cane or bone 1 $\frac{1}{2}$" long. A chicken or turkey leg bone can be cut with a hack-saw and used to make the tube, if river cane isn't used.

Use a small drill bit to bore the holes at the base of the tube. These holes are made so that the tube can later be attached to the center of the rosette with a needle and thread. Next, clip off the end of the feather at the quill point and then slip on the cane or bone tube as shown. Then push a small piece of cork up into the quill. Glue may be used to hold the cork in place. Cut a tie string 3" long and fold it in the middle, pushing a tack or stick pin through the middle and into the quill end of the feather as shown. Attach the ends of the tie strings through the holes punched in the rosette near the center of the disk. Pulling the slack out, tie the ends of the leather string together on the other side of the disk or rosette. Now slide the cane tube back down the quill to the rosette using a needle and thread to attach the cane tube to the disk. Horse hair can be glued to the feather and a very small white fluff, as seen in the sketch on the preceding page.

The two long tie strings are used to tie the rosette with the feather to the hair on the crown of the dancer's head. In the older times, a hole was made in the rosette base so that a braided portion of the scalp-lock could be pulled through the hole. Then a wooden peg was pushed through the braid to hold the rosette onto the scalp-lock.

PREPARING THE SINGLE EAGLE FEATHER

strip of leather

opening

Fold and glue a $^1/_4$" wide strip of leather over the end of the feather

2"

1"

Tied to hair by tie strings

Glue and wrap a red piece of cloth around the end of the feather, sewing the seam of the cloth together on the backside.

Cut a tie string about 8" long by $^1/_4$' wide. Insert this string through the loop on the end of the feather. The string is used to tie the feather to the hair.

This method of attaching the feather allows it to be on an angle in the scalp as it is worn. The feather will also move with the wind.

This is the most simple way to tie a feather to the hair - using tie strings.

Another method is to attach a feather to a wooden peg, as in the prior illustration.

THE LEAD EAGLE DANCER'S BREECHCLOUT

The sketch above shows the front flap of the lead Eagle Dancer's breechclout. I made this using the patchwork method. The ideal piece of material is red flannel cut to the dimensions shown below.

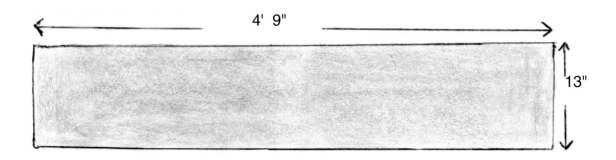

Draw the designs on the red cloth using a pencil and then cut a piece of black cloth the shape of the black design, allowing $^1/_4$ " extra in the material for hemming the design all the way around while turning the edges under.

The white strips of cloth used to form the lightning design is 3" long by 2 $^1/_2$" wide. Place these strips of white cloth where they belong as shown below. Use stick pins to hold the pieces of cloth in place. As the edges of the white pieces are turned under, use a whip-stitch to hold them in place.

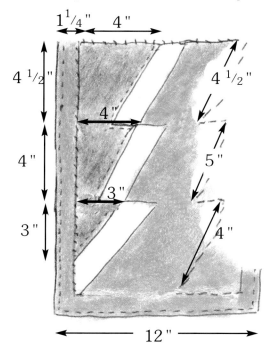

The sketch to the left shows the measurements of my breech-clout.

Your own measurements may differ, but use your own judgement in sizing the designs.

Further details on making a breechclout can be found in my book, *How to Make Cherokee Clothing*, pages 84-89.

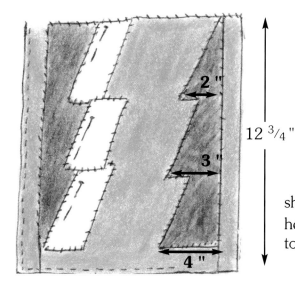

Cut a piece of black cloth like the one shown, allowing $^1/_4$ " extra for the hemming, when the edges are turned under to be whip-stitched.

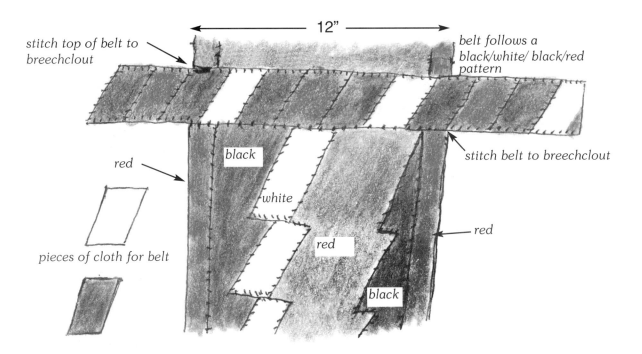

stitch top of belt to breechclout

12"

belt follows a black/white/ black/red pattern

red

black

pieces of cloth for belt

white

stitch belt to breechclout

red

red

black

To make the belt for the breechclout, use red flannel to make a belt 3" wide by 42 inches long. The belt needs to be made two or more layers thick so that it will hold it's shape when worn.

Cut out several black squares 4 $\frac{1}{2}$ " by 3 $\frac{1}{2}$ ". Also cut out several white pieces of cloth to the same dimensions. Next, sew the squares of cloth onto the belt like the pattern in the illustration above. These squares of cloth are laid on the red belt background at an angle, as shown. When sewing the squares of cloth in place, be sure to turn each edge of the square under, as you use an over-cast or whip-stitch.

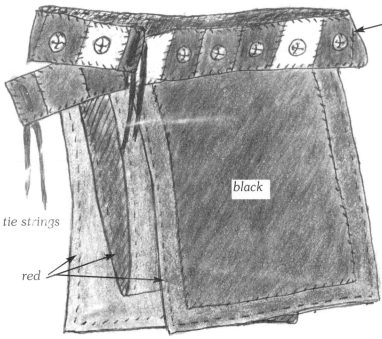

small bells are sewn onto the belt

black

tie strings

red

Sew a large piece of cloth on what will be the back-flap of the breechclout, as shown.

After the front flap has been aligned to the belt and sewn into place, align the back flap as shown. You may have to model the breechclout while getting it to fit.

118

THE COMMON EAGLE DANCER'S BREECHCLOUT

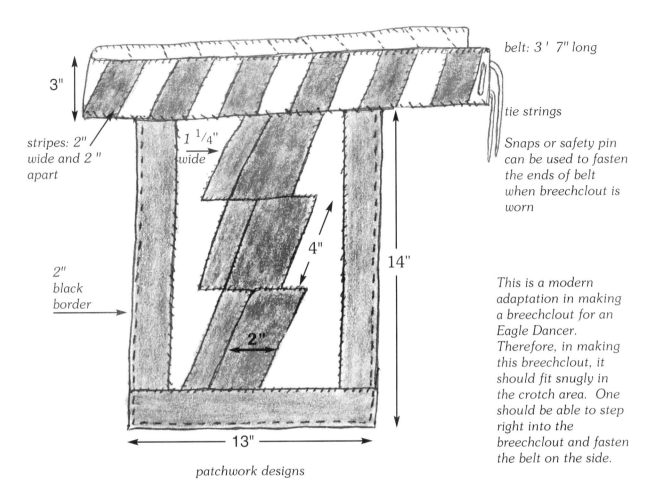

belt: 3 ' 7" long

3"

tie strings

stripes: 2" wide and 2 " apart

Snaps or safety pin can be used to fasten the ends of belt when breechclout is worn

1 ¼" wide

4"

14"

2" black border

2"

This is a modern adaptation in making a breechclout for an Eagle Dancer. Therefore, in making this breechclout, it should fit snugly in the crotch area. One should be able to step right into the breechclout and fasten the belt on the side.

13"

patchwork designs

The breechclout above is made of white material 13" wide by 4' and 6" long. These measurements can vary according to the dancer's size. A strip of 6" wide black material is sewn around the sides and ends of the white material. Hem the black material until the stripe is reduced down to 2" on the front and back side of the breechclout.

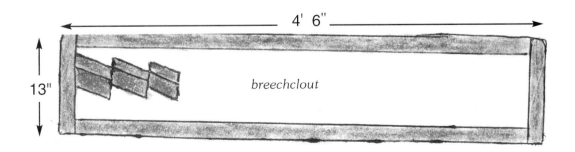

4' 6"

13"

breechclout

With a pencil, mark 2-inches back from the edge of one side of the breechclout. This serves as a guideline when sewing on the black strip of cloth to keep it straight while hemming.

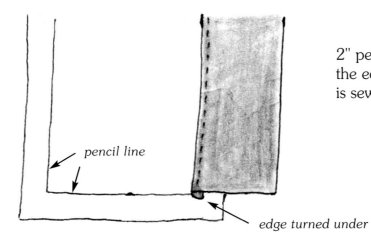

pencil line

edge turned under

Sew black strip along the 2" pencil marks, as shown. Fold the edge under as the black cloth is sewn in place.

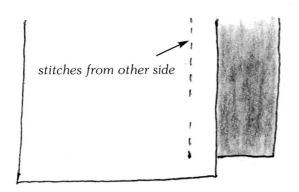

stitches from other side

Turn the breechclout over, as shown. Follow the stitch marks, hemming the black cloth on this side. Keep the edge of the material turned under, as done previously.

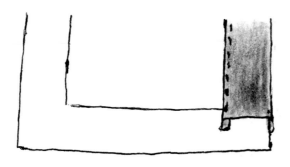

Try to keep the black stripe two inches wide as your hem. Now hem the left side of the breechclout, the same as the right side was done.

To hem the two ends of the breechclout, turn the edge of the black cloth under, sewing it along the pencil line on the white cloth.

Flip the breechclout over, folding the excess black cloth on the sides, as shown

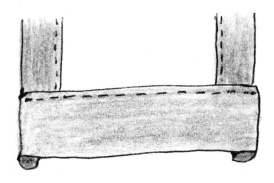

Hem the black cloth on the back side of the breechclout, following the stitch marks which show through the white cloth.

Hem the other end of the breechclout in the same way. You are now ready to sew on the black and red patchwork designs to what will be the belt of the breechclout.

TO MAKE THE BELT FOR THE BREECHCLOUT:

The belt to the breechclout is made of white material, such as that of a blanket. Cut a strip of white cloth 7 " wide by 3 ' and 7 " long. Then fold the strip down the middle length-wise. Sew at the top, hem the ends and bottom of belt, as shown. Hem the bottom and end edges of the belt

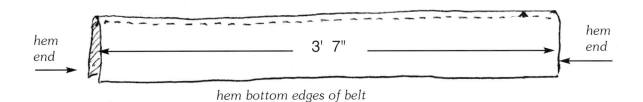

hem end →   3' 7"   ← *hem end*

hem bottom edges of belt

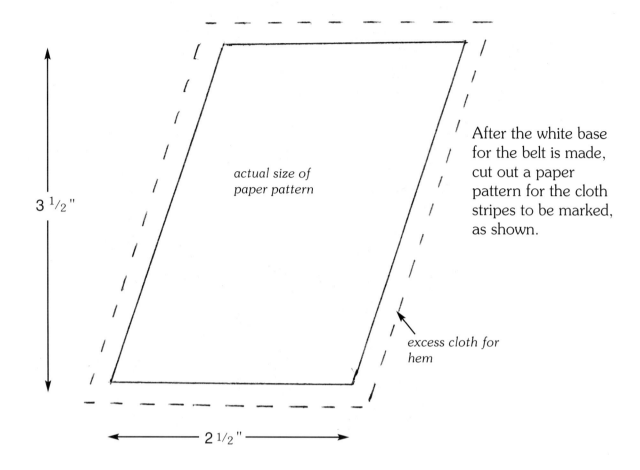

3 ½"

2 ½"

actual size of paper pattern

After the white base for the belt is made, cut out a paper pattern for the cloth stripes to be marked, as shown.

excess cloth for hem

Lay paper pattern on the white belt and mark out the slanted vertical lines with a pencil, as shown below.

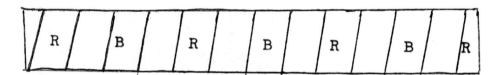

| R | B | R | B | R | B | R |

The stripes follow an alternating order, red, white, black, white, red, white, etc.

Next, cut out an ample amount of red and black pieces of cloth using the paper pattern to span the length of the belt. The white background of the belt is used for the white stripes. Allow about a ½" extra cloth around the pieces to be turned under as they are sewn onto the belt.

When the belt is finished, the next step is to align it to the breechclout as it is sewn into place. The following page will explain this process.

ATTACHING THE BELT TO THE BREECHCLOUT

Mark a pencil line across the breechclout 14" up from the bottom of both ends. Extend the belt 4" to 5" past the edge of the breechclout at the pencil line. Then sew the bottom edge of the belt across the pencil line, as shown.

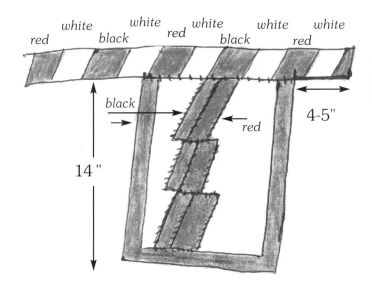

Extend the belt 4" to 5" past the edge of the breechclout. Then sew the front flap of the to the belt along the 14" line, as shown.

Thunder and lightning designs are patch-worked onto the front flap last.

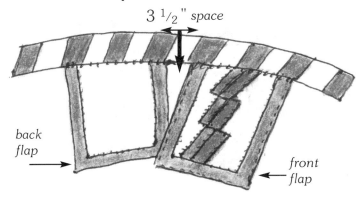

Next, place a mark 3 ¹/₂ " to the left of the front flap.

Align the 14 inch line on the back flap to the belt, allowing for the 3 ¹/₂" space, as shown.

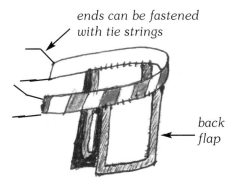

Sew back flap to the belt's bottom edge.

Final sketch demonstrates how breechclout will look when attached to belt.

123

AN EAGLE DANCE BREECHCLOUT

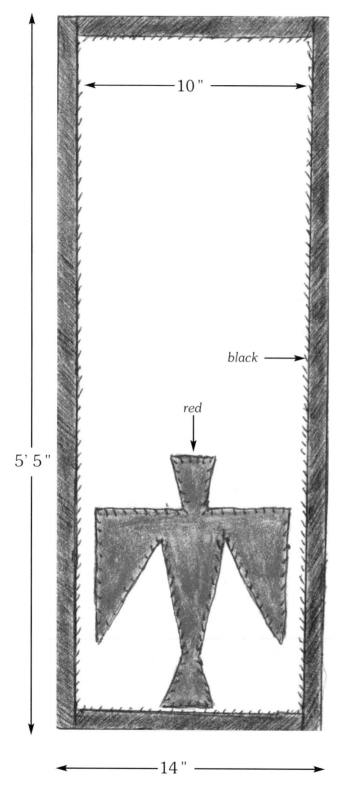

10"

black →

red

5' 5"

14"

The breechclout in the sketch has been worn in the past as part of the Eagle Dance costume in North Carolina at the outdoor drama.

I have seen other versions of breechclouts worn for the Eagle Dance through the years, but this one is particularly beautiful.

The red emblem is a symbol of the eagle.

When I started making this breechclout, I didn't stop until I had made enough for a whole group of dancers to use!

First, cut a white sheet or any thick white cloth to the length and width given in the illustration. Measurements will vary according to size.

Use black cotton cloth to form the 2" black border that goes around the outer edges of the breechclout.

Red cotton, or flannel cloth can be used to make the eagle. The edges of the red cloth should be turned under and then stitched all the way around the edges, as shown.

More details follow.

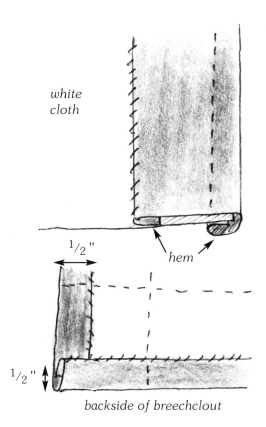

white cloth

hem

$^{1}/_{2}$"

$^{1}/_{2}$"

backside of breechclout

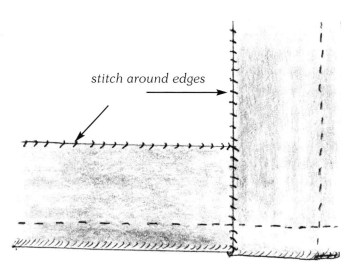

stitch around edges

3" strips of black cloth are hemmed on both ends, along the sides of the breechclout, as shown, turning under. When hemming is done, these black strips of cloth will have narrowed down to a 2" stripe around the border of the front side of the breechclout.

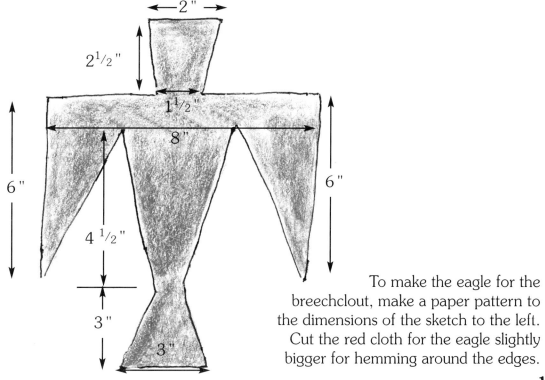

2"

$2^{1}/_{2}$"

$1^{1}/_{2}$"

8"

6"

6"

$4\,^{1}/_{2}$"

3"

3"

To make the eagle for the breechclout, make a paper pattern to the dimensions of the sketch to the left. Cut the red cloth for the eagle slightly bigger for hemming around the edges.

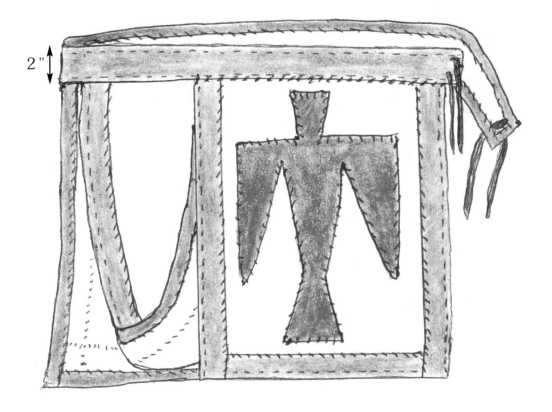

The sketch above shows how the breechclout can be sewn directly to a 2-inch wide black cloth belt. Then, when it is worn, all that is required is to step into it, fastening the ends of the belt on the side with the tie strings.

If you choose not to use the above method, this breechclout can be worn the traditional way, by using a smaller belt to hold it on the body. A black cloth belt is then worn over the belt.

BELLS USED IN THE EAGLE DANCE

The use of bells on leather or cloth garters would appear to be an item that has been added to the dance in more modern times for special effect. The sound of the bells is one of the first things that catch one's attention in the North Carolina drama.

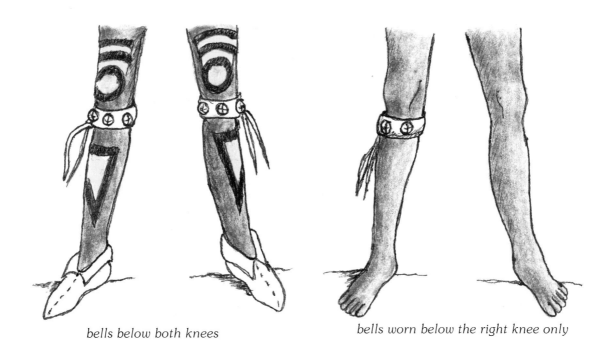

bells below both knees

bells worn below the right knee only

The optional bells can be worn below the right knee only, or below both knees.

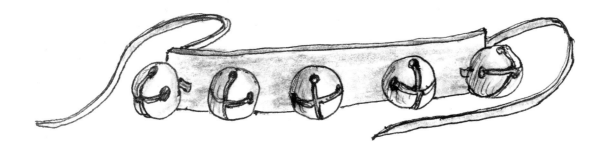

The dance bells below are a typical type. They are quite simple to assemble onto a leather strap.

HOW TO MAKE GARTERS WITH BELLS

Two strips of stiff leather 8" long by 1 $^1/_4$" wide are needed. A leather belt can be cut to make the base if no other kind of leather is available. Scissors or a utility knife can be used for cutting the leather.

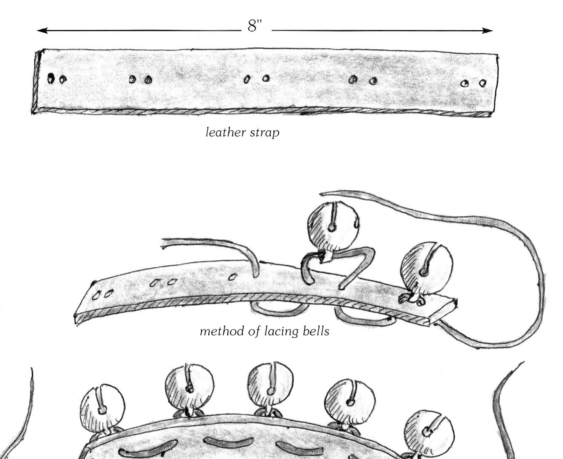

leather strap

method of lacing bells

completed bell strap

Holes can be punched using a large nail and hammer. The holes are punched in $^1/_2$" sets, 1" apart, as shown.

As illustrated, 5 large 1 $^1/_4$" bells are laced on each leather strap. The strings are 28" long.

There are other styles of bell garters that can be made to wear with the eagle costumes. Following are two other options to consider.

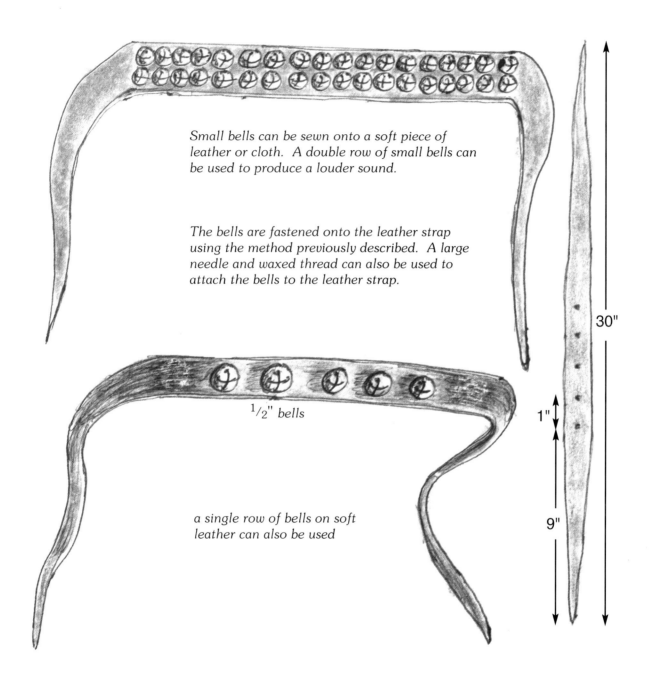

Small bells can be sewn onto a soft piece of leather or cloth. A double row of small bells can be used to produce a louder sound.

The bells are fastened onto the leather strap using the method previously described. A large needle and waxed thread can also be used to attach the bells to the leather strap.

30"

$^1/_2$" bells

1"

a single row of bells on soft leather can also be used

9"

To make the garter shown above with the 5 bells, cut a piece of soft brown leather 29" to 30" long. The middle section, where the bells are to be attached should be 1" wide, tapering down toward the ends, as shown.

BODY PAINT FOR THE EAGLE DANCE

The use of painted designs on a dancer's body are as old as the Native American dances themselves. In early prehistoric times, judging from engravings found on shell gorgets, dancers decorated themselves with various bird costumes, arm, wrist and leg bracelets or bands of white shell beads, more so than body paint. The body paint, in my opinion, came into more regular use after the dances began to alter due to cultural changes.

In 1730, when Alexander Cummings visited the Cherokee, he reported Eagle Dancers having blue curlicues, red circles and white hand prints painted on their bodies.

Evans, in 1835, observed Eagle Dancers painted in a similar fashion to the way ball players painted their bodies.

The dancers in the Cherokee drama "Unto These Hills" also use body paint. Given that thousands of people have viewed this dance in North Carolina, this style could be accepted as the evolution of Eagle Dance body paint for the 20th century.

When the Cherokee, in earlier times, made their own paint for dances, it was in a powdered form, stored in containers. Before use, bear fat or other animal fat had to be mixed with the desired color of powder.

There is little need to go into detail on how each color was made since there are many colors of body paint available today. The Halloween season is a good time to find a wide variety of body paint from most stores. I sometimes use water color or tempera paint if the proper paint is unavailable. One must be careful, in choosing body paint, to consider skin irritations or allergies.

If you are a non-indian doing these dances, and wish to achieve a Native American look, you'll have to get a good tan or use a dark pancake make-up . But if you are dressing like an Indian for fun, or because of special personal interest only, skin color is not important. Dress up, and be an Indian in your heart!

The series of sketches on the following pages will help you to paint your body the way the Eagle Dancers in North Carolina do when the dance is presented to the public.

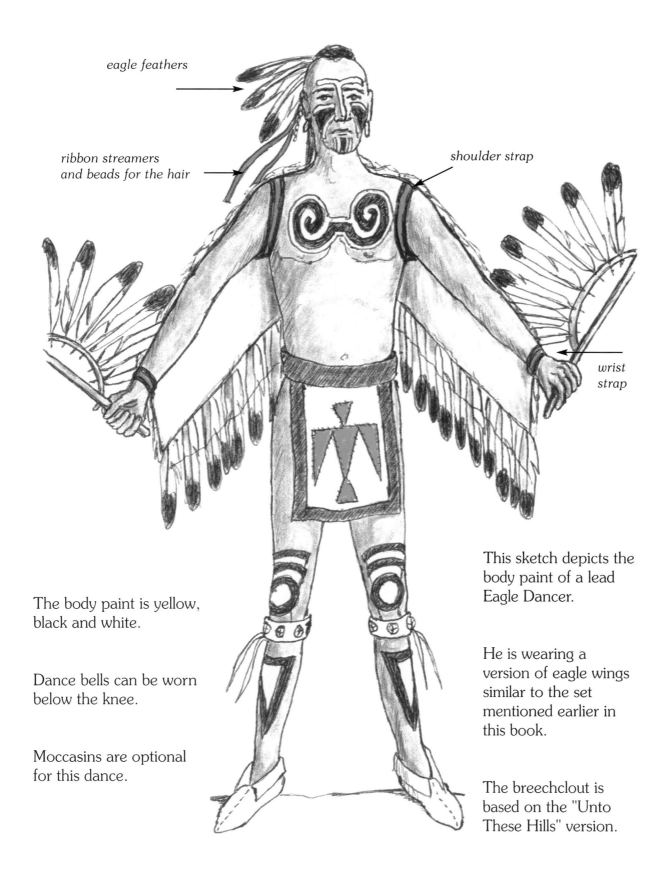

eagle feathers

ribbon streamers
and beads for the hair

shoulder strap

wrist
strap

The body paint is yellow,
black and white.

Dance bells can be worn
below the knee.

Moccasins are optional
for this dance.

This sketch depicts the
body paint of a lead
Eagle Dancer.

He is wearing a
version of eagle wings
similar to the set
mentioned earlier in
this book.

The breechclout is
based on the "Unto
These Hills" version.

This sketch depicts one of the common dancers of the Eagle Dance.

His body paint is done in yellow, black and white paint.

Feathers, ribbon streamers and beads are attached to his scalplock.

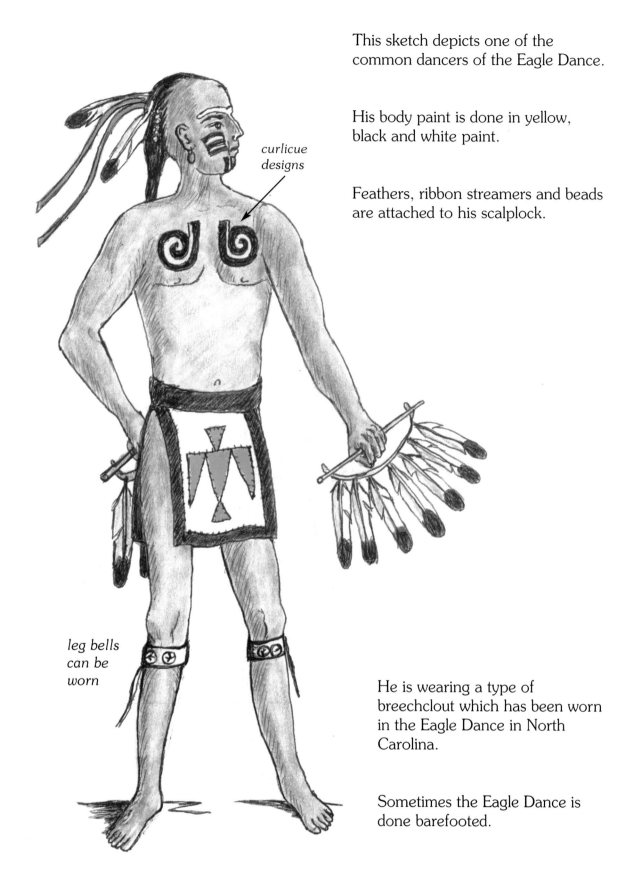

curlicue designs

leg bells can be worn

He is wearing a type of breechclout which has been worn in the Eagle Dance in North Carolina.

Sometimes the Eagle Dance is done barefooted.

132

roach headdress

This lead Eagle Dancer has black and white painted designs on his body.

Breechclout similar to North Carolina version.

See wing design on earlier page.

leg bells

Eagle Dancers in the outdoor drama, "Unto These Hills", sometimes paint their bodies as shown here.

133

The man pictured here is one of the common Eagle Dancers. He is wearing black and white body paint.

This type of breechclout, which I highly admire, is also worn in the outdoor drama, "Unto These Hills".

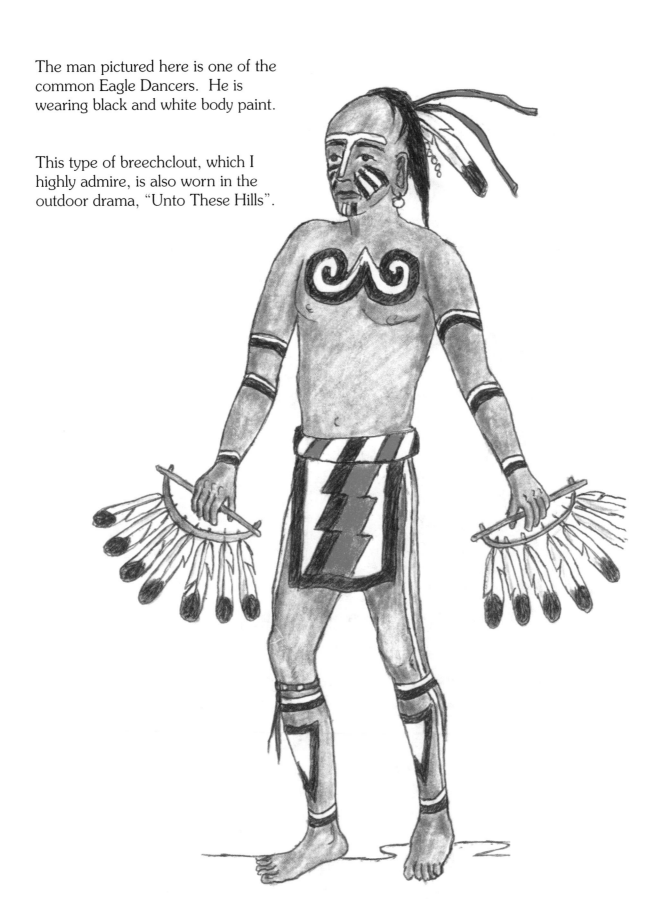

WOODEN MASKS FOR THE EAGLE DANCE

There is evidence that long ago, ceremonial masks were worn during animal and bird dances of the Cherokee. This would have been true of the Eagle Dance as well, at least by the lead dancer. When a mask was worn by an Eagle Dancer, it helped to further represent the eagle in an abstract way.

In studying the shell gorgets of the prehistoric Southeast, it is observed that men dressed in bird costumes. Some gorgets depict men with bird-like noses which suggest a facial mask worn by the dancer. In historic times, men like Sir Alexander Cummings of the 18th century and J. P. Evans of the 19th century, witnessed the Eagle Dance on separate occasions, but neither mentioned an eagle mask being worn by the dancers they observed. Perhaps the eagle mask was diminishing as a vital item at this point in history due to the great cultural changes of the Cherokee.

During the past century and in this century, the costumes for Cherokee dances have no longer been in use. As for facial masks of the Eagle Dance, James Mooney collected some masks which were said to have been worn in the Eagle Dance around the turn of the century. These masks and others were obtained from the reservation in Cherokee, North Carolina, and are presently on display along with others at the Smithsonian Institute.

The mask illustrations on this page and the next are based on the Mooney masks.

A mask for the Eagle Dance is no longer a vital item, as observed in the Cherokee drama, "Unto These Hills". Face paint is now used instead.

To make a mask, refer to the section in this book on the "Booger Dance Costume".

How to do the Eagle Dance

The Eagle Dance is done to celebrate victory or peace. It was a winter dance held sometime after the first frost.

The dance begins with two single file rows of dancers, proceeding side by side toward the danceground. With the men in one row and the women in the next, there can be up to 4 to 6 rows of dancers, much like a platoon of soldiers. The male dancers hold a gourd rattle in their left hand and an eagle wand in their right, while the female dancers hold an eagle wand in both hands. The women are led by a Beloved woman wearing tortoise shell leg rattles. It is noted that in some Eagle Dances, both men and women carry sets of eagle wands without gourd rattles.

In the 1820s, J.P. Evans described the dancers, moving toward the danceground chanting a chorus in response to the chanter. They moved in quick motions, but proceeded slowly, taking three short quick steps, pausing, and then repeating the pattern again and again. The drummer would direct the tempo of the pattern by hitting the drum once and pausing, then hitting the drum three more times quickly. Each time the dancers paused, they would sound out a long shrill war whoop. Then as they proceeded forward, they would stretch their arms like an eagle in flight and shake their wands to the beat of the drum.

The above procession would begin a fair distance away from the danceground. But as they entered the danceground, the following procedure took place.

An equal number of male and female dancers, in separate lines running east and west, face each other in pairs. Then the dancers advance a pace, turn and retreat, circle counter-clockwise, stop and then resume They then circle the dance fire while extending their arms like an eagle and shaking the wands to the rhythm of the drum and rattles. Then the female circle and male circle move in opposite directions, with the males moving clockwise and the females moving counter-clockwise. Now as they circle the fire, they jump up and down and move in crouching postures, bending one knee to the ground and the other at a right angle. The body movements vary at this point with the jumping and dancing. The male dancers hold the wand and gourds close together, waving them up and down as they circle. The next phase of the dance is also known as the Peace Pipe Dance and was done close to morning.

With the male and female dancers facing each other in opposing lines, the males take a step forward and wave their wands horizontally over the women's heads. They then step back to their original position. Then the women perform the same movements, waving their wands over the mens' heads. This process of alternating between the male and female dancers is repeated several times.

137

As the song changes, the complete male and female lines switch places as they wave their wands over the heads of the opposite line. Then the lines move back to their original positions. This process of line-switching continues until the end of the song and ultimately returns to the starting position.

Next, the two lines continue waving the wands over heads as they both back up to create a space of approximately ten feet between them. Then the two circles rotate in opposite directions again for $1/2$ rotation, giving everyone a new partner. The dancers then all face outward, back to back, and wave their wands in the air to the beat of the music for about ten minutes.

To conclude, the dancers form one single file line with the women following the men, circling counter-clockwise. Holding their fans and gourds vertically, they wave them up and down to the music. Sometimes the women carry empty baskets instead of wands, to symbolize feeding the eagles in gratitude for their feathers.

The different phases of the Eagle Dance can be done all at one time, as a complete dance, or separately at different times, to suit particular occasions of varying rituals and ceremonies.

The Eagle Dance song has been passed down through the generations to men like Will West Long, Walder Calhoun and others. The song goes something like this:

"Ha na ti Yu way ha na ti" (repeated 14 times)
"Wah he ye Wah he ye" (repeated 24 times)

For further details on the Eagle Dance, see *Cherokee Dance and Drama* by Speck and Broom, pgs. 39 - 44, and *The Cherokee Perspective* edited by Laurence French and Jim Hornbuckle, pgs. 128 - 129.

Costume for the Peace Pipe Dance

The costumes for the male dancers are simple. White swan down covered the tops of their heads. These fine white feathers of the swan can be substituted with white turkey fluffs. Another alternative would be white rabbit fur. I'll describe later how this hair ornament can be made.

Also, a white breechclout and moccasins are worn.

The body is streaked or painted with white clay paint. Theatrical paint, white shoe polish, or white water color paint may be substituted. Again, the Halloween season is a good time to stock up on these types of paints.

Other items the male Peace-Pipe dancers would have worn were necklaces, earrings, arm or wrist bands and garters. They also carried gourd rattles in the left hand and eagle wands in the right hand.

This costume is further described in the *Timberlake Memoirs*, pgs. 36 - 39. Also see the *Payne Papers*, Vol.3, pgs. 176 - 177.

The Peace-Pipe dance is a part of the Eagle Dance, but can be performed separately. In the old days, when the dance was used to honor someone in friendship or to seal a peace agreement, the dancers were all male. However, in *Cherokee Dance and Drama* by Speck and Broom, both men and women are described to participate in the dance.

When women take part in the dance, they should wear white deerskin or cloth dresses with moccasins, plus their jewelry. These women , long ago, were probably some of the Beloved women and took part when the complete Eagle Dance was performed. The lead woman wears terrapin shell leg rattles. The women also carry eagle wands, and sometimes empty baskets.

The costumes worn in this dance depend largely on whether the dance is done by men only, or if women are included, as in the version described in "Cherokee Dance and Drama".

The Peace Chief should wear his white ceremonial outfit during this dance. Other pages in this book give information describing his outfit.

An honored leader or visiting chief should wear some type of white outfit suitable in portraying his role when the Peace-Pipe Dance is performed especially for him.

THE WHITE SWAN'S DOWN HEAD ORNAMENT

This type of head ornament was worn by the Peace Messenger and the Peace-Pipe dancers.

Originally, it was made of white swan's down and dancers used it to cover the tops of their heads during the peace rituals and dance.

Swan's down is the soft or fine feathers of the swan found underneath the body. White turkey fluffs or white rabbit fur can be used to imitate the swan's down.

James Adair hints at how this ornament was made. He reported that the band of the Peace Chief's hat was made of folded swan's skin. If the band is made this way, a portion of the swan's skin with the feathers still intact can be used to make the hair ornament.

In current times, the substitute of white turkey fluffs must be used to make the ornament. They are sewn or glued to a leather disk base, and are made with two tie strings.

To make this ornament, cut two soft leather disks $2 \frac{1}{2}$" in diameter. Felt or imitation leather can also be used. Make two slits in 1 disk and insert a 10" leather string, as shown. This will become a tie string to later attach the ornament to the hair.

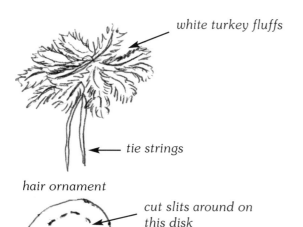

white turkey fluffs

tie strings

hair ornament

cut slits around on this disk

cut hole in the center of top disk

$2 \frac{1}{2}$" leather disk

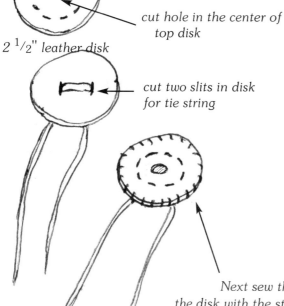

cut two slits in disk for tie string

Next sew the other disk on top of the disk with the string as shown.

140

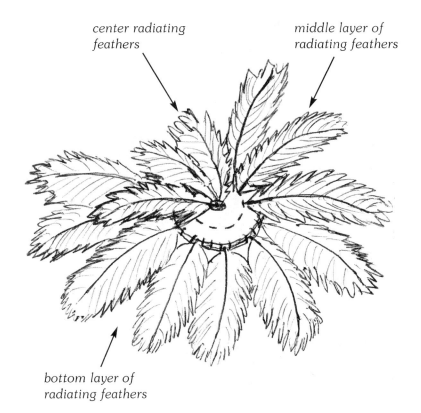

center radiating feathers

middle layer of radiating feathers

bottom layer of radiating feathers

Now put a little glue on the tips of the 5-6" white turkey fluffs. Insert the tips of fluffs between the 2 disks where they are stitched together. Radiate the fluffs around the disks, turning the bend of the fluffs down. You may have to pry the layers apart at the stitches using a large needle. Then insert the feathers. Refer to the sketch.

Next use a pair of small sharp pointed scissors, or a utility knife to make a series of slits on the top disk, as shown.

Now insert more fluffs into the slits on top of the disk in a radiating pattern, turning the bend of this circle of feathers up.

Then make a hole in the center of the top leather disk using the scissors. Put a little glue on the tips of the 3-4" fluffs and insert them in a radiating pattern in the hole in top of the disk. Turn the bend of these fluffs down.

When the entire leather disk is concealed, the feather ornament is finished. The tie strings are used to tie the ornament to a plaited lock of hair on the head.

When a Peace Messenger was sent out, he carried a white swan wing fan. The fan was an emblem of peace, and was akin to a flag of truce. It was well respected by other Native American tribes, thus giving the messenger safe passage on a peace mission. A fan of this type is illustrated in the sketches of a commission paper given to Oconostota in 1761. It is located in the National Archives in Washington.

The Peace Messenger's body was streaked or painted with white clay paint. His head was probably covered with white swan down or fluffs. His breechclout and moccasins would have been made of white deerskin.

Shown here, the Peace Messenger has been sent to a town to notify the chief of a desire for peace and friendship. If all went well, the Peace Messenger's chief, along with a delegation would arrive the next day. If there was to be peace between the two peoples, peace talks, rituals and ceremonies would take place, followed by the Peace-Pipe Dance.

The Peace Messenger costume. Note the white fluffs on the head and the white fan in his hand. He holds a wampum belt on his arm. Other items of his costume include the white breech-clout, belt, garters and moccasins

(modeled by Jimmey Gwinner)

How To Make A White Swan Wing Fan

The Swan Fan was a very sacred and well respected emblem of peace.

The fan had several purposes. It was carried by peace messengers. Such a fan could be exchanged during peaceful meetings, as pictured in the Oconostota Commission Paper.

The Beloved Woman had another use for the fan. She used it in a ritual, flourishing the fan over a brewing pot of the "Black Drink". This was witnessed by Timberlake, and is described in his memoirs. Also see *Nancy Ward - Cherokee Chieftainess* by Pat Alderman, pg. 6.

The White Swan Wing Fan probably had other uses in Cherokee rituals and culture.

It may be interesting to mention that the white fan of Oconostota had a red handle. In this case, "red root" or blood root may have been used to color the handle. This type of red was used on sacred objects. Vermillion was another type of red used on things dealing with war. In making this fan, one may choose to color the handle, or leave it plain.

Since a white swan wing may be difficult or illegal, to obtain, white turkey feathers or white rooster wing feathers may be used.

I have found no instructions on how to make this fan, so the following method is my own.

NOTE: *Many birds are protected by law and the use of their feathers forbidden. Check the laws, both federal and state ,before using bird feathers in any of your projects.*

If a bird wing is used, use the section down to the first joint of the wing.

Treat the joint of the wing with salt and borax and allow wing to completely dry.

If white turkey feathers are used, you may wish to trim the sides to make them look more like swan feathers.

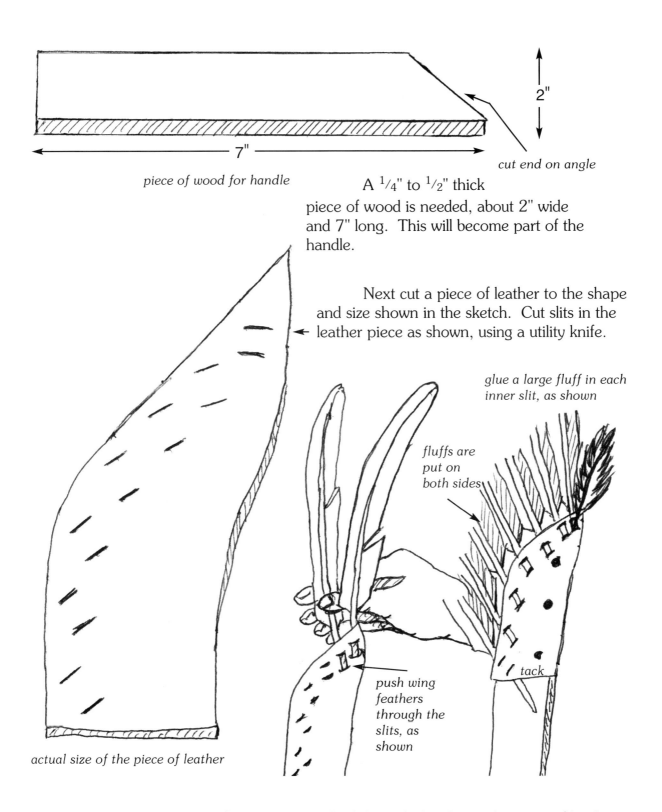

2"

cut end on angle

piece of wood for handle

7"

A $^1/_4$" to $^1/_2$" thick piece of wood is needed, about 2" wide and 7" long. This will become part of the handle.

Next cut a piece of leather to the shape and size shown in the sketch. Cut slits in the leather piece as shown, using a utility knife.

glue a large fluff in each inner slit, as shown

fluffs are put on both sides

push wing feathers through the slits, as shown

tack

actual size of the piece of leather

The large white wing feathers are pushed through the slits in the piece of leather. Next, the leather piece, with the wing feathers is tacked onto the piece of wood. Brad the sharp ends of the tacks where they protrude on the other side of the wooden handle.

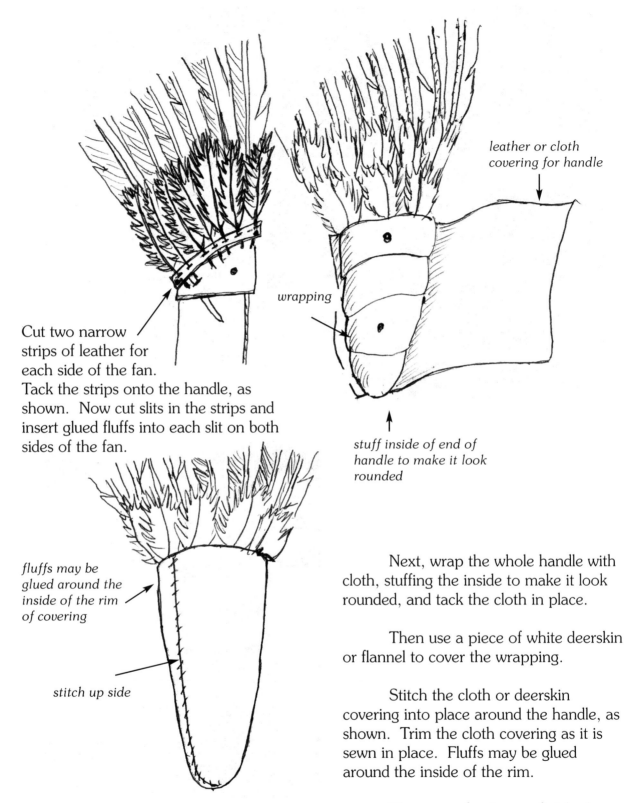

leather or cloth covering for handle

wrapping

Cut two narrow
strips of leather for
each side of the fan.
Tack the strips onto the handle, as
shown. Now cut slits in the strips and
insert glued fluffs into each slit on both
sides of the fan.

stuff inside of end of handle to make it look rounded

fluffs may be glued around the inside of the rim of covering

stitch up side

Next, wrap the whole handle with
cloth, stuffing the inside to make it look
rounded, and tack the cloth in place.

Then use a piece of white deerskin
or flannel to cover the wrapping.

Stitch the cloth or deerskin
covering into place around the handle, as
shown. Trim the cloth covering as it is
sewn in place. Fluffs may be glued
around the inside of the rim.

The peace fan is now finished.

146

Below is a depiction of a Peace-Pipe Dance as described by Henry Timberlake, in the mid 18th century. Head Chief Cheulah and one of the dancers are shown

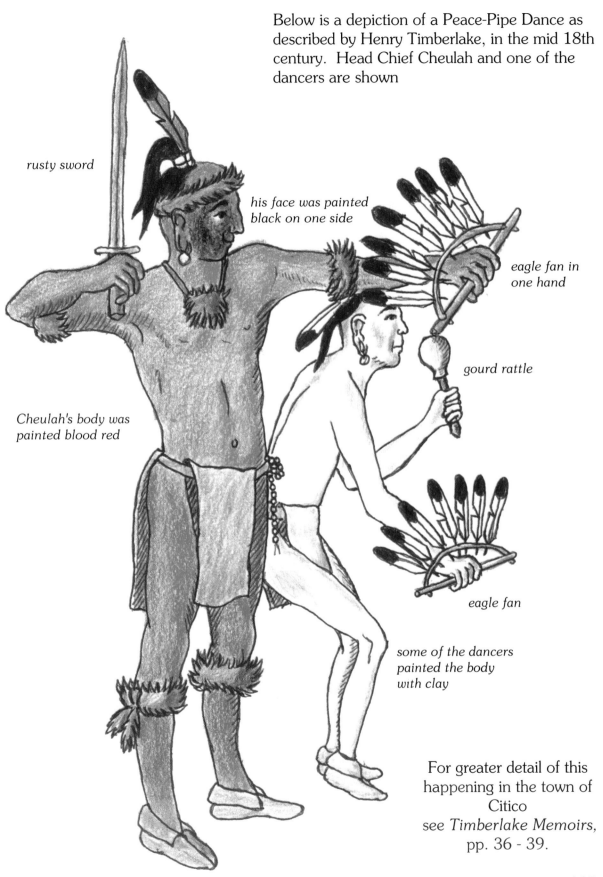

rusty sword

his face was painted black on one side

eagle fan in one hand

gourd rattle

Cheulah's body was painted blood red

eagle fan

some of the dancers painted the body with clay

For greater detail of this happening in the town of Citico
see *Timberlake Memoirs,* pp. 36 - 39.

147

How To Do The Peace Pipe Dance

This particular dance was the Cherokee way of making peace or friendship with other nations. It was also used to honor an important person as a friend.

When the Cherokee held this ritual and dance, it was done before The Great Man Above. This is shown in the dance when the dancers look upward waving their fans. Smoking the white peace pipe sealed this friendship between the two parties.

The Cherokee did not need a treaty paper to show peace or friendship. All the Cherokee needed to confirm peace and friendship was the Peace-Pipe Dance.

This ritual and dance was performed as follows: On day one, a peace messenger was sent to the town. He was like an ambassador from his chief. He notified the leader of the town of the intention of peace and friendship. You may ask,"Why was the messenger not killed as he entered the village?"

First of all, the messenger carried a white swan wing fan in his right hand. Secondly, his body was painted all over with white clay paint. These were emblems that were respected, keeping him from harm. Most Southeastern tribes knew at a glance when they saw a peace messenger and would let him pass freely.

On day two, if the mission of the peace messenger was positive, his chief and a delegation entered the town. They went to the square grounds where the chief of the town met them. No weapons were carried by them. The two chiefs approached each other with a slight bowing posture. Both leaders now made vows and pledges of peace and friendship to each other. As they made their vows, the sacred name of "Yo Ho Wah" was invoked to show their truthfulness and sincerity.

According to the *Timberlake Memoirs*, pgs. 36 - 39, a string of white wampum beads was given to the visiting leader at this time by the town chief.

Once the vows had been made, the chief of the town grabbed the wrists of the visiting chief. Then he proceeded with a series of grasps moving up the arms. This was the Native American way of showing greeting and friendship between two leaders, rather than the white man's handshake.

Next, the chief of the town would wave an eagle fan or wand over the visiting chief's head as a pledge of good faith. Then they would proceed to the council house. With their delegations with them inside the council house, they both would sit side by side on the white throne seats at the west end of the house. The town chief took his place on the center throne seat. In my opinion, the visiting chief probably sat down in the speaker's seat at the left of the chief among the three throne seats, with the chief's "right hand man" taking a place elsewhere for this occasion.

148

The delegation of the visiting chief and the town officials found their places to sit on the other white seats. As everyone was seated, the two chiefs would smoke the peace pipe, eat together and then drink the "White Drink". As they drank this mixture, they would use the ancient invocations as described in the *Howard Payne Papers*, Vol. 3, pgs. 176 - 177. The white people called this liquid the "Black Drink". This drink was believed to purify the body and *etc.* A complete ritual and invocation formula of the Black Drink Ceremony can be found in James Adair's *History of the American Indians*. Also James Hudson's *The Southeastern Indians*, pgs. 226 - 229, 372, 373, and 398 give good information on the Black Drink.

A visiting leader is honored with the Peace Pipe Dance inside the council house

After the prior mentioned rituals were completed, the actual Peace Pipe Dance took place. The dance was a part of the Eagle Dance, but could be used separately.

To do this sacred dance of peace:

Six or more of the town chief's young warriors are chosen and they come into the council house dressed in white breechclouts and moccasins. Their bodies are painted with white clay. White swan down or fluffs cover the tops of their heads. In their left hand they carry a gourd rattle and in their right hand, an eagle fan.

To begin, they draw near to the visiting chief and wave their fans back and forth over his head. They do this in time to the music, taking a step forward and then a step back, repetitively. They then bow and wave the fans, and then stand up straight and look toward the heavens. As they look up, they wave their fans in a slow movement followed by a quick movement. The gourd rattles are held close to their chest, and all of the dancers move in unison, with their fans and steps to the beat of the music. To conclude, the dancers wave their fans over the visiting chief's head again and leave the council house.

All of the dances had songs which were chanted during the dance. In the Peace Pipe Dance, "Yo" is often repeated over and over again. It is part of the name of the Great Man Above, "Yo Ho Wah". In the bowing portion of the dance, a solemn song is sung. The song was handed down by one of the traditional elders to Walker Calhoun, in North Carolina, who sings the song as follows:

"Hi no he ye ni" (repeated approximately 12 times)

Cherokee dance songs can be heard on the cassette, "Where the Ravens Roost" by Walker Calhoun - a Mountain Heritage Center recording of Western Carolina University, Cullowhee, N.C.

For further studies on the Peace Pipe Dance, which includes men and women, see "Cherokee Dance and Drama" by Speck and Broom, pgs. 40 - 43, "The John Howard Payne Papers", Vol. 3, pg. 63, and pgs. 176-177, and the "Timberlake Memoirs", pgs. 36-39.

Phase 1
of the Peace Pipe Dance

(demonstration by Jimmey Gwinner)

Phase 2
of the Peace
Pipe Dance

151

Phase 3
of the Peace Pipe Dance

(demonstration by Jimmey Gwinner)

THE PIGEON DANCE COSTUME

As settlers moved into this country, they reported that, in some areas, such great numbers of Passenger Pigeons would fly over that the sky would darken until they had passed. These birds were a source of food to the Native Americans. But the settlers killed the pigeons, mostly for sport, until they became extinct.

The Cherokee had a dance called the Pigeon Dance. This dance was most likely done for success before hunting the bird. Some Indians in the Southeast hunted the bird at night during the winter. They used torches to blind the pigeons where they roosted, and then knocked them off the roost with long wooden poles.

To prepare for the Pigeon Dance, a man will have to be selected to portray a pigeon hawk. Using body paint, his arms are painted brown to represent a pigeon hawk's wings. His upper body is painted red as shown on the prior sketch. Other items of his costume were the breechclout and belt or sash. If the weather is cool, then leggings are added. Armbands and wristbands may have been worn as well. Garters worn below the knees were an item often worn during dances. Moccasins are also a part of the costume. There is no evidence that a hawk mask was worn.

Given that the man represents the pigeon hawk, imitation hawk feathers or other feathers can be added to the costume or his hair as ornaments.

The male dancers in the dance circle can wear pigeon feathers in the hair. Also they may wear a necklace, breechclout, belt, garters and moccasins. They may also wish to wear arm or wrist bands with pendants of small pigeon feathers.

Women dancers may wear their best deerskin dresses. Small fluff type pigeon feathers can be attached to the hair. Earrings, bracelets, necklaces and moccasins are also worn.

The man who does the chanting positions himself at the outside of the dance circle. He uses a gourd rattle to provide music.

Two women are chosen to wear terrapin shell leg rattles. They are positioned behind the lead dancer in a double circle.

The dancers carry hemlock limbs in both hands. The limbs can be about 8 inches long and can be used to represent the wings of the pigeon. The hemlock limbs are placed at the side of the dance circle so that the dancers can pick them up during a certain phase of the dance.

In *The Eastern Cherokees*, by Gilbert, pg. 266, is told how the man in this dance representing the Sparrow Hawk paints his face red, wears feathers, and carries a buckskin. Naked to the waist, he waits in a dark corner ready to capture the dancer in the group that is representing a pigeon. Also see *Cherokee Dance and Drama*, by Speck and Broom, pgs. 72 - 73.

The Pigeon Hawk dancer, His arms are painted brown to represent wings, and his face and chest are painted red.

(model, Frankie Mafnas.)

HOW TO DO THE PIGEON DANCE

To do the pigeon dance, the lead dancer is followed by the two women with the leg rattles. They are followed by alternating men and women dancers in a single file line moving counter-clockwise in a circle. The dancers go into a trot. They do not carry the hemlock wings at the beginning. This means the pigeons feel safe and at ease, with no need to spread their wings for flight.

After they dance for a while , the dance changes. Each dancer grabs a pair of wings from the pile of hemlock limbs and waves them up and down. This signifys that they know their predator is close and they need to fly to safety.

The chanter sound out the words, "Tconi:hawo". This tells the pigeon hawk to come out of hiding from the side of the dance ground. He quickly runs toward the dancers, grabbing and carrying one of the pigeon dancers away.

This move by the pigeon hawk cuts the dance circle in half. The dancers then pretend to be afraid, by turning their heads left and right as birds do when watching for the enemy. The pigeon dancers make a noise like "Gee gee gee", and then a louder sound like "Ga ga ga!". These sounds imitate a pigeon being attacked.

After the pigeon hawk has left with it's victim from the dance circle, the circle of dancers regroup, forming a complete circle again as before. They continue dancing in a counter clockwise direction.

As the pigeon dancers continue dancing and waving their hemlock wings up and down, other attacks are made on the pigeon dancers by the pigeon hawk. The pigeon hawk sometimes grabs at a dancer just to tease him. Other times he circles the dancers continuously until he picks a victim.

When the dancers are finished with their dance, they throw their hemlock wings down on the ground and leave the dance ground. The pigeon hawk also retires.

This dance offers a lot of fun for young and older people alike!

THE QUAIL DANCE COSTUME

Little is known of the costume dancers wore for the Quail Dance. In the book, *Cherokee Dance and Drama*, there is a photograph taken in the 1930s that depicts the male dancers wearing a headband with an upright feather at the forehead, and the women wearing native dress. However, the costume worn in this dance centuries ago can only be left to conjecture.

This sketch depicts a projection of how a male dancer may have dressed long ago.

He is wearing a headband with an upright quail feather with a necklace and earrings, which were most always worn. Without a doubt, armbands were worn, along with bracelets which were also very common for men to wear at dances. In my opinion, a shirt and leggings with a breechclout were proper for this dance, if the dancer preferred. Otherwise, he would have worn a breechclout and belt, as shown. A braided sash was probably part of the costume as well. Garters worn below the knees and moccasins would have a part, as well as body paint.

Today, the important thing to achieve with this costume would be to wear traditional Native American clothing portraying the quail in some way. To do any Indian dance in non-Indian clothing diminishes the effect of the dance. When Cherokee men and women, as well as those depicting the Cherokee culture, dress in a native way while doing these dances, great meaning will once again be portrayed.

*This outfit is suitable for the Quail Dance as
well as other dances.*

(Modeled by author's sister, Myrtle)

The typical outfit for the female dancer of the Quail Dance may have been similar to that shown above. A deerskin dress would have been the main part of the costume. This one is made of imitation leather cloth. The basket designs are formed with black yarn embroidery and red flannel on a white cloth strip.

Other items a female dancer would wear for this dance are earrings, necklaces, bracelets, small fluffs in the hair and moccasins.

Dresses similar to the one shown can be adorned in many ways to enhance the Quail Dance.

How to Do the Quail Dance

The Quail Dance was sometimes referred to as the Pheasant Dance or the Partridge Dance. At one time, it was performed during the Green Corn Festival.

The Quail Dance is done today for fun and entertainment. Although it accomplished the same purpose in the old days, it could have had greater meaning. Little is known about it's original purpose, but it may have been done to help bring the hunter success who needed the quail for food.

In this century, the chanting is provided by the drummer, who stands off to one side of the dance circle.

In the first phase, the male dancers follow their leader in a counter-clockwise circle. The female dancers then follow their leader around the men in a clockwise fashion. The dancers beat their feet against the ground with dance steps that imitate a quail beating the ground with his wings. These movements stay in time with the drum for several minutes.

When the chanter says "Yo hyo", the dance changes. Both circles stop moving, and then the two circles take turns moving forward and then backward for a few steps. These movements are repeated several times and will last for several minutes.

Next the two dance circles exchange places. They pass each other, with the men moving to the outer circle and the women becoming the inner circle. Each circle now moves in opposite directions as they did originally.

This whole process can be repeated over and over until the dancers decide to stop. It can be challenging and fun trying to keep in beat with the drum and stay in unison with the other dancers.

This song is sung for the Quail Dance in North Carolina:

> Wo he ya hay
> Wo he ya hay
> Wo he ya he ya

THE CHICKEN DANCE COSTUME

Since the Chicken Dance was held to show friendship, it is considered a social or fun dance. At such a dance, participants may wear common clothes as long as they are well dressed.

The male dancer of the Chicken Dance may wear an eagle feather in his hair. Earrings and a necklace are almost always worn. His armbands may have a pendant such as a chicken feather to represent the fowl being honored. In the old days, tattoos and body paint were displayed at such dances as well as wrist bands or bracelets. A belt, breechclout, garter and leggings could also be worn, as well as a shirt if preferred. Moccasins were worn, but some may prefer to go barefoot. One could also use vermillion in his hair.

Whatever is worn, male or female, for this dance, a feather or two from a chicken is very symbolic.

The costume for this dance is left mostly to one's own conjecture. A short feathered cape for the women and long feathered capes for the male dancers, made of various colors of chicken feathers would add to the effect of this dance. In this dance, common people wore feathered capes too.

How to Do the Chicken Dance

This isn't a very old dance of the Cherokee, since chickens were introduced to them by the white traders.

One of the old "Stone Coat" legend prophesies was about the coming of a strange people bringing new kinds of animals and birds. The chicken was thought to be included in this prophesy.

The Chicken Dance was done to inspire friendship with strangers and animals, including the chicken which they brought. This became a social dance for the people to enjoy.

In the old days, this dance would have been done at the Square Grounds, in front of the council house. It is now done in any large open space.

A chanter using a rattle or drum is needed for this dance. He will stand at one side of the circle of dancers. The female dancers represent the hens. The male dancers represent the roosters. The dance is made up of male and female partners. The man's partner is behind him in the circle. There is an even number of partners.

The dancers begin by moving in a counter-clockwise direction. Then the chanter signals the male dancers to turn and face their partners. At this point, everyone begins dancing on their left foot. As the men lift their right foot, the women place their right foot on top of the male partners, in step. The dance can last for several minutes, as they continue to dance in this counter-clockwise fashion. The two phases of the dance can be alternated several times.

During the second phase of the dance, in which the dancers are moving on one foot, the Chanter sings these words over and over:

"Wi: a' ska le lat o,
Wi: a' ska le lat o,
....."

NOTE: To add to the effects of this dance, the arms may be held out or moved to imitate wings.

THE BOOGER DANCE COSTUME

An audience sitting and watching a "Booger Dance", will not only be spell-bound by the actions of the dancers, but will also be fascinated by what the "boogers" wear.

In 1714, Lawson observed a Booger or Mask Dance, as did later observers up to the 1930s. From these reports we can gather the information necessary to reconstruct the dance costumes.

Lawson observed men at this dance wearing gourd masks, probably similar to the masks pictured. Masks at that time in Cherokee culture were also made of bark or a hornet's nest. The hard wooden masks were made of soft woods such as buckeye and poplar. Wooden masks at that early time were fewer in number as compared to the abundance of masks today that are made by the craftsmen in North Carolina. Such masks were difficult to make and took a lot of time to complete. After the Cherokee obtained better tools made of metal, masks could then be made easier.

It should be remembered that masks were also worn during other dances, as well as for hunting certain animals, and even for the curing rites of the medicine men. During the Buffalo Dance, a buffalo mask would have been worn. During the Beaver Dance, a beaver mask would have been worn, etc.

Most masks were about 7 - 8 $^1/_2$ " wide, 11 - 12 $^1/_2$ " in height and 2 - 7 " deep. These measurements are based on rough measurements taken from various masks I own and have seen. Others could be larger.

During the time of Lawson and before, booger masks were made to represent the faces of indian tribes who were enemies to the Cherokee. When the white men came, often creating chaos, the Cherokee started making masks having large eyebrows, mustaches, beards, bald-heads, etc. to represent their new white enemies in the Booger Dance.

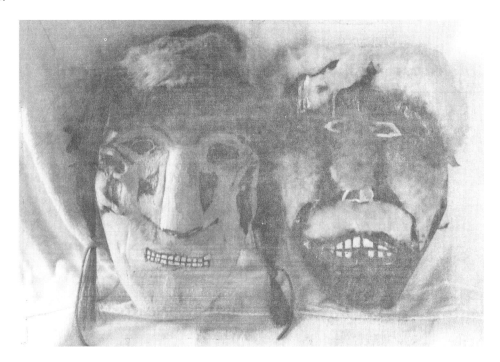

The two wooden masks in the photograph above are Booger Masks. An Indian woman is represented by the mask on the left, and an old Black man by the other mask. Both masks were made by the author.

When I made my first Booger Mask, I split a block of poplar wood in half with an ax. My dad and I had used a cross-cut saw to cut up a tree into blocks of wood for winter stove wood. Most people use a chain saw, these days.

After drawing an outline of the intended mask on one of the halves of wood, I used a hatchet to chip away the areas forming the sides of the forehead and chin of the mask. Next, a wood chisel was used to form the nose, cheeks, mouth and other features. A crooked knife is useful, At times I used a pocket knife to get a better finish. A hand-drill made the openings for the eyes, nose and side holes for tie-thongs.

See source page in back of this book for "crooked knife".

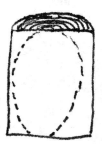

Draw an outline of the mask on the block of wood, front and back.

Use a hatchet or ax to chip away the unnecessary wood on the sides.

A wood chisel or spoon gouge is used for the facial features, starting with the nose.

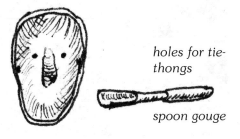

holes for tie-thongs

spoon gouge

Carve out the back of the mask using a drill and wood chisel or spoon gouge.

When carving the hollow for the back of the mask, I used a hand-drill to make holes around the back of the mask so that I could chip away the unneeded wood. While using the drill, great care must be taken to keep from drilling all the way through the mask. Now, a wood chisel, crooked knife or gouge may be used.

Once I finished all of the carving, I used sandpaper and a sandstone rock to smooth the surfaces of the mask.

I used flat red-orange paint on the mask, and to get the facial features to stand out, I used a flat dark brown paint. The teeth were painted white.

Horse hair was used by sewing it to a piece of black cloth, as a wig would be sewn. Then, small tacks were used to attach the hair-piece and a portion of rabbit fur to the top of the mask. Leather tie-thongs are then inserted through the holes on each side of the mask. Attaching the hair-piece and thongs in this way aides one in the wearing of the mask.

I created the second mask in the same manner. Having no instruction, other than a picture of the masks, I learned by trial and error. I learned of the detail and difficulty that was involved for the early Cherokees in carving these masks. Once it is finished, however, there is the realization that the effort was worthwhile.

Once you have made a dance mask, you will want to make others. There are quite a few examples of masks still being made. Such models may be seen at museums in North Carolina or in various books of the Cherokee.

Below, and on the following page are some various wooden masks which can be carved from buckeye wood and worn during the Booger Dance.

Hand-made masks are available. See "source page" in back of book.

166

The Booger Dance was done at night, in homes, during the winter months, or at times around an outdoors fire. At one time, it was probably done in the council house or in the town square.

A leather shirt, leggings and moccasins would have been worn during cold weather. The clothes were intentionally worn several sizes too large in order to stuff them with rags and such. The belly was made to look larger than normal, as well as the buttocks, to create a look of deformity.

Since the Cherokee had, at one time, dyed their leather clothing black, it stands to reason that some of the Booger dancers would have worn dark leather clothing.

Men of the Iroquois, farther north, as well as Tuscarora and the Southeast Cherokee, would sometimes wear a wrap-around fringed skirt. The skirt was tied at the waist with a belt or sash, as shown.

It is probable that such a skirt was worn by the men of the Booger dance in early times up to the 18th century. Such an article of clothing would have made it easier for the dancer to flap back, exposing a large gourd phallus worn underneath the clothing. This was a common gesture of the Booger dance.

During the early 18th century, Lawson observed that it was common for a Booger dancer to wear a mantle or cloak made of feathers. Also, other dancers would have worn mantles or robes made of buffalo, bear or deer hides.

Wooden curved bladed sword-like weapons were carried in the hand of some Booger Dancers in the 18th century. At one time, these items were probably made of flint. In the early 20th century, a chicken or rooster was carried in the hand, and others would carry a small rifle

Later, as the dance costume went through various changes with more contact with the white people, old quilts and sheets were used for wraps during the dance. Such drapes were worn over the shoulders, tied or knotted on the chest and just below the waist. This allowed the Booger dancers to hide their arms and hands underneath, to create suspense.

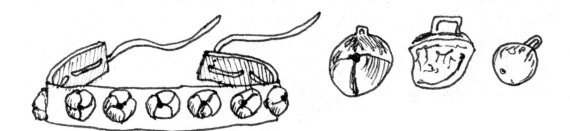

In the early 18th century, bells were worn around the ankles and above the knees. A leather strap or sash can be used to attach the bells, as shown.

Typical smaller bells of the 18th century. Those women joining the men in dance wore small hawk-bells around the neck. They also wore horse bells around their legs.

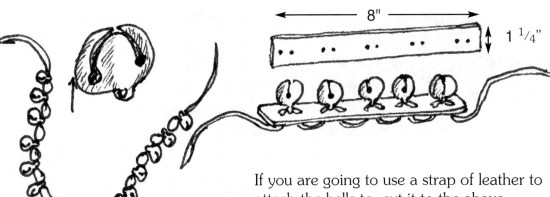

A necklace of bells mixed with beads would have been an item worn by a woman, when dancing with the boogers, in the bear dance.

If you are going to use a strap of leather to attach the bells to, cut it to the above dimensions. The series of holes are evenly spaced, 1 $\frac{1}{4}$" apart.

The leather lacing string is $\frac{1}{8}$" wide and 20" long. You can use a utility knife or scissors to cut the leather. A nail or punch is used to make the lacing holes.

Since finger-woven garters were worn by both men and women, as a part of normal dress, such garters with bells attached much in the same way as depicted in the sketches above, would have also been a part of the costume.

A leg sash with bells; 34" long by 1 $\frac{3}{4}$" wide.

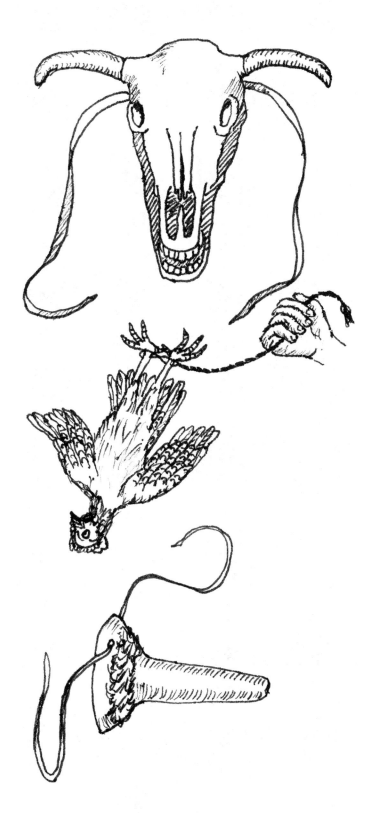

A cow or horse skull was sometimes worn in front of the chest by booger dancers.

I found a cow skull in a field, where the animal had died several years earlier. Skulls of this type can occasionally be found around farm areas.

The leather strap is inserted through two holes located directly behind the forehead of the skull. This enables one to hang the skull from the neck, over the shirt of the costume.

A booger dancer, wearing a hunting mask, sometimes carries a chicken tied to a string, as depicted. The people in the audience of the square ground are told by the "Booger" that he is carrying a turkey.

Also shown, is a phallus made from a gourd handle with fur glued on. This costume item was worn beneath the clothing, in the appropriate location, to be exposed to the women during the dance. This is often left out if thought to offend the people watching. Discretion should be used.

169

How To Do The Booger Dance

The Booger Dance or Mask Dance was done to teach the people about strangers coming to the Cherokee country. These strangers did not always have the best intentions. Sometimes they came wanting land, taking away the women and children and destroying the Cherokee way of life.

The dance taught children to beware of strangers, and gave them an abstract idea of the enemy. The dance also depicted the foolishness of the white man's ways, as he destroyed the environment.

To conduct a Booger Dance, the following is needed: a dance ground, an audience, chanters, rattles, a water drum and costumes. Following, is a description of how the dance is performed.

The dancers with masks can number from four to eight or more. Each of the Boogers have names, which are usually obscene, such as Big Butt, Sooty Butt, Long Phallus, Sweet Phallus, Big Balls, etc. If you wish, make up your own name.

A drummer usually sits to one side of the dance area and the chanters, and those using rattlers, on the other side. The dance moves in a counter-clockwise circle.

170

If the dance is to be done indoors, a wooden mortar is made from a section of a log and then placed in the center of the dance ground. The dancers will dance around the mortar. If done outside, a fire is built for the dancers to encircle.

The dance steps should be practiced prior to the dance. These steps can be done as follows: First, stomp the ball of the right foot, then lower the heel to the ground. This movement is then repeated with the left foot. These steps are done repeatedly, in a hopping motion, to the beat of the drum and rattle music. The body is bent or slightly stooped over. The dancers arms may be kept to the side or allowed to move with the movements of the body, for drama.

wooden mortar

dance step

In teaching this dance to some neighborhood children, I omitted certain portions for obvious reasons. Before they entered, I had the audience doing some of the more common dances of the Cherokee, such as the Friendship dance, the Women's dance, and lastly, the Beginning dance. Everyone was instructed to pretend, even though they knew the "Boogers" were about to enter, as if they were unaware of the odd intruders.

As the Beginning dance is concluded, the musicians and chanters start the Booger Dance songs, which is the signal for the Booger dancers to enter the dance ground.

As people are finding their seats, the Boogers enter, acting very mean. Some may hit at people and push the men around, while others may hit at the air or run after and grab at the women and young girls as they flee for a safer spot.

It is common for a Booger to suddenly fall to the ground, spin around, and to expose their buttocks or phallus, to the dismay of female onlookers. This gesture is often omitted to prevent offending onlookers, but is included here to be true to historic references.

When all of these entrance actions are done, the dancers sit down side by side on a bench or log. The dance scene changes, now that the Boogers have relaxed a little.

The chief or leader of the people will make himself known by announcing that "we have strange intruders who have come among us". They then ask the Boogers, "Who is your leader?" The Boogers only talk in loud whispers and sometimes with their words distorted. When the lead Booger makes himself known, the Chief asks questions. "Where is your homeland? Where are you going? What is your purpose here? The answers from the lead Booger are repeated loudly to the people by the Chief.

The answers are usually, "We have come from far north, we are on a southward journey, we need some women and girls!"

The people are amazed and afraid at the Boogers' demands. The Chief tells them that they cannot have any women or girls. The Boogers now pretend to want to fight, hitting at the air, etc., while still sitting on the benches. The Chief then tells them, "We are at peace and do not want to fight you, but we will if we must." The Boogers back down, probably realizing that they are outnumbered. The lead Booger talks it over with the other Boogers, then he tells the Chief, "We have decided to dance for your people". Now, the Chief relates the Boogers decision to the people, which is found more sensible than fighting, and it is agreed.

The scene of the drama changes again, as the Chief asks the lead Booger, "What is your name?". "My name is Sooty-Butt", may be the reply. As the name is repeated to the people, laughter and emotions are shown by the people along with clapping and yelling.

As the musicians and chanters begin their songs of the Booger Dance, they say the name of the Booger at the beginning of the verse, as the lead Booger starts to dance. The song is repeated four times for each Booger as he takes his turn dancing. Each time a new Booger's name is announced in the chant, the people shout and clap their hands.

The lead booger does a dance in a counter-clockwise circle, around the mortar or fire, in this fashion: He begins by stomping his right foot on the ground (ball then heel), while the left leg is lifted to a horizontal position. Then the same is done with the opposite legs. While repeating these steps, sometimes an odd or incorrect step is added to mock the enemies.

The lead dancer will try to imitate the character represented by the mask he is wearing. If he is portraying a white farmer, he may carry a crooked pole for a plow, wearing dirty clothes, a straw hat, no shoes, carrying a blanket. He may scratch in the dirt with the crooked pole, acting stupid, dumb and ignorant, mocking the intruding farmers. He hobbles along doing odd gestures and acting out his part. When he is finished, he sits back down on the bench as the people clap their hands.

The next Booger is asked his name by the Chief, who then tells the name to the people. Again, as this booger starts his dance, the chanters start a song using his name in the verse, and repeating it four times. Suppose this dancer is wearing a devil mask. He too will by hopping, twirling, and making obscene gestures. He may dance a few steps in a stooping posture with his hands on the upper thighs. He may stop now and then, and move very close to the onlookers making fun of the whites by coughing, grunting, and passing gas, etc. When he is finished, he sits down with his Booger buddies. Each Booger takes a turn dancing from right to left.

172

The Chief then asks the Boogers if they would like to join in a dance of their choice, the Bear, Eagle or Pigeon dance. If the Boogers chose the Bear dance, a rest period is likely needed for everyone. As the Bear dance begins, the women join the Boogers in dancing. This dance is described in the following section. As the dance ends the Boogers might try to dash out, taking a female with them, but without success.

The people may wish now to do other dances for the night, or close the night of dancing with the following rituals:

The pipe smoking in this ritual is done by the chief, by filling a stone pipe with tobacco and lighting it. Probably a white stone pipe with an eagle image is used. The chief faces the fire, perhaps eastward, taking a puff from the pipe and exhaling the smoke. Then he goes to the drummer and holds the stem of the pipe to the drummer's mouth allowing him to take a puff from the pipe, as he does for all the musicians. Then he will go do the same for the singers on the other side of the room, after which he will put the pipe away.

The chanters are usually singing a song all during this ritual, which the word for "Smokes or it's tobacco" is used. My version of the song is:

> "Yo Yo,
> ats legi ss ki, yo
> ats legi ss ki, yo
> ats legi ss ki, yo
> ats legi ss ki, wa
> Yo"

This song can be sung over and over until the smoke ritual is finished.

The above ritual is done to show honor and gratefulness to the ones doing the singing and making music. Then the dance is over for the night, as the Chief gathers up the rattles and the drum, putting all of the musical instruments away.

The following Booger Dance Song is sung in North Carolina:

Yo wah he Yo wah he yuh nah	(four times)
Ni ge he He guh ti yo nah	(ten times)
He yo ho He yah he yo ho	(ten times)

THE BEAR DANCE COSTUME

The Bear Dance was one of the winter night-time dances held by the Cherokee. It would sometimes follow the Booger Dance, when the Booger dancers selected this particular dance. Since some Booger dancers were masked and dressed as bears, we are given some hints regarding the Bear Dance costume.

The bear mask marked the true representation of the bear, and several types were worn. These masks were carved of buckeye wood and dyed black by placing the mask in a boiling mixture of sumac berries or bark and walnut roots or bark. Others achieved this black coloring by using a mixture of charcoal and water. Dark fur may be attached to the top of the mask, as shown. The number of bear masks for the dance depended on the number of male dancers, for participating females wore no masks.

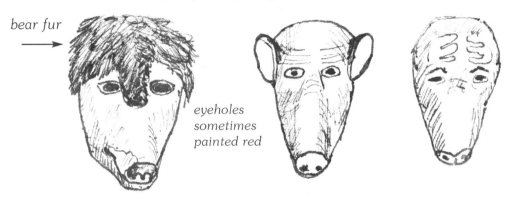

bear fur

eyeholes sometimes painted red

Bear Masks

A bear-claw necklace would have been a very suitable item for a male bear dancer

When carving a bear mask, it may be helpful to refer to the previous section of this book on how to carve a booger mask.

In the old days, a real bearskin was worn on the body of the dancer in a mantle or draped fashion. Presently, a fur coat or imitation fur may be made into a robe. It is proper for the lead Bear dancer to wear a white fur mantle or robe for the dance. In *Cherokee Dance and Drama* by Speck and Broom, there is an old Cherokee legend on page 86 about a White Bear Chief.

NOTE: For ready-made masks, see "source-page" in back of book.

Since the Bear Dance was done during the winter months, a logical assumption would be that the dances wore their ordinary clothing underneath the fur robe or mantle, as part of the dance costume.

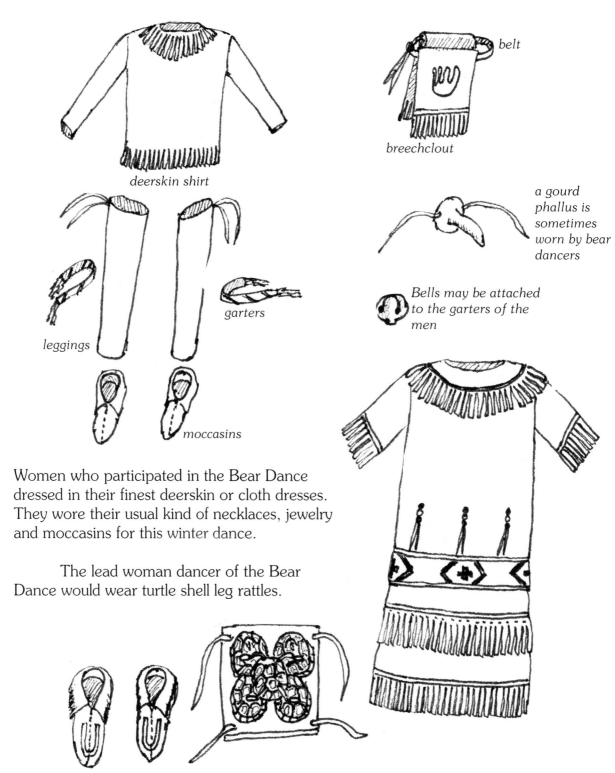

belt

breechclout

deerskin shirt

a gourd phallus is sometimes worn by bear dancers

leggings

garters

Bells may be attached to the garters of the men

moccasins

Women who participated in the Bear Dance dressed in their finest deerskin or cloth dresses. They wore their usual kind of necklaces, jewelry and moccasins for this winter dance.

The lead woman dancer of the Bear Dance would wear turtle shell leg rattles.

176

A Bear Dance Costume
note the wooden mask and fur robe

HOW TO MAKE A BEAR ROBE

Real bear fur may be difficult to obtain for most people in the making of this robe. Imitation black fur may be used, or a fur coat can be taken apart and reassembled to create the robe.

The robe I made for this dance is fashioned similar to one that is exhibited in the Museum of the Cherokee Indian in Cherokee, North Carolina

First, cut a piece of fur to the shape of a hide as it would appear when taken directly from the animal. It should resemble the form shown below.

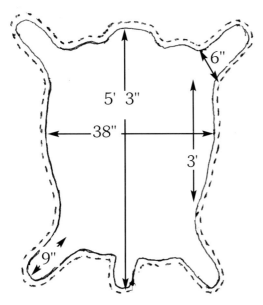

Use a utility knife to cut the fur from the backside of the skin or imitation fur.

If real fur is used, it may not be necessary to line the back of the fur with cloth. Since I used an imitation, I chose to line the backside of the fur with red cotton cloth.

After you have cut the fur to the proper shape, lay it on top of a large piece of red cloth. A table or floor are good areas for this project.

Use scissors to cut the cloth to the same shape as the fur, allowing an extra $1 \frac{1}{2}$" to form a red border around the fur, as shown. Scissors with a jagged cutting edge (pinking shears) can give the red border an outstanding effect.

The fur may then be machine or hand-stitched to the red lining. Stick pins should be used to hold the fur in place as the sewing is done. Keeping the fur pushed back a little during the sewing will keep it from becoming entangled with the thread.

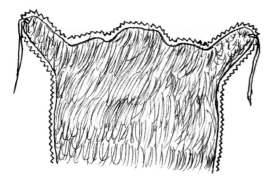

Leather tie strings can be used to hold the bear robe in place as it is worn by the dancer.

A wooden bear mask is worn with this robe.

An ordinary leather or cloth outfit can be worn underneath the fur robe.

178

HOW TO DO THE BEAR DANCE

The Cherokee Bear Dance did not portray the hunter in pursuit of bears, as seen in the Bear Dance of the Western tribes. Rather, it was done to show how the bear timidly pursued a mate. Women dancers portray the bears that the males are seeking to mate. I believe the dance is derived from the old legends, in which bears were at one time believed to have been humans.

Men intending to do this dance should carefully study the movements of the bear in order to impart the bear's body movements into that of their own during the dance. Some of the actions of a bear are as follows: Bears walk on all fours or on their hind feet erect, using a loose shuffling walk. A bear stretches out it's forearms, as shown. The paws of the bear hang loosely while stretching out the arms. At other times, the bear raises it's forearms upward, bent in a "V" fashion with it's paws hanging loosely downward. Also, a bear will lean forward and backward in a swinging motion as it walks. The bear dancer should execute these body movements in time to the drum music.

The women dancers should equal the number of male dancers. There may be 4 or more couples. However, the female dancers remain seated during the first part of the dance.

A man using a water drum and another shaking a rattle, sit to one side of the dance ground. The Bear Dancers enter the dance ground when the chanter begins the first song.

The song may be sung over and over during the first part of the dance. To begin, the men dance around the fire in a counter-clockwise direction. If inside, a mortar is used rather than a fire.

179

The dancers use the shuffle dance step, moving the feet on the floor or ground with a dragging step, without lifting the feet too high. Starting with the right foot, the steps are alternated right and left repeatedly.

1. Strike the ball of the foot first, lowering the heel
2. Drag the whole foot back a little on the ground
3. Repeat the same process for the left foot

As the dance steps above are done, the dancers should watch the lead Bear Dancer, as he slowly swings his body forward and back in time to the drum beat, and do the same. He may also extend his arms lowered in front with the hands hung loosely, or draw his forearms up about chest level. The dancers should do the same. See the illustrations on previous pages.

When the song is chanted during this part of the dance, certain syllables of the song words are accented louder and pitched differently. When this happens, the man with the rattle shakes his instrument rapidly, similar to the sound of a rattlesnake. The lead dancer growls at this point and the other dancers grunt like bears.

All of these gestures are repeated and continued throughout the first part.

In the second phase of the Bear Dance, the second Bear Song is chanted and the women dancers enter the dance circle. The lead woman dancer, wearing the turtle-shell rattles, takes her place in front of the Lead Bear Dancer. The other women become partners then take their places in front of the other bear dancers (see prior illustration).

The women dance in a dignified manner, with their arms hanging free at their sides. Their dance step is accomplished by dragging the ball of the foot 3 or 4 inches on the ground, then lowering the heel as they do the same with the other foot. As the women begin this phase of the dance, the male partners behind them begin to make sexual advances by motioning the gourd phallus to depict sexual acts from the rear. Each woman continues to dance, not paying any attention to her partner behind. After some time, the women turn to face their partners and dance backwards. Her partner should be more polite at this point as they continue to dance counter-clockwise for several more rounds. Next the women turn back around to their original positions as their partners place their hands on them from behind. After a few rounds in this manner, the dance concludes and the dancers leave the way they came. The woman may then take a seat, or go about their business.

180

I think the intention of the Bear Dance was to denote courtship which leads to mating. It stems from an old legend of the Cherokees, in which a Bear Man who mated a she-bear, and had to defend their bear cubs from hunters.

If the dance was done before a bear hunt by Cherokee hunters to help them kill a bear, then perhaps only the first part was performed. Other tribes have used hunters in the dance instead of women. The Cherokee version of the dance may have gone through alterations as the bear became more scarce and therefore hunted less. Women could have then replaced the hunters in the dance, making it a form of entertainment to be used during night-time social dances.

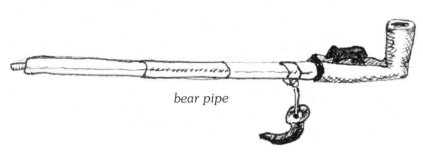

bear pipe

I think if the Bear Dance is done as a separate dance, at the conclusion, as the host or Medicine Man gathers up the musical instruments, he should smoke from a sacred Bear Pipe, facing the fire. He should then place the stem of the pipe to the mouths of the drummer, the rattler and singers, allowing each of them to take a puff. This would show the honor and respect as exhibited at the conclusion of the other dances. The host then takes the pipe and does a brief Pipe Dance around the fire. He shouts, "aya'hi:sta-ti:yi'" which means "stop" or "end". He then puts the pipe back in place and gathers all of the musical instruments to put them away.

BEAR DANCE SONG

Way hi Way hi
Way hay we hay Way hay we hay (sing twice)

Ha yah tuh ha ni He ho

He yo hah yah tuh ha ni He yo (sing 12 times)

Heee
Yo Nuh wa ti ga
Ni ga ya he say
O na ta si ha
Gu la o sho hi
Ni ga yuh he say

Ya he ya go way ya he (sing 16 times)

The song above is used by Cherokees in North Carolina . Other bear songs are mentioned in the writings of James Moody

NOTE: The phallic, sexual aspects of this dance are included to be true to historical references to the dance and could be eliminated, of course, if found offensive or if children are involved.

The Buffalo Dance Costume

The Buffalo have disappeared from the land of the Cherokee in the Southeast. These were mountain buffalo, which were scattered in numbers, but used to the forests, hill-country and grazing areas of this section of the United States.

With good reason, the Cherokee honored the buffalo with a special dance. When the hunter brought in a buffalo, several important uses were made of it. The meat provided food. The hide was used for clothing, such as moccasins, fur blankets for the beds, and robes to be worn during the winter. Even the hoofs could be melted for glue, and the horns could be made into spoons. So one can see that the buffalo indeed deserved great respect.

Hunters usually offered certain prayers or used formulas to ensure a successful hunt, and then asked the forgiveness of the slain animal by saying a prayer. This was done to ward off misfortune by the spirit of the animal.

A feast of the meat was common in those days, as people of the village believed in sharing. Since the women prepared the meals from the hunter's catch, it stands to reason that they were included as dance partners in the Buffalo Dance.

In the 20th century, animal dances of the Cherokee have been done at night. The Buffalo Dance is saved until the other dances are finished, which would be in the early morning before dawn.

In the old days, before the 19th century, the Buffalo Dance was probably done before the hunt and perhaps, at times, afterwards at the village when the people would celebrate the good fortune of the hunters.

It is well known that when a Cherokee hunter went to hunt a buffalo, he wore a wooden mask resembling a buffalo face. He also wore a tanned buffalo skin over his body. All of this was done in order to deceive the animal into thinking the hunter was just another buffalo.

Now let's consider some of the pieces that were worn as part of the buffalo costume.

A wooden mask can be carved from buckeye wood, the face stained with sumac dye, or red clay. In keeping with Cherokee tradition, the eye holes should be outlined in black.

If you, for some reason, cannot carve a mask from wood, try making one from paper mache, as described in the "Booger Mask" section of this book. You could also visit Cherokee, North Carolina and buy one that is already made (*see sources list at end of book*).

Before the 18th century, the buffalo mask was probably made from real fur, just as the other animal masks were.

The women that participated in the Buffalo Dance probably wore masks as well, representing the cow buffalo. But there would have been a difference in the design, which would depict a female. Women were associated with buffalo and deer in the old tradition, because the men were always hunting them, just as they did the game animals.

It should be remembered that dance masks for this dance were absolutely worn by the male dancers. This was one of the main items worn. I might also mention that in James Adair's *History of the American Indian*, he mentions an Indian wearing a leather headband with buffalo horns attached to it. The same Indian also carried a gourd rattle. This could have been part of the old-time buffalo dance costume for Southeastern Indians.

To portray a buffalo in dance, a man would wear a buffalo robe draped around his body, as shown in a prior sketch. This was common practice by Cherokee hunters when trying to fool the buffalo in order to get close enough to kill the animal

Modern-day buffalo robes are not often made of authentic buffalo fur. However, it may be constructed from an old brown fur coat, or from imitation brown fur.

Some basic things for the man's Buffalo Dance costume are:
1. a wood or fur mask
2. a buffalo tanned hide, or brown imitation fur
3. the tail, or an imitation tail

Accessories worn beneath the costume were:
1. necklace
2. breech-clout and belt
3. garters
4. leggings, moccasins and shirts
   (optional if weather conditions were cold)
5. jingle bells (perhaps added to the garters for a modern touch)

Since few people today know the old Cherokee dance songs, it's a good idea to use a cassette tape to play during the dance. One such tape, which I highly recommend, is "Where the Ravens Roost", by Walker Calhoun. Some things of the past must be revived and adapted for modern times. Likewise, not everyone willing to do a Cherokee dance will have a drummer or song leader, so a recording is well suited for the purpose. Once the songs are learned, they can be sung to the length needed for the duration of the dance.

From all that I have studied about the Buffalo Dance, the women that participated, during the early 20th century, wore dresses common to the time when performing the dance. However, the lead woman wore turtle-shell rattles on her legs and took her position behind the lead male Buffalo Dancer. The other female dancers wore no rattles.

All of this knowledge tells us a lot! In the early times, before the 19th century, when Cherokee dancers would have worn more meaningful things during this dance, this is what they may have worn.

It is sure that the women wore dresses to represent the female buffalo. Since most all Native Americans believed in the "White Buffalo Legend", the lead woman Buffalo Dancer may have worn a white leather dress, possibly ornamented with buffalo symbols and tassels of buffalo hair. She would also wear leg-rattles as previously mentioned.

The other women dancers would have worn light or dark brown dresses of leather, ornamented in a similar fashion. These dresses were most likely made of tanned buffalo hide to correspond with the dance.

Another item all of the women would have worn, is a braided garter made of buffalo hair. This string for a garter was worn by the women of many Southeastern tribes.

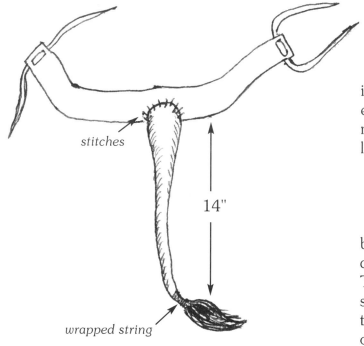

stitches

14"

wrapped string

Other dance apparel would include necklaces, bracelets, earrings and moccasins made of the same color leather as the dresses worn.

This illustration depicts a belt which can be worn during the Buffalo Dance. The belt part is made of a strip of brown leather with tie strings. The tail is made of a piece of tapered black leather, with black hair attached to the end

HOW TO DO THE BUFFALO DANCE

The Buffalo Dance was done by the Cherokee people to ensure a successful hunt, celebrate the occasion, and to appease the spirit of the slain animal.

To do the dance, a drummer is needed, and it is necessary to learn the sequence of the song. As the dance is progressing, the lead male dancer chants the words: "Hano he". Immediately, the other male dancers respond by saying, "Hu' hu". These words are chanted over and over, in this manner, throughout the entire dance.

This dance would have been originally done outdoors in the square grounds, near the council house. All of the people of the village could watch the dance in this setting.

The drummer would sit off to the side at his appointed seat.

The lead male dancer may have worn a white buffalo robe to distinguish him from the other dancers. This is conjecture on my part.

As the male dancers enter the dance ground in a single file, they dance in a counter-clockwise circle, as was common in Cherokee dancing.

The sketch above is drawn from a description given by James Adair in <u>History of the American Indian</u>, page 33. In the Cherokee Buffalo Dance, the dancers moved their feet by using the "Stomp and Shuffle" dance steps.

The lead woman dancer, wearing the ratties, takes her place behind the lead male dancer. She keeps perfect time to the drumming with the rattles.

Other women who take part in the dance, take their place behind a male dancer.

Keep in mind that during this dance, the men are portraying the bull buffalo, and the women dancers are portraying the cow buffalo. The appropriate parts must be played.

Male dancers sometimes pawed at the ground, just like a buffalo. During this century, dancers pretend to use imaginary buffalo hoofs where their hands are. At one time, long ago, actual buffalo hoofs were used for this mannerism. Occasionally, the male dancer might bump into the female dancer in a flirting gesture that buffalo sometimes do. Dancers also would sound out a bellowing sound like a buffalo. This may be learned by visiting the zoo, or by viewing a helpful video.

Dancers would also drop their heads down like a buffalo, and sometimes charge their slayer. Another buffalo posture would be achieved by stooping at the shoulders and waist. Some dancers curve the fingers of their right and left hands and hold them to the sides of their head, imitating the horns of the buffalo. This practice was adopted during the early part of the 20th century due to old dance items and costumes no longer being used for the dance.

References to the costume and dance:

The Cherokees, by Grace Steele Woodward, pg. 50

Cherokee Dance and Drama, by Speck and Broom, pgs. 71-72

League of the Iroquois, by Morgan, pg. 287 (This dance was borrowed from the Cherokee)

History *Myths and Sacred Formulas of the Cherokees,* by James Mooney, pgs. 27, 263, 293, 352, 410, 412, 443, 485

Cherokee Perspective, edited by Laurence and Jim Hornbuckle, pg. 132

History of the American Indians, by James Adair, pg. 33

The Southeastern Indians, by Charles Hudson, pg. 247, 269, 366

Sun Circles and Human Hands, by Emma Lila Fundaburk and Mary Douglas Foreman, pg. 204

Letters and Notes on the North American Indians, edited by Michael M. Mooney, pg. 172 (George Catlin)

George Catlin and the Old Frontier, by Harold McCracken, pgs. 38, 108

THE HORSE DANCE COSTUME

In prehistoric times, the Cherokee did all of their traveling by foot. Their possessions had to be carried upon their backs when moving to a new location. Even during war, the men traveled on foot, or by dugout canoe when possible.

The horse was introduced to the southeast around 1540, when Hernando de Soto entered the area, by way of Florida. The years passed, and by the late 18th century, the horse had become very familiar to the Cherokee.

The foot trails from one village to another, began to look more like roads. This new phase of Cherokee culture brought many changes. Fields could now be plowed using the horse, and traveling great distances became easier.

It's no wonder that, as the horse became so important to the Cherokee, the animal was honored with the Horse Dance. There is no existing reference to a costume that might have been worn for this dance. As early as the first half of the 20th century, the dance was performed by the Cherokee men and women in the plain clothes that they had adopted from the white men.

In my opinion, this casual manner detracts from the intended effect of the dance. To reconstruct a Cherokee Horse Dance costume, one might study early historic writings of the horse as well as related costumes from other indian tribes. Following, is a description of my own such reconstruction.

In 1730, a London newspaper reported of some visiting Cherokee men who wore breech-clouts with horses tails hanging down behind. Their faces, shoulders and other body parts were painted with streaks, whirls and spots of red, blue and green. They carried bows and wore painted feathers in their hair and were practically naked except for the breech-clout and moccasins. See *Tennessee's Indian Peoples* by Ronald N. Satz, pgs. 18-19.

According to other newspapers of the time, and *The Cherokee Crown of Tannassy* by William O. Steele, pgs. 109-110, the men also had long black hair that was gathered into strands and tied with ribbons in such a manner that the hair arched up at the back of the head, resembling a horse's tail. One man wore a turkey feather in his hair, while others wore the feathers of the Carolina parakeet and the wood duck. These are all good suggestions for items to wear for the Horse Dance.

All Cherokee dancers, as well as dancers from other Southeastern tribes, always dressed in great detail. The Horse Dance costume must have looked outstanding in it's earliest form.

It's also interesting to note that in a George Catlin painting of a Choctaw ballplayer, as depicted in the book, *George Catlin and the Old Frontier* by Harold McCracken, the subject is wearing a collar made of horse hair along with a beaded belt with an odd looking horse tail attached. It stands to reason that these items could have been borrowed from the Horse Dance costume of another era. In this sketch, taken primarily from the Catlin painting, the face is painted red from the tip of the nose up to the hairline. Feathers are in the hair, and a horse hair mantle, dyed red, yellow and white, is worn.

The following depiction is a version of the Horse Dance costume that I crafted in the process of teaching neighborhood children what I know of the Dance.

One feather or more from the turkey, parakeet, wood duck, etc., sometimes painted, may be worn in the hair

In historic times, the scalp-lock was worn in several strands in a high arch, resembling a horse's mane

A belt with a horse's tail is worn

The dancers' naked body is painted in whirls, streaks and spots using colors of blue, green and red. I am of the opinion that these colors were used for entertainment dances, such as the animal dances of the Cherokee.

A breech-clout and moccasins are worn.

Garters are an option as well.

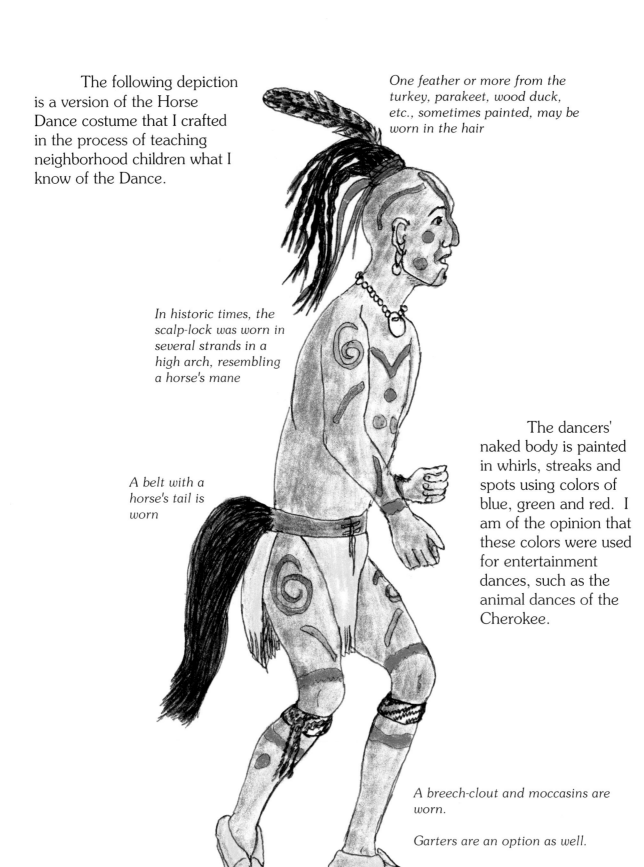

190

Some Cherokee men shaved their heads, except for the decorated scalp-lock. Currently, most dancers have a full head of hair, therefore, adaptations can be made. A headband can be worn with a feather stuck behind the band at the back of the neck. Or, a feather may be tied with ribbons to the hair on the crown of the head.

Sometimes the Cherokee men would arch the scalp-lock by pulling the hair through a large bone tube, as shown. Feathers and ribbons can then be tied to the hair.

In the photo above, a frontal view of the costume is shown.
(models are Jimmy Gwinner & Frankie Masnas)
Below, is a side view.

From all of the previous descriptions, one can get a good idea of a potential Horse Dance costume. These descriptions are, however, my own speculations and represent an educated projection as to what the men might wear for this dance.

A woman would wear her best dress for this dance, along with turtle shell rattles tied to the leg below the knee.

If you wish to perform this dance, consult *Cherokee Dance and Drama* by Speck and Broom, pgs. 74-75, and *The Cherokee Perspective* by Laurence French and Jim Hornbuckle, pgs. 132-133. The Horse Dance is explained in these books.

To prepare a feather to be worn in the hair for the Horse Dance, select a wing feather and paint sections of the quill with enamel paint, as shown.

Painted Feather for the Horse Dance Costume.

glue

horse hair

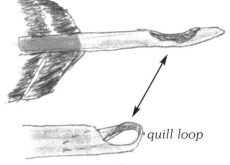

quill loop

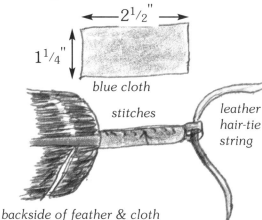

2¹/₂"

1¹/₄"

blue cloth

stitches

leather hair-tie string

backside of feather & cloth

When the painted feather is dry, follow these steps:

a. Use a single edge razor blade to cut out a section of the quill tip.

b. Put a small amount of glue in the opening. Flatten and bend the quill tip back into the opening and wait for the glue to dry

c. Cut a piece of blue cloth 2¹/₂" long by 1¹/₄" wide. Put a little glue down the center of the cloth and place it around the quill as shown. Keep the seam of the cloth on the backside of the feather as the cloth is sewn.

d. Cut a leather string ¹/₄" wide by 8" long to insert through the quill loop

HORSE TAIL BELT

I suggest a belt, such as the one shown above, to be worn for the Horse Dance. Even though this belt is essential in the portrayal of the horse, there is no existing example of a horse tail belt, to my knowledge. My rendition is based on the belts that the Choctaw ball players were wearing in the painting by George Catlin. The belt was worn during ball play to represent swiftness.

To make this belt, cut a strip of black or brown leather to the desired width and length, as shown.

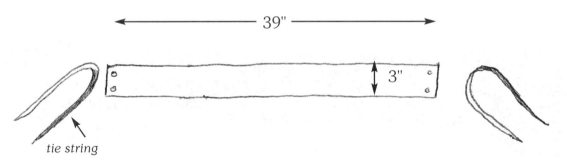

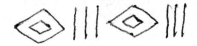

tie string

The length, of course, will depend on the waist line, and the width can be from 3" to 5". The Choctaw belts appear to be about 5" wide and decorated with white pony beads, forming diamond and line designs, as seen below.

Two holes are punched on both sides of the belt, as seen in the prior sketch. Through these holes are inserted tie strings, which are $1/4$" wide by 16" long.

This particular belt is tied at the front of the waist line, due to the fact that the tail attachment is at the back. Ordinarily, most belts were tied at the back and sashes were tied at the side.

The base of the tail attachment for this belt can be made of black leather or layered cloth. In the old days, the tail attachment was probably cut from the horse's mane and tail from time to time until there was enough to make a complete tail.

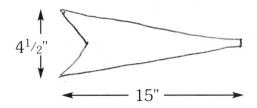

Base of black leather or layered cloth.

The hair from a long wig is ideal to use when making this tail. Black yarn or unraveled black dyed grass rope can also be substituted.

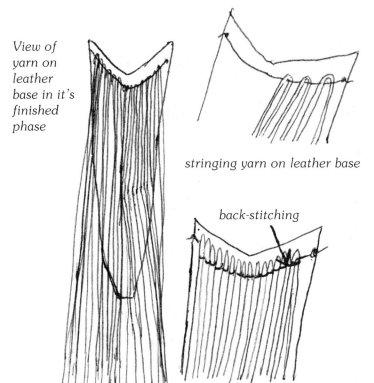

View of yarn on leather base in it's finished phase

stringing yarn on leather base

back-stitching

Fold a bundle of 52" black yarn strings in half, and hang them on a string, as shown. Keep the strands very thick and close together along the string.

Once all the black yarn strands are in place, use a needle and thread to back-stitch each strand of yarn to the leather base, as shown.

The doubled strands of yarn should make the tail 26" long.

Now sew the horse tail base to the middle half of the belt, as shown below. After tail is completely sewn to the belt, flip it over in a normal hanging position.

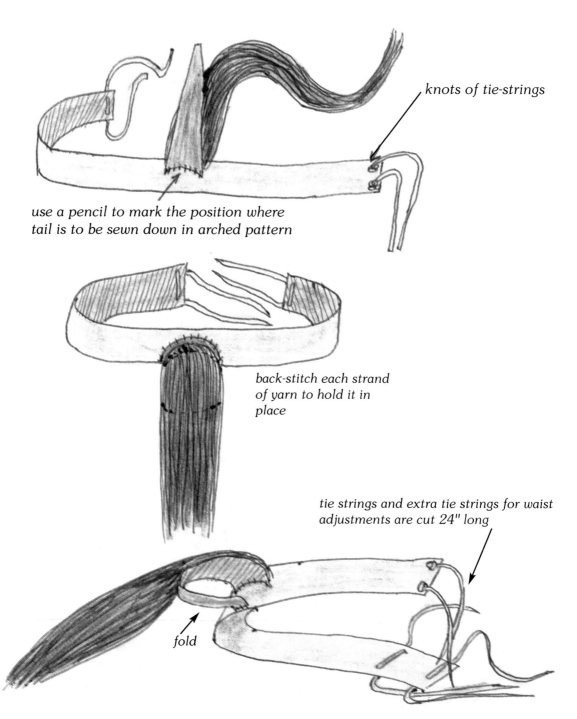

knots of tie-strings

use a pencil to mark the position where tail is to be sewn down in arched pattern

back-stitch each strand of yarn to hold it in place

tie strings and extra tie strings for waist adjustments are cut 24" long

fold

If you would like the tail to have more spring or motion to it during the dance, sew the other end of the leather base to the bottom of the belt, as shown above. The tail will then move up and down with the dance movements

A simpler type of horse-tail belt that can be made for younger dancers who wish to learn the dance can be made using imitation leather cloth for the belt with black yarn and painted designs for decorations.

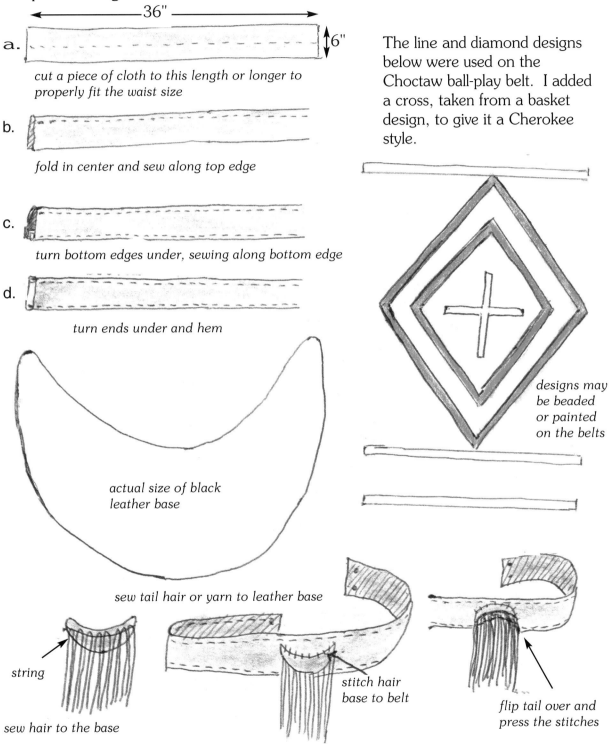

a.

cut a piece of cloth to this length or longer to properly fit the waist size

36"   6"

b.

fold in center and sew along top edge

c.

turn bottom edges under, sewing along bottom edge

d.

turn ends under and hem

actual size of black leather base

sew tail hair or yarn to leather base

string

sew hair to the base

stitch hair base to belt

flip tail over and press the stitches

The line and diamond designs below were used on the Choctaw ball-play belt. I added a cross, taken from a basket design, to give it a Cherokee style.

designs may be beaded or painted on the belts

NOTE: add tie strings to ends of belt

How To Do the Horse Dance

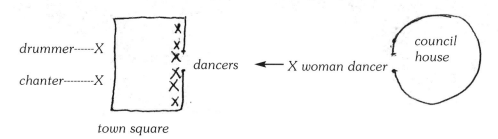

town square

Let's say this dance is held at the town square in front of the council house. For modern purposes, the dance can be done in a yard or a large room. There must be plenty of space.

The drummer and chanter sit off to one side of the dance ground, as shown above.

The male dancers enter the dance ground from the direction of the council house. They then form a straight line, standing side by side.

As the drummer begins, the chanter yells "Yo Ho". The dancers stomp the right foot and then the left, trying to imitate the way a horse walks. These dance steps are slow and short, as the dancers step in unison. The drum beat is slow.

The dancers keep stepping forward toward the chanter until they are close to where he sits. The chanter yells "Yo Ho". The dancers respond by saying, "Ye hye", and as they say these words, they suddenly turn around and dance back to where they started. This advancing and returning to the starting place is repeated four times in succession.

As the second phase of the dance begins, the drum beat becomes faster.

A woman, wearing her best outfit with turtle-shell rattles on her right leg, enters the middle of the line of male dancers. All of the dancers stand side by side as they dance and hold hands with each other. The steps become short and quick, in time with the drum. As the woman dances with them, the dancers beside her will sometimes make a flirtatious kicking gesture toward her. This returning and retreating process of the dance is performed as in the first phase, except faster.

Some dancers make horse sounds as they advance and retreat.

Kid's love doing this dance, and the reconstructed costumes will make it come alive for them.

198

The Horse Dance

THE BEAVER DANCE COSTUME

The Beaver Dance costume must have been quite simple. The lead male dancer would symbolize the hunter by wearing regular hunting clothes, such as a hunting shirt, belt, breech-clout, leggings and moccasins.

A female dancer represented the hunter's wife, wearing her regular deerskin dress and moccasins. The other dancers would have dressed in similar clothes. Fancy ceremonial costumes were not important in this dance.

The only ceremonial object in this dance was a wooden club from a sumac tree, which was stripped of it's bark. The club was carried by each dancer, male and female.

In the Beaver Dance, there is a man who works a rope with a beaver skin attached to it. As he gives the imitation beaver motion, the other dancers strike at it with their clubs. For added flavor, he could wear a brown fur hanging from his back or waist. An imitation beaver tail could also be added for effect, along with his breechclout, belt and moccasins. In cooler weather, a shirt and leggings may be added.

ROBE FOR BEAVER DANCE

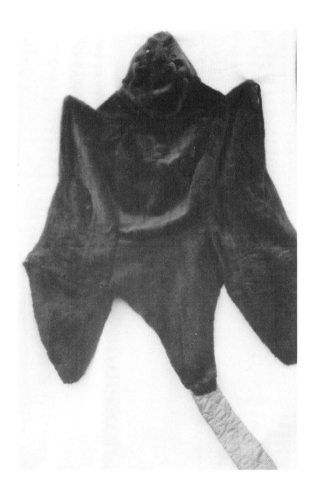

I designed the robe pictured above to be worn by the man who works the rope during the Beaver Dance. In my opinion, he should look the part.

Long ago, when there were beaver in the Cherokee country, hunters sometimes wore furs as a disguise during the hunt, to deceive the animal they were trying to kill. This robe is of my own conjecture, but I feel it gives the dance a more realistic effect.

A large piece of fur can be fashioned to make this robe. However, I used a brown coat with the sleeves removed, sewing the openings shut. I had to rework the shoulders for a better fit, and I added fur to the collar to form a hood. It's important to get a good loose fit for the robe. Placing the robe on a person while making it is a good idea, pinning up any excess and cutting them with scissors. These reworked areas can then be stitched up.

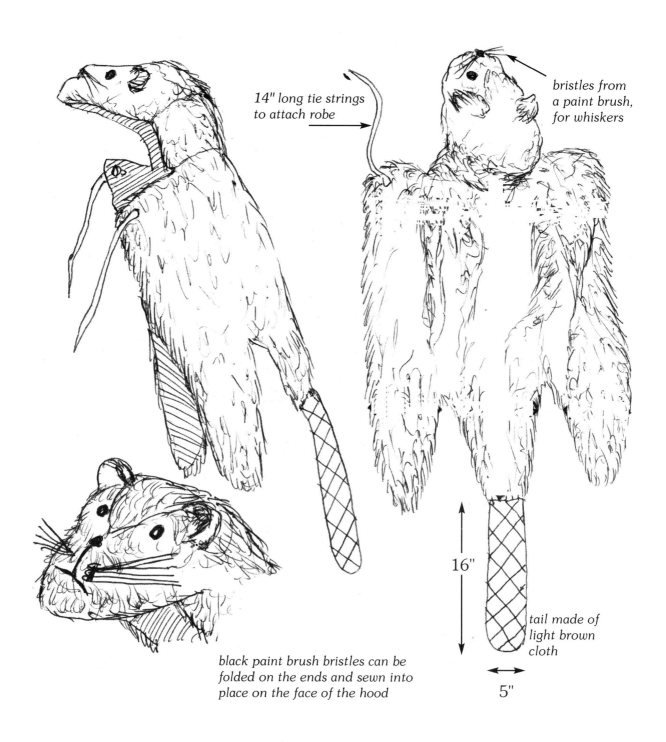

14" long tie strings
to attach robe

bristles from
a paint brush,
for whiskers

16"

tail made of
light brown
cloth

5"

black paint brush bristles can be
folded on the ends and sewn into
place on the face of the hood

The hood is made to resemble a beaver's head and face. Black yarn is sewn on to resemble a nose and mouth. Several adjustments should be made to make the hood look and fit correctly.

MAKING AN IMITATION BEAVER

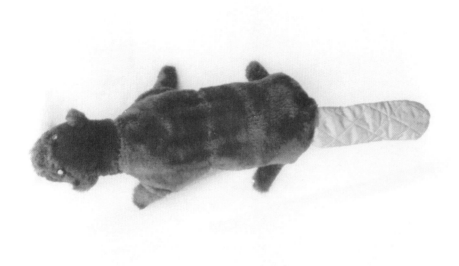

The photograph above shows an imitation beaver that was made for the Beaver Dance.

During the early part of this century, the Cherokee in North Carolina attached a piece of fur to the rope used in the dance. Others used a stuffed beaver skin. If neither were available, they then resorted to using a bundle of rags with feathers attached.

I created my beaver by using a brown fur lining from an old coat. Following, are the instructions on how I made this effigy.

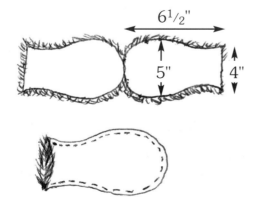

To make the head portion, cut the fur as shown. Next, fold the two pieces together with the fur on the inside and sew around the edges. Now turn inside out, so that the fur is on the outside.

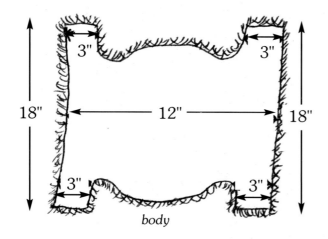

body

To make the body part of the beaver, cut a piece of fur, as shown.

Always cut and stitch the fur from the back side.

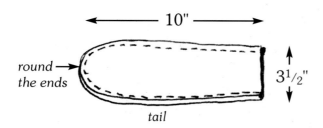

round → the ends

tail

turned inside out

The next step is making the tail.

For this, I used the light brown quilted lining from the coat.

Cut two pieces of material to the shape shown. Then turn the outside of the pieces in and stitch around the edges. Once this is finished, turn the tail right side out, as shown.

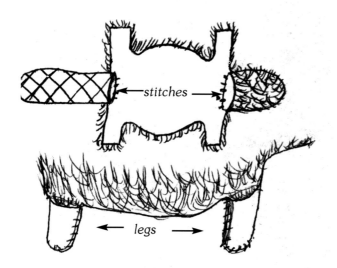

←stitches→

← *legs* →

Sew the head and tail on as shown.

Next, fold the leg portion like a tube, with the fur on the inside. Stitch along the sides and bottom. Do the same for the all legs, then turn them fur side out, stuffing them with rags, cotton, etc.

Stuff the head of the beaver with rags, cotton, or whatever is available and shape it to a desirable shape. Then cut a piece of fur big enough to be sewn between the back legs and at the abdomen area. Sew the "belly" part. Any available soft material was probably used for stuffing. I used some of my old socks as a padding for this purpose.

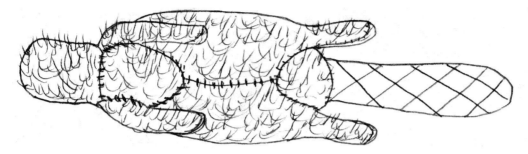

Now, cut a piece of fur to fit the chest region between the front legs, and sew it into place. Most of the stitching may have to be done on the fur side, as the belly and chest region is closed. To cover this stitching, rub the fur around the seams.

triangle of fur

After the beaver has been sewn together, cut a piece of fur in a triangle shape and sew it to the forehead region. A layer of padding underneath it will give it more shape.

Paint brush bristles, folded at the end, can be sewn on for whiskers, as shown.

Small pieces of fur are sewn on for the ears.

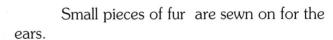

Black buttons are used for the eyes.

White tube beads are used for the teeth.

When finished, the beaver is tied to the middle of a rope for the Beaver Dance

HOW TO DO THE BEAVER DANCE

Before the end of the 18th century, there were plenty of beaver in the Cherokee country. The furs from these animals made soft robes and cover for beds. Other uses would have been food and perhaps warm hats for winter.

Cherokee hunters always believed in good luck for a hunt. They would say prayers during the hunting process, so as not to offend the spirit of the animal to be killed. They asked the animal to allow itself to be killed and not to be angry, because it was needed for food and skins. Hunters would sometimes wear the skin of the animal, or a mask resembling the animal they were hunting.

The beaver dance was done to determine if the hunt was going to be successful or not. After a good hunt, the dance was done again as entertainment for the people of the village.

Usually, the Common Dance, as described elsewhere in this book, was performed prior to the Beaver Dance on the hunter's return.

The photograph above illustrates how the rope is worked with the imitation beaver attached. This procedure is done near the end of the Beaver Dance.

(demonstrators are Sonny Eagle Eye Miller and Carol Sizemore)

Both men and women dancers alternate in a dance circle that moves counter-clockwise. They carry the wooden Sumac clubs in their left hands. The clubs can be around 2 feet long with a few dancers, but with 20 dancers or more, the clubs should be shorter.

At the center of the danceground, a wooden stake is driven. A grass rope, about 16 feet long is looped around the stake, and the imitation beaver is tied to the middle of the rope.

There is one man who is appointed to see-saw the rope around the stake, and he stands to the inside of the dancers to keep them from tripping on the rope. He stands waiting, holding the ends of the rope in each hand, for his function in the dance.

The dancers use a shuffle step, which involves stepping out with the right foot, touching the ground with the ball of the foot, and then sliding or lowering the heel to the ground, and repeating with the left foot. This step is similar to the toe-heel step, but adds the sliding motion.

As the dance begins, the dancers hold their clubs in the left hand and then switch to hold the clubs horizontally, touching the person's club to the left of him. The hands of each dancer grasps the tips and ends of the clubs, as shown in the photograph below.

This photograph shows how to hold clubs inside the dance circle.
(Sonny Eagle-Eye Miller demonstrates how to work the rope)

During the first part of the dance, the dancers dance in time to the drum beat, using the shuffle step in a clockwise direction. The clubs are held horizontally outside the circle. This part of the dance can last up to five minutes. 20 dancers would be a good amount of people for this dance.

The second phase of the dance is done the same as the first, except that the clubs are switched to the right hand, forming a stick circle to the outside of the dancers. This portion can also last around five minutes.

Photograph above illustrates how to carry wooden clubs outside of the dance circle.

In the third phase of the dance, the dancers hold the clubs over their left shoulders, as one would hold a rifle. They continue their counter-clockwise movement using the shuffle step. After about five minutes, a man and woman enter the middle of the circle and begin yelling "Beaver, Beaver!" about four times. The man and woman, representing the hunter and his wife, then go and stand near the wooden stake where the rope and beaver fur are attached. The man yells "Hyu!" (or here) as he raises his club to strike the beaver. He then attempts to strike the beaver as the rope-puller tries his best to cause the hunter to miss. The dancers all yell "Yo hyo". Then, whether he has hit the beaver or not, he throws the stick down and leaves the danceground. His wife then comes to take her turn.

Each dancer then takes a turn striking at the beaver, while the other dancers respond with the vocal chant. They each throw their club down and leave until no more dancers are left.

In the last part of the dance, the dancers circle with their clubs on their shoulders. Each person gets a chance to strike at the beaver

Hitting the beaver during this dance determines whether or not the hunt will be successful. If too many of the dancers miss the beaver, the hunt might have been called off.

This would be an excellent fun dance for children today, as they can take turns striking at the beaver.

BEAVER DANCE SONG

Yo ha he yo ha he yo ha he yo ha he

He ya he yo he yo ni tu wa yo ha he yo ha he (2 times)

Hi ya ti ga na wi gi na (3 times)

Yo ha yo ha

Hi ya ti ga na wi ga na (3 times)

Yo ha yo ha

Hi ya ti ga na wi ga na (3 times)

Ho he yo wa hi ye wa hi ye

To yi to yi he no he ya

Hi ye hi ye hi no way (repeat last 2 lines until dance is completed)

THE RACCOON DANCE COSTUME

This sketch is drawn from a shell gorget located at the Craig Burial Mound-Spiro Mound in Le Flore County, Oklahoma. This gorget is in the University of Oklahoma, Stovall Museum. It is called the raccoon gorget.

On the actual piece, there is an identical dancer facing the other direction on th left side.

See "Sun Circles and Human Hands", edited by Emma L. Fundaburk and Mary D. Foreman, pg.60.

The men in the Raccoon Dance should wear a tan leather or cloth fringed hunting shirt, breechclout, leggings and moccasins. They might also wear their eagle feather, jewelry, knife and holster.

The male dancers might carry a short wooden club to represent the tool used to kill the raccoon. The knife and holster represent the tool used to skin a raccoon.

The women may wear tan leather dresses, or dresses made of cloth, as seen elsewhere in this book. Moccasins and jewelry are also an option.

Since the women did most of the tanning of hides, perhaps they could carry miniature tanning frames to represent their duty after the hunter-husband brings the hides home. Raccoon hides can be bought at pow-wows, trading posts and Indian craft shops. It would be a good idea to lace a piece of fur to each of the miniature frames. Such items will make the dance more meaningful since the dance is a thing of the past, and the dancers would only be going through motions of pretense otherwise

This tan outfit consists of a fringed top and wrap-around skirt.
(The model is Elizabeth Mafnas)

A suitable tan outfit which can be worn by a male dancer of the Raccoon Dance

(The model is Terry Collins)

HOW TO DO THE RACCOON DANCE

This dance symbolizes a raccoon taking shelter in a tree and being killed by the hunter. It also portrays how the animal is skinned, and the hide tanned. This dance was done both for fun and to celebrate a successful hunt.

In parts of the dance, the male dancers tease and joke with their female dance partners, as in the Bear Dance. The male dancers pretend to rub raccoon grease on the women as an adornment feature. See Gilbert, *The Eastern Cherokees*, pg. 266.

Phase 1 of the dance represents the hunt. Male and female dance partners form a circle, going around in a single file counter-clockwise direction. They use a shuffling trot or a fast moving dance step. At the head of the dance circle is the male leader who is followed by a woman wearing tortoise shell leg rattles. The chanter is at one side of the dance circle, using a gourd rattle.

Phase 2 of the dance represents the killing of the raccoon and the tanning of it's hide. In this part, the leader at the head of the line dances backwards facing the woman behind him. The other male dancers then do the same.

The male dancers pretend to strike the raccoon with a wooden club. This gesture can be done for one complete round of the circle. Next the pretense of stretching the hide on a wooden frame is done. They pretend to scrape the hide with a knife or their fingernails. The men pretend to rub the raccoon grease on the front and sides of their female dance partner.

In **phase 3**, the dancers return to their positions as in phase 1 and repeat.

For more details, see *Cherokee Dance and Drama*, pg. 79.

In Oklahoma, some of the Lenape or Delaware Indians still do the Raccoon Dance and sing it's songs. Their dance is similar to the Cherokee version. It starts with only the men in the dance circle in facing pairs, as in phase 2 of the Cherokee Raccoon Dance.

Then the women join the dance circle by picking out a dance partner in this counter-clockwise circle. The female partner faces her male dance partner, while the males dance backwards.

When the song changes, the pairs of dance partners whirl around. As they switch positions, causing the women to be dancing backwards with their male partners facing them.

The dance is done until the chanter stops

THE GROUND-HOG DANCE COSTUME

During the 1930's when Speck and Broom studied the Groundhog Dance, the Cherokee dancers wore white men's clothes for most of their dances. One may assume that in early times, when this dance had more meaning, the dancers wore their best common clothes.

Male dancers would have worn feathers and ornaments in their hair, along with earrings, necklaces, and arm and wrist bands. A belt or sash with the breechclout would also have been a part of the costume. Since the dance was performed for the Green Corn Festival, leggings were probably not worn since it was so warm. Garters and moccasins may have been worn.

The female dancers fixed their hair according to status. Young women wore their hair loose, while older women fixed their hair in a coiled up fashion on top of the head. Of course, there were other hair styles too. Some women daubed vermillion along the hairline or a spot of it on the cheek. Earrings, necklaces and bracelets would have been a part of the costume as well, along with deerskin dresses and moccasins.

We can learn certain things about the costume from the legend of how the wolves tried to kill a groundhog, and the origin of the Groundhog Dance, as related by James Moony. In the legend, the singer or chanter of the dance was the groundhog. In the dance, the man who does the singing for the dance should wear a tanned groundhog skin or the tail, to represent the animal. The whole hide could be worn in a hooded fashion on the head, as was popular among Native Americans.

Also, the legend describes the dancers as wolves. This leads me to believe that the dancers should wear a symbol of a painted wolf on their body, or some representation of the wolf as part of their costume. Since the Cherokee at one time believed if they killed a wolf, misfortune would befall them, I doubt seriously that the hide of a wolf was ever used in this dance.

The representation of the groundhog and wolves by the singer and dancers would add a great visual effect to this dance, giving the audience a better understanding.

Wrap-around skirt and jacket. Note the ribbon-work at the bottom of the skirt.

(Model is author's sister, Lucy)

Beaded jacket and velvet wrap-around skirt.

(Model is author's sister, Myrtle)

215

HOW TO DO THE GROUNDHOG DANCE

This dance should be done in a large open space. Normally it was performed in the "square grounds" in front of the council house.

There should be an equal number of male and female dancers to be partners. The men form a circle and their women partners form a circle inside of the men's. The circles both move in a clockwise direction as they dance.

The men's circle has a leader whom they follow. He carries a gourd rattle and chants the song. One or two of the women wear terrapin shell leg rattles and lead the women's' circle. The men and women leaders should be paired, side by side as they dance.

As the male and female dancers go around, the chanter chants:

> "Ha' wi ye' ehi Ya ha' wi ye' ehi
> Ha' wi ye' ehi Ya ha' wi ye' ehi
> Yu-u"

When the signal "Yu-u" is given, the male and female dancers switch positions, positioning the women on the outer circle. Meanwhile, the chanter sings the second verse:

> "Hi' ya gu' we Ha he' ya gu' we
> Hi' ya gu' we Ha he' ya gu' we
> Yu-Yu"

When the signal "Yu-yu" is given, the first verse is repeated as the male dancers turn and dance backwards. They can then face their women partners. Then, at the Yu-u" signal, the male dancers turn and face forward again during the second verse.

During the dance, the dancers make scooping motions toward their chests, imitating the ground hog digging his den in the ground.

The Groundhog Dance should be done seven consecutive times to be true to the old legend of how the Groundhog Dance began. This legend was recorded by James Mooney. It tells of how the wolves danced seven times for the groundhog, until at the end of the seventh dance, the groundhog got away.

In the legend, the groundhog told the wolves they should do this dance to show thanksgiving as people did at the Green Corn Festival. This dance is now done by people as a fun dance.

THE ANT DANCE COSTUME

In this dance, the men may wear their tan colored leather outfits, or those made of cloth. One might choose to wear a fringed hunting shirt, or go without a shirt. Leggings, breechclout and moccasins are other possible items, along with braided garters, necklaces, armbands and feathers for the hair.

The women of this dance may wear their tan colored dresses and moccasins, plus their jewelry.

Chief Oliver Collins of the Talligee Cherokees in Portsmouth, Ohio, says that their dancers sometimes have worn small antennas on their heads. Antennas can be fashioned very simple from wire fastened to a headband.

Another addition one might consider when dressing for the Ant Dance, is to use some body paint, as mentioned in the James Mooney account of "Nun Yunu wi or Stone Man". The red ant is sometimes referred to as "nun yunu wi". In this legend, the medicine man told the people to paint their face and breast with red paint. In doing so, whatever the person prayed for while he was being painted would be granted - hunting success, working skill, or for a long life.

*Typical tan colored outfits which can be worn by women
doing the Ant Dance.*
(models are Lisa Howard and Carolynn Mills)

A typical tan colored outfit suitable for a male
Ant Dancer.
(modeled by Jimmey Gwinner)

HOW TO DO THE ANT DANCE

The Ant Dance is done today primarily for fun and entertainment. During the dance, men and women move in a snakelike procession like a colony of ants. A good reference is Gilbert's *The Eastern Cherokees*, pg. 260.

James Mooney's *History, Myths and Sacred Formulas of the Cherokees*, pgs. 309 and 319, mention the red ant, also referred to as Nun Yuni Wi, or Stone Dress. These myths are worthy of study as the old legends sometimes contain information to help in understanding the meaning behind the dances, and they give clues to the make-up of the costumes.

It is surprising what can be learned in observing a colony of ants. They all labor and work together as a unit, performing difficult tasks in gathering food and working for the good of the group. In a way, this is very symbolic of how the Cherokee people worked together in their tasks for the village and their families.

Following is a description of the Ant Dance performance:

In this dance, the singing or chanting is done by the men. The dancers use a fast moving shuffling trot. The men and women represent ants, forming two single file lines, side by side, moving in a circle, one inside the other. The circles move in opposite directions.

Each circle has a male leader or priest carrying a gourd rattle. Behind each leader is a woman wearing tortoise shell leg rattles. The rest of the dancers are in an order alternating men and women.

As the circles revolve, the leaders quickly bow to each other and take a few steps backward to show respect. This movement causes the other dancers to back up as well, creating a little confusion and laughter before proceeding. This is repeated over and over for several minutes. For more details, see *Cherokee Dance and Drama*, by Speck and Broom, pg. 76.

Note: In other versions of the Ant Dance, opposing dancers, when stopping to move backwards, will look at each other directly in the eyes with their faces close together. Then they will flick their forefingers close to their opponents eyes. This imitates the antenna movements of ants, as they pause to meet another ant in line.

THE WAR DANCE COSTUME

A typical warrior's outfit.

The War Dance depicted the advance of warriors, the battle and the victory against the enemy. Three phases or movements of the actions of warriors on the warpath can be seen in the dance.

This dance gave each warrior a chance to show off his outfit and status. Most Native American tribes wore very beautiful costumes to a War Dance. Cherokee warriors wore costumes during this dance closely resembling that of the actual war costume.

The war costume consisted of the following items: feathers in the hair, war paint, earrings, necklace, breechclouts, pouch and moccasins. The weapons carried consisted of warclubs, hatchets, knives, spears, shields, bows, arrows, quivers, and in certain periods, guns. A blanket was carried for warmth. Leggings were worn only if the weather was cool or the area traveled was rough. Parched cornmeal or cornbread cakes were stored in the pouch carried by the warrior. To see how a common Cherokee warrior may have looked, refer to the previous painting.

Any of these items can be worn as part of the War Dance costume, with the exception of the pouch or pack in which the food supply was carried. The most prominent weapon appears to be the warclub.

A warrior dressed in his ceremonial shirt.

Warriors of greater status sometimes wore elaborate ceremonial war costumes during the dance. When the dance ended, such outfits were taken off and given to their women to be put away. The lighter costume of the warpath was then put on before heading off on the war trail. As seen in the previous illustration, the ceremonial shirt and outfit can be very beautiful.

The above outfit depicts a War Chief's outfit as was worn during ceremonies, councils, dances, etc.

(model is author's brother, Tom)

How to Do the War Dance

When war was declared, a red pole stripped of it's bark, was set up in front of the council house. Fastened to the upper part of this red painted pole was a flag made of red dyed deerskin. The length of the flag was 4 or 5 yards long. Later, it was probably made of red cloth. On the very top of the pole a carved wooden eagle was mounted. When the flag was raised, everyone in the village knew that war had been declared. Warriors interested in going on the warpath ran up to the pole and gave out a war whoop.

Next, the Great War Chief gave a pep talk to the warriors concerning the enemy and why they should go to war. His war speech excited the warriors and inspired them to volunteer. Those going to war had to show that they had accepted the invitation by picking up the red war club belonging to the Raven, as the Great War Chief was now to be called.

This ritual went something like this: A large bonfire was started near the war pole. Next, seven advisors from a group of warriors came and stood before the fire as the war chief lay his warclub on the ground in front of the fire. As they stood looking at the war club, the councilors sang:

"Yo wi hi, hi yo wi ye
Yo wi hi, hi yo wi ye
Yo wi hi, hi yo wi ye
Yo wi hi, hi yo wi ye"

The verse was sung 6 times. As it was sung, a speaker or leader of the seven counselors picked up the war club and walked around the dance grounds with it. This demonstrated that they were willing to pick up the warclub against their enemy. This ritual formalized their agreement, as a body of warriors, to perform as a team going to war.

After the ritual was finished, the War Dance could begin. The dance was sometimes called "Ti ge yo hi" or "Te you hi", which meant going in a circle. The dance was usually done at night with large bonfires providing light.

The principal assistant to the Great War Chief led the dance and did the chanting. A drum made of a large clay pot and covered with raccoon skin was used. It had a leather string with bells attached to it which went around the brim of the drum.

Each warrior who took part in the war dance carried a red war club made of hickory or some other hard wood. After the dance was over, warriors would go dip themselves seven times in a creek or river before they went to bed.

Following is an explanation of the War Dance with directions and illustrations:

The dancers first stand side by side facing east, and as they begin to dance, they have a leaning posture as shown. A red warclub is carried in the right hand, while the left arm and hand is extended toward the red war pole. They then step slowly forward and backward to a slow drum beat. The warclub is held passively as the chanter sings "He ha li". The warriors then shout "ye ye!" as they dance.

    Now the drum beat changes to fast time and the feet movements also pick up
pace. The dancers raise their warclubs and pretend to strike at the enemy, symbolized by
the war pole. The facial expressions are fierce with anger, as in battle. This part of the
dance portrays the actual encounter with the enemy.

Next, the dancers turn about with fast dance steps and rapid drum beats. After dancing in this mode for a while, the dance ends with the warriors sounding out four war whoops, "Ye Ye". For more detail on this dance, *see Cherokee Dance and Drama*, pgs. 63-64, by Speck and Broom.

THE ORDINATION OUTFIT OF THE NEW GREAT WAR CHIEF

This costume is similar to the one worn by the New Great War Chief, as he took office at the National Capitol in his ordination.

His scalp lock was pulled through a large tube made of deer antler, so that the hair arched upward. A 2" red painted cane tube was tied to this large tube. And a red dyed eagle feather was inserted into the tube, as shown. He also wore a cape made of red dyed eagle feathers. The armbands and wrist band were also red along with his garters, belt, breechclout and moccasins.

Seven red and black alternating stripes were painted across his face. Red stripes were painted around the crown of the head. A vertical red stripe was drawn down the nose, chin and neck to the chest. Then, red lines were drawn from the thumbs back up the arms and across to the line on the chest. Next, from each big toe, a vertical line was drawn back up the legs to the line on the chest. Refer to the drawing.

The chief carried a red war club at his ordination. This was a ceremonial club made of polished red stone. During war, his costume was also red, including his bow, arrows, club, quiver and shield.

Other war chiefs dressed differently. One example would be brown turkey feather capes.

COSTUME OF THE
GREAT WAR CHIEF'S COUNSELORS

There were seven counselors who helped the Great War Chief to carry out his orders during war time. They made sure the other warriors knew what to do.

The counselor wore his scalplock arched up with a tube made of deer antler. A shell gorget was attached to the tube with two short red dyed eagle feathers.

The breechclout and other articles of his clothing were lighter red than that of the Great War Chief's. Head warriors wore red moccasins to show their status.

As shown, a turkey feather cape or mantle was worn as a status symbol for leaders of the tribe.

During colder weather, shirts and leggings would also have been an addition. At a War Dance, many warriors went without shirts and leggings, probably to keep cool and show their tattoos and battle scars.

COSTUME OF A WARRIOR'S WIFE

For ceremonies and dances, the wives of warriors put traces of the red war color on their white deerskin outfits. Red cloth, seed beads or paint can be used to make the designs. Feathers can be woven or sewn onto a strip of cloth and sewn onto the dress as shown.

A finger woven belt can be worn with this dress.

Important women usually added a beautiful short feather cape as part of the costume.

Boots which reached halfway up the lower leg were commonly worn by wives of the warriors. Their ceremonial dresses during peace time were made of white deerskin, but a darker color, such as tan, may have been worn during war.

The dress was knee-length with longer sleeves during cooler weather. A petticoat or wrap-around skirt could be worn underneath, reaching down below the knees. Or, a strap dress could be worn underneath, instead of the petticoat or wrap-around skirt.

Wives of high-ranking warriors might wear their hair fixed up high on the head. A bone comb or shell hair pin would hold it in place.

ceremonial outfit.

(modeled by Frankie Mafnas)

these outfits would be suitable for war dances.

THE SCALP DANCE COSTUME

The Scalp Dance costume for men is quite simple. The dancer, Mooney mentioned, was wearing only a breechclout, and wore no shirt. A warrior's breechclout was decorated with designs, beads, quillwork, etc. to suit his own medicine power. In the old days, the breechclout was made of buckskin, but later with the coming of the Europeans, trade blankets were used.

Moccasins of the center-seam style would have been worn as part of the outfit for this dance as well. Ceremonial or dance moccasins were worn which were beautifully decorated with designs done in bead, quillwork and paint.

Necklaces, wrist and armbands, and earrings were also a part of the dance costume. Feathers in the hair usually consisted of swan down or fluffs or eagle tail-feathers, and covered the head attached to the warrior's scalplock.

Since most of the warrior's body was exposed during this dance, body paint would have been used. Red paint symbolizing success and bloodshed may have been one of the colors used. Yellow stood for trouble and calamity on the victim. This may have been another color used. See *The Cherokee People*, by Thomas E. Mails, page 101. He talks about the color meanings of the Cherokee. Painting the body for dances was common all through the Southeast in those days. It added flavor to the appearance of the dancer and was believed to help one's medicine power.

Designs painted on the body could have been painted on the face, arms, chest and legs. Tattoos were also a body decoration.

A beautiful belt, knife holster and knife decorated with beads, tin cones, paint, etc. would have been very suitable for items of this costume. The knife was a tool used for scalping, so logically it would be carried during the dance. It might be helpful to read James Mooney's account of the Scalp Dance. See *History Myths and Sacred Formulas of the Cherokee*, pages 170, 371, 377, 390-391, and 496.

In the following sketch of a male dancer in his Scalp Dance Costume, the warrior is shown holding a scalp pole and an eagle wand. Another useful illustration can be found in the book, *Sun Circles and Human Hands*, page 205.

The sketch of a female dancer depicts what a woman would wear for this dance. She would have dressed in her finest ceremonial dress with vermillion on her face. Bracelets, earrings and necklaces would be worn as extras. Moccasins or short boots were also worn. These women dancers also were permitted to carry a gun or scalp during the dance. For more information, see Mooney's *History Myths and Sacred Formulas of the Cherokee*, page 496.

Shown below is a depiction of the male Scalp Dancer's costume.

white swan fluffs and
long feathers decorate
the scalp-lock

body paint

earrings and necklace

armbands

knife,
holster
and belt

scalp
pole

eagle wand in right hand

breechclout

garters

center-seam moccasins

232

This sketch depicts items a woman could wear when participating in the Scalp Dance.

vermillion on the face and hairline

women who joined in the dance sometimes carried guns or scalps

earrings

necklace

a tan colored buckskin dress

white dresses were worn for religious dances, which were related to peaceful purposes

bracelets

bells sewn on clothing

woven feather strips on clothing

moccasins or short boots

To take a scalp, a Cherokee warrior would put his foot on the slain enemy's neck. He then grabbed the hair of the slain one, and using his knife he cut through the skin around the top of the head, removing the scalp very quickly.

A scalp was a trophy brought back from battle to prove to the people that the warrior had killed an enemy. Scalps were displayed on a pole in front of the homes of the warriors and were also carried during Scalp Dances on short cane sticks about 5' long.

234

A typical outfit which could be worn by a male dancer in the Scalp Dance.

(modeled by Frankie Mafnas)

How to Make a Scalp Pole

The last scalps taken by the Cherokee were during the Civil War. It was reported that a couple of Union soldiers were killed in 1862 at Baptist Gap, Tennessee and scalped. Refer to James Mooney, *History, Myths and Sacred Formulas of the Cherokees*. However, those days are gone forever.

In our time, if a scalp pole is needed when the Scalp Dance is performed, the pole for the scalp can be real, but the scalp must be imitated. Following, is my version of a modern day Scalp Pole.

In the old days, when a scalp was taken, it was stretched on a cane or hickory hoop. To make a hoop of cane, a trip to a creek or river bank is necessary. Green cane is preferable because it is very pliable. While there, cutting extra cane can is beneficial for future projects. The cane selected should be about $^1/_2$" thick and the pole or handle for the scalp hoop should be about $^3/_4$" to 1" thick. If hickory is more available to you, use it.

If river cane is not available, then green limbs from willow, elm or hickory should suffice. Some scalp hoops, such as those made of hickory, can be made by splitting the limb down the middle. This makes it even more pliable to bend when shaping the hoop. Hoops can also be bought premade at craft stores.

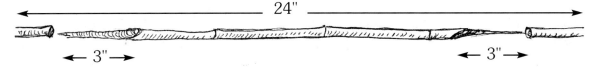

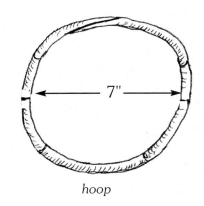

hoop

Using a pocket knife, cut a piece of $1/2$" green cane, 24" long. Taper a 3" portion on the top of one end of the cane. Then taper a 3" portion from the bottom of the other end of the cane. These tapered cuts should be made between two joints of the cane, as shown. The tapered ends form the splice where the hoop is joined together.

Bend the cane slowly along the shaft while forming a circle. Then fit the ends together to see how it looks.

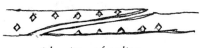

side view of splice

top view of splice

Now, with the knife, cut a series of notches on both sides of the splice, where the hoop is joined together. These notches are grab spots where twine, rawhide or sinew string can hold the splice. See the illustrations.

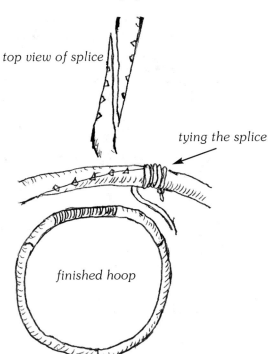

tying the splice

finished hoop

While sitting, place the bent hoop between your legs, holding the splice together with one hand, while wrapping the twine around the splice with the other hand.

The finished scalp hoop should look as shown here.

Now a long leather string is needed to lace the scalp to the hoop. Cherokees probably used rawhide string for the lacing.

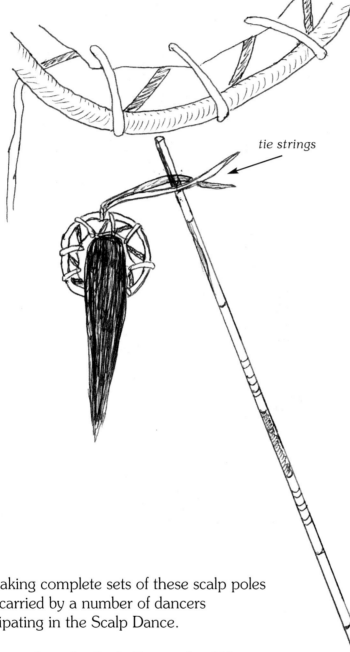

tie strings

This sketch demonstrates the technique of lacing.

Once the scalp is laced to the hoop, the backside is painted red.

The purpose of tie strings is to attach the hoop to the end of a 5' long, $^3/_4$" thick cane pole.

Designs of stripes or bands can be painted on the cane pole.

Try making complete sets of these scalp poles to be carried by a number of dancers participating in the Scalp Dance.

Dances such as the Scalp Dance should be carried on purely for the interest in Native American culture, and to insure that they are not forgotten.

238

To make a base for the hair to be sewn, one must cut a disk, 3 $\frac{1}{2}$" in diameter, made of soft leather, such as suede.

Then cut a tan colored disk from cloth, 4 $\frac{1}{2}$" in diameter. Lay the smaller disk on top of the cloth disk, as shown.

Next, cut the edges of the cloth disk under the edges of the leather disk, whip-stitching around the edge of the disk.

Now that the base has been made, some long hair will be needed. A cheap wig works nicely, and can be found in stores such as Walmart or Kmart around the Halloween season. Next, cut a 2 - 2 $\frac{1}{2}$" section from the wig as shown below.

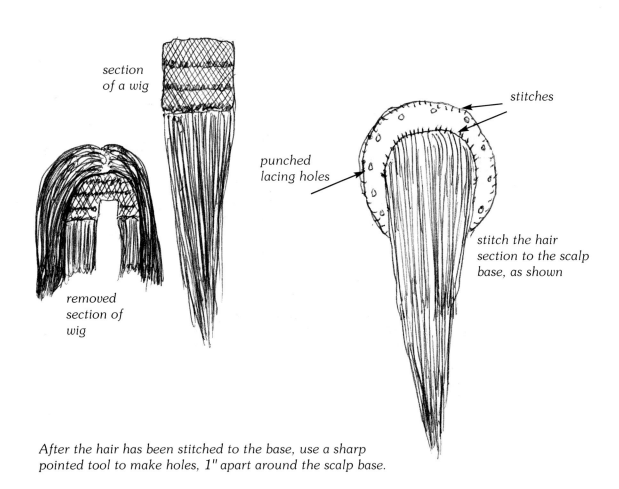

section of a wig

removed section of wig

punched lacing holes

stitches

stitch the hair section to the scalp base, as shown

After the hair has been stitched to the base, use a sharp pointed tool to make holes, 1" apart around the scalp base.

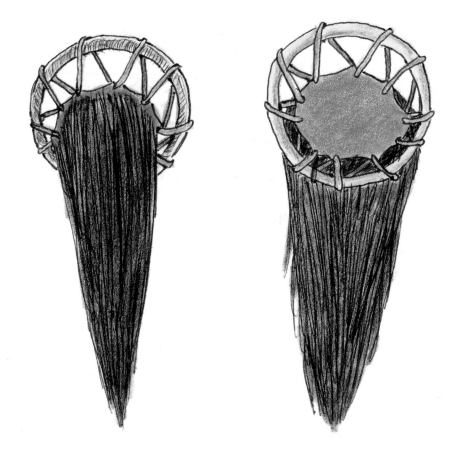

A Cherokee warrior cleansed any remaining flesh from the scalp he had taken. Then he made the hoop of river cane. The scalp was then laced to the hoop, and after it was dry, he painted the skin side red. This can be imitated by using a long-hair wig and sewing a piece of soft leather or cloth to the underside before painting. *See The Cherokee Crown of Tannassy*, by William O. Steele, pgs. 45-46.

COSTUMES OF THE FOUR SCOUTS
ATTENDING THE SCALP DANCE

After a war party returned from battle, cleansing rituals were performed by the warriors who had shed blood. A Scalp Dance was held soon after. The dance was performed at night and attended by the four spies, or scouts.

One of these scouts was called the Raven, known also as the Great War Chief. The other three were known as Owl, Wolf and Fox.

The Raven wore a raven skin around his neck. The head of the skin hung down on his chest, while the wings spread out over his shoulders. The tail hung down the back with red leather strings. This necklace piece tied behind the Great War Chief's neck and was always worn when he attended the Scalp Dance.

Other items he may have worn, would be a red painted eagle feather, otter skin headband, armbands and garters, his crystal, a red breechclout, a knife and holster, and red moccasins. Most of these items were included in his everyday wear, but all are also suitable for the Scalp Dance. The other warriors simply wore the breechclout and moccasins only.

The scout known as the Owl wore an owl skin around his neck in much the same fashion as the Raven scout. He probably wore an eagle feather in his hair, armbands, belt and breechclout, knife and holster, garters and moccasins.

The Wolf Scout wore a wolf skin around his neck. A slit or opening was made near the neck of the wolf skin to put his head through. The rest of the skin hung down his back. He also wore the other basic articles, similar to the other scouts.

The Fox scout wore a fox skin around his neck, in the same manner as the Wolf scout. He wore the other basics as well.

Body paint may have also decorated their bodies in some way to show their status as warriors. The designs, painted on breechclouts and moccasins, were left up to the owner of the items.

The following sketches depict how the scouts may have dressed. For further study on the four spies or scouts, refer to *The Cherokee People*, by Thomas E. Mails, pgs. 49 and 105. Also, *The Southeastern Indians*, by Charles Hudson, page 249 is helpful.

Costume of the Raven Scout

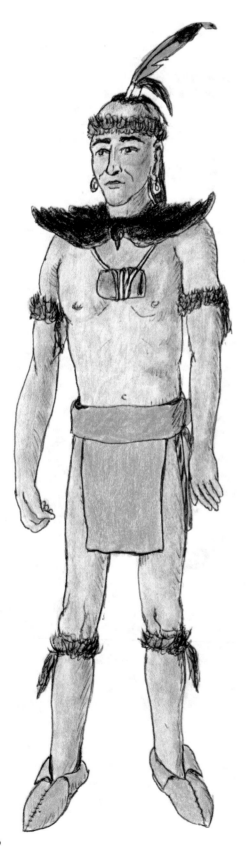

red painted eagle feather

otter skin headband

earrings

raven skin necklace

His crystal, carried in a leather packet, hung from the neck

otter skin armbands

red breechclout

otter skin garters

red moccasins

242

COSTUME OF THE OWL SCOUT

a depiction of the Owl Scout

COSTUMES OF THE WOLF AND FOX SCOUTS

a depiction of the Wolf and Fox Scouts

How to Do the Scalp Dance

During the first part of the Scalp Dance, the warriors who have returned from battle are the participants. They form a single file line and circle around, while sounding out war whoops, pausing, then sounding out more war whoops. Each warrior in the dance, as shown, carries an eagle wand in his right hand. In the left hand, he carries a cane stick about 5' long. The scalps are attached to hoops on the tops of the cane poles. The chanter, who is also the drummer, is in the center of the line.

In the second phase, when the song stops, the warrior at the beginning of the dance line will tell about his war deed and might even act it out. The other warriors walk slowly behind him as he does this. When he is finished, he gives the eagle wand to the dance leader. The other warriors then have a chance to tell their story and act out their war deeds, each giving the eagle wand to the dance leader as they finish.

After relating their exploits, the warriors would go to the back of the dance line. As the next warrior moves to the head of the line, the Scalp Dance song is sung again until he starts to tell of his experience. The war whoops are usually sounded out at the start of the song, and at the conclusion of each warrior's story. The chanter/drummer stops beating the drum as each warrior speaks, and resumes as the next man moves to the head of the line.

After the first Scalp Dance was held, a second dance usually followed in about seven days. Sometimes they were performed every few days, as the warriors returned home from a victorious battle. According to tradition, each warrior told or sang his tale first to the drummer, who then helped him sing it. Some warriors would exaggerate to the degree that all the people would burst out in laughter. Their stories of each exploit could last several minutes.

A Scalp Dance song or exploit story might begin like this song of my own creation:

> "Hi! I have killed one of our enemy in a far away land.
> Yu! His scalp I now hold for all to see!"

Mooney, in *History, Myths and Sacred Formulas of the Cherokees*, has another account on pages 376-377. Speck and Broom, in *Cherokee Dance and Drama*, pg. 64, make no mention of women participating in the Scalp Dance. However, according to Mooney, women did take part. They carried a gun in one hand and a scalp in the other. Scalps were waved or shook as they danced. They would dance wildly and yell out war whoops as the men and women danced together. See also, *The Cherokees* by Grace Steele Woodward, pg. 50.

When the women took part, they first danced in a circle holding the scalps. Next, they went into the Snake Dance. Then the women would form a circle while the men joined in and formed another circle around them. They then danced side by side as partners.

Usually, the War Chief and his wife would lead the dance couples as they danced around the fire in the square grounds. Torches also added light.

After the Scalp Dance, warriors would sometimes receive new war names such as Raven, Wolf, Fox, Owl and other related titles. Other warriors received rewards such as eagle feathers and such. See *History, Myths and Sacred Formulas of the Cherokees*, by James Mooney, pg. 496, or *The Cherokee People*, by Thomas E. Mails, pg. 111.

Junaluska received his new name at a Scalp Dance after the Creek War. He had tried to kill all of the Creeks, but failed. At the dance, he whispered a few words of his song to the drummer: "detsin' lahungi", meaning "I tried, but could not". His name then became "Tsunu'lahun'ski", meaning "One who tries but fails". See *History, Myths and Sacred Formulas of the Cherokees*, pg. 164.

246

A portrayal of the Scalp Dance.

The red ribbon dress is a very suitable outfit for this dance.

(modeled by Kathy Ferris)

THE SNAKE DANCE COSTUME

a warrior wearing a snake mask

The warrior that leads the Snake Dance wears a mask, similar to the one shown above. These types of masks can be bought in Cherokee, North Carolina. To make such a mask, it should be carved from buckeye wood as shown in the photograph. The face is painted a medium red with areas of flat black. If this mask cannot be easily bought or carved, one could try making one from paper maché

The lead warrior, as well as the others, wear a war uniform. The uniform basically consisted of a breechclout and moccasins. One feather in the hair would denote an ordinary warrior, while warriors of higher status may wear extra feathers slanted backward. Eagle and hawk feathers were worn in the old days, but imitations must be used in modern times. Some warriors wore hoods made of animal skins, along with other types of hats. One must keep in mind that whatever a warrior wore on his head was a symbol of his status.

Other items to be worn for this dance include a necklace, belt, knife, holster, armbands, head-bands, garters, sashes, earrings and body paint.

The women in this dance should wear a dress, as illustrated in the dance sketches. She might also wear a necklace, earrings, bracelets and moccasins of the center-seam style. Her hair-line can be lined with vermillion and her cheeks decorated with the same red coloring. On the right leg, below the knee, turtle-shell rattles are attached.

suitable dresses for the Snake Dance

(models, Chastity Ramey and Carol Sizemore)

HOW TO DO THE SNAKE DANCE

This dance was done when the warriors returned home from the warpath. Usually, the Scalp Dance was combined with it, but the two dances could be performed separately as the occasion called for it.

The Snake Dance served to demonstrate that the warriors were fearless, and not afraid of the enemy, or even ghosts.

The lead warrior, wearing the snake mask, was followed by a man with a gourd rattle. He, in turn, was followed by a woman wearing the tortoise shell rattles. The rest of the dancers then followed in this single-file line, alternating with partners if desired.

A lesser detailed form of this dance can be found in *Cherokee Dance and Drama* by Speck and Broom, pgs. 62-63. Also see *Cherokee Perspective* by French and Hornbuckle, pg. 130. In these versions, the dancers move in a single-file counter-clockwise circle. The lead man eventually takes his place behind the woman with the leg rattles, as the other warriors follow behind him.

250

The *John Howard Payne Papers*, Vol. 3, pgs. 71-80, describe further details. In his version, the warriors first perform the Scalp Dance as they return home. Then the women join in, with a certain signal from the drummer, doing the Snake Dance. They move around the fire with a stooped posture, using slow dance steps in time with the drum. They sang this song, which was probably the Snake Dance song:

"Hu ya nv ni yo
Hu ya nv ni yo
Hu ya nv ni yo
Hu ya nv ni yo"

The female dancers occasionally raise their hands and pretend to strike at the enemy. Eventually the warriors join in the dance with their scalp poles, and form a circle around the women. They then dance side by side with their partners in a stooped position singing a war song, which was more than likely the Scalp Dance song:

"Hi no nu
Hi no nu
Hi no nu
Hi no nu

Ya a ho yi ne
Ya a ho yi ne
Ya a ho yi ne
Ya a ho yi ne"

So, we surmise from the Payne Papers that the Scalp Dance and the Snake Dance were sometimes performed as a single dance. Following, is a description of the Snake Dance only.

20 or more dancers are needed to form a single file line alternating male and female. At the head of the line is the man with the gourd rattle and the snake mask. Behind him, is the woman with the tortoise shell rattles, and then the rest of the alternating dancers.

In the first phase of the dance, the line enters the danceground doing a slow stomp step. They are led in a large counter-clockwise circle around the inside boundaries of the danceground. As they go around again, the circle becomes smaller and smaller, until they reach the center circle. At this point, the dancers have formed a very tight circle. The leader yells out, "Yo Ho!" and raises his left arm pointing backward, as the drum beat stops. This part of the dance represents a rattlesnake coiling up, ready to strike at the enemy.

As the second phase of the dance starts, the leader yells "Yo!" and turns right. The drumbeat is now fast and he leads the dancers clockwise going from a small circle to larger circles, until they are dancing around the inside boundary of the danceground again. This fast unwinding represents the quick uncoiling of the rattlesnake when it strikes the enemy. The dance can then be repeated several times in other areas of the danceground.

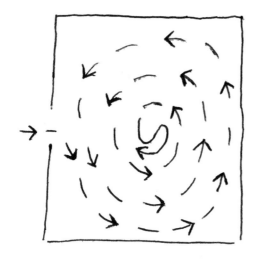

phase one: counterclockwise

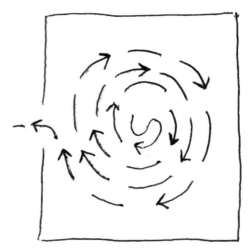

phase two: clockwise

dancers in the first phase of the Snake Dance

dancers in the second phase of the Snake Dance

a typical costume worn by the lead dancer in the Snake Dance

THE BALL PLAYER COSTUME

This sketch depicts women and men doing the Ball Player's Dance. There is a drummer, seated and beating a water drum. Directly behind the drummer, are seven of the "Beloved Women", one from each clan. They are wearing white deerskin dresses, which later on in history would have been made of white cloth. Necklaces and bracelets were worn by these women, and their hair is fixed in a coiled fashion with several beautiful colored ribbons. Given that they were wearing their finest clothes, it stands to reason that they would be wearing moccasins as well. Their hairline and cheeks would have been dabbed with vermilion.

The ball players are shown behind the women wearing groundhog skin head-bands, and feathers fastened to the scalp-lock with a high waving feather. The players also wore armbands, gorgets made of silver, wampum necklaces and beautiful beaded moccasins. However, the moccasins weren't worn during the ball game, if the weather permitted. This team is wearing red breechclouts with the flaps tied between the legs, while the other team wore yellow breechclouts, trimmed in red. A wide leather belt was worn over the breechclout as shown. They were often beaded in beautiful designs, consisting of vertical and horizontal lines with diamond shapes spaced evenly apart.

At the back of this broad belt, a tail attachment was added. Usually, this tail was chosen by the player and could be one of the following: a deer tail, a feather tail made of eagle, hawk or even white goose feathers. If falcon feathers could be obtained, some players used them for a tail. These same types of feathers were also worn in the scalplock.*

The players were sometimes given sacred feathers, which were dyed red by the Medicine Man. Such feathers were worn in the hair on the day of the game.

The dancers also painted their bodies with symbols of good luck. Shown, are two such designs, usually painted on the forehead, cheek, back or chest.

In the George Catlin paintings of ball players, the face is painted, and the legs and forearms are painted also, with stripes. It is also knowledge that one team would paint themselves white, and the other team would paint themselves primarily red. The medicine man would then put scratches on the upper and lower arms, the chest, back, thighs and lower legs. These scratch marks were not meant for the dance and were done just before the ball game.

The male ball players carried their sticks, or rackets, during the dance. The sketch on the previous page depicts a scene with the ball sticks on a hanger, and a scene with the players carrying the ball sticks during the dance.

The costumes depicted in the sketch demonstrate what was worn from about 1775 - 1835. The players later began wearing shorts and other "non indian" styles. The sketch of the Ball Players Dance on the previous page exhibits the late 18th century Native American costume.

>   *NOTE: *Many birds are protected by law and the use of their feathers forbidden.*
>   *Check the laws, both federal and state, before using bird feathers in*
>   *your projects.*

Body paint was used to some degree by most male dancers.

Scratch marks were put on the players bodies by the Medicine Man prior to the game. Such marks were made on the upper and lower sections of the arms and legs, and also on the chest and back.

belt

feather tail

One team at this particular village wore breech-clouts made of yellow cloth, trimmed in another color, like red.

Cherokee ball players tied their breech-clout flaps between their legs.

Players did not wear moccasins during play.

In 1797, Louis Philippe traveled among the Cherokee. He described the players and their costumes in his diary. This sketch is drawn from that description.

Eagle feather with red dyed

Dyed horse hair was worn by some tribes, around the neck.

A deer tail, representing swiftness, is attached to the back of the belt.

He is wearing a black belt with white beaded designs.

A red breech-clout is also worn, tied between the legs.

ball player of an opposing team

How to Make Ball Dance Breechclouts

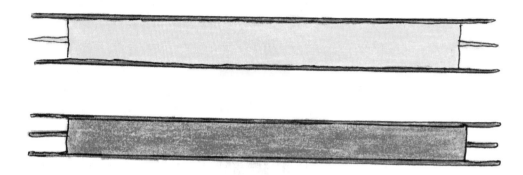

The illustration above exhibits two breechclouts worn by ball dancers of opposing teams in 1797, when Louis Phillipe visited a Cherokee village. One team wore breechclouts made of yellow cloth trimmed in another color, and the solid red breechclouts were worn by the other team.

It was noted by George Catlin and John Howard Payne, in their studies, that the breechclouts were tied between the legs and at the sides. This gave them the appearance of a pair of shorts.

Around 1904 - 1905, Frank Speck collected a Yuchi Indian breechclout which had strings at the bottom of the front and back flaps. A belt was worn at the waist to hang the breechclout.

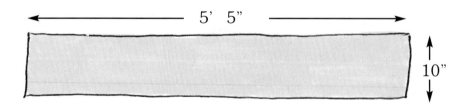

To make the yellow breechclout for the ball game or dance, cut a thin yellow cotton blanket to size, as shown. Then cut red flannel strips of cloth about 2" wide and long enough to reach from one end to the other, with 5" extending past the ends. The 5" of excess are used for tie strings once the strips are hemmed onto the breechclout.

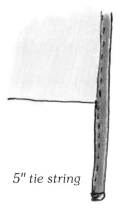

5" tie string

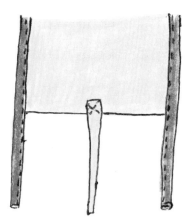

Sew on a 5" yellow tie string on the ends of the front and back flaps, as shown.

A belt can be made from the same yellow blanket cloth.

Each dancer of the team should wear a breechclout, yellow for one team and red for the other. The women wear white deerskin dresses during the dance.

 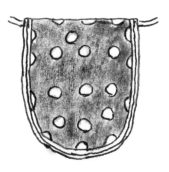

This illustration depicts two breechclouts seen in an old James Mooney photograph from 1888.

In the late 1880's, James Mooney observed Cherokee men in North Carolina doing the Ball Dance. These men were wearing white colored shorts with patchwork designs, similar to the following sketches. The only other items of their costume for the dance and stickball game, were the feathers in their hair. No shirt or moccasins were worn. Times had changed and the dancers were then wearing clothing similar to their white neighbors.

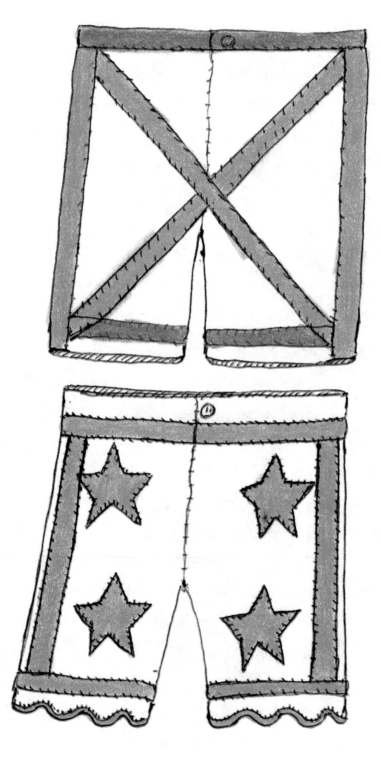

ball-play shorts worn by the men in the 1880s

The women doing the Ball Dance in the 1880's, as James Mooney observed, wore long white dresses like the white women. Their native deerskin dresses were fast becoming a thing of the past.

261

HOW TO MAKE A METAL GORGET

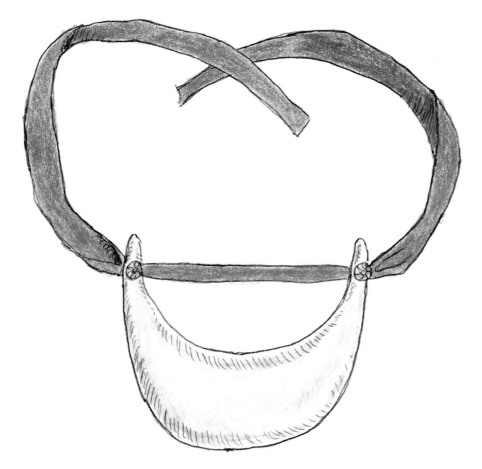

During the 18th and 19th centuries, the Cherokee sometimes wore a necklace made similar to that shown here. Such necklaces were obtained from the white men, either in trade, or as medals of honor when they were allies. British and French officers often wore this type of necklace as well.

To make the above gorget, I used a wide piece of chrome from a car. This type of metal can be found at a junk yard. The old gorgets were made of German silver. Aluminum can be used as a substitute, but will not have the same shine as chrome.

Make a pattern on paper, cut and lay it onto the metal. Trace around the pattern with a marker. Next, use a pair of tin-snips or heavy duty scissors to cut the shape of the gorget. Other possible tools to use in cutting metal would be a jig-saw or coping saw, which have metal cutting blades.

Once the shape has been cut, use a pair of pliers to bend $1/8$ th of the edge up all around the gorget. This edge should be on the back side of the gorget.

Source: James Townsend and Son, Inc. See source page in back of book.

Continue to bend the edge down flat around the gorget, as shown below.

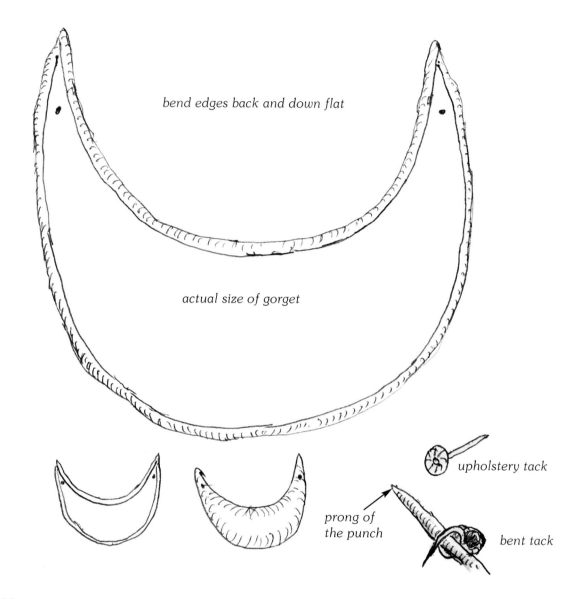

bend edges back and down flat

actual size of gorget

upholstery tack

prong of the punch

bent tack

Next, use a punch or nail to make two holes through the gorget near the top points. Use pliers to bend more of the edges back about $1/2$" all around to start the concave shape. Now lay the face of the gorget on a block of wood and use a ball-peen hammer to pound the back side to form the concave shape.

As shown, an upholstery tack is bent around the prong of a punch or large nail. To do this, insert the upholstery tack through the hole of the gorget, and then use the punch as shown. Hammer a curve in the tack prong. Remove the punch and do another tack the same way for the hole on the other end.

Position the bent parts of the tacks as shown below. Use a soldering gun to melt solder around the points of the tack, then let the gorget cool. The brackets are now formed.

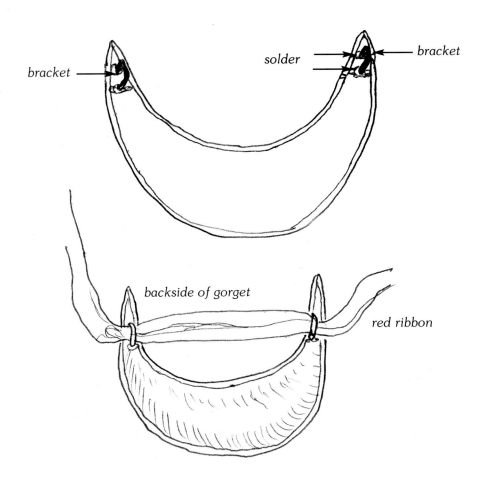

Lace a colored ribbon through the brackets on the backside of the gorget. This ribbon should be long enough to suspend the gorget just above the chest. The ribbon ends tie behind the neck.

Several styles of metal gorgets can be made this way. A piece of wire may be soldered and substituted for the upholstery tacks for the brackets.

This method is of my own design, and doesn't necessarily reflect the old way that it was done.

Reproductions of metal gorgets can be purchased in some shops dealing with Native American crafts.

FEATHER ORNAMENTS WORN IN THE HAIR

*various types of feathers that can be worn in the hair by
ballplayers or dancers*

In the old days, the ball players usually wore feathers attached to the hair or scalplock, in the same fashion as the warrior. In one of George Catlin's paintings of a Choctaw ball game, the players are wearing feathers in their hair. The same is true in an old James Moody photograph. John Howard Payne also reported ball players wearing feathers in their hair along with a 3" or 4" red fluff or feather attached to the end of the bigger feather. This type of feather was worn by both the warrior and ball player. Feathers of the the White Heron, or American Egret, along with other various types of feathers were also worn. Feathers were thought to help the players by giving them speed and powerful movements during the ball-play. Such feather ornaments were also believed to raise the person's ego.

←white
fluffs

Some players wore head-bands made of groundhog skin. These head-bands had feather attachments or pendants. Such feathers can be worn attached to a tuft of hair on the top of the head, or to the hair at the back of the head. Some prefer to stick their feather at the back of the headband.

265

How to Make the
Ball Player's Feather Ornament

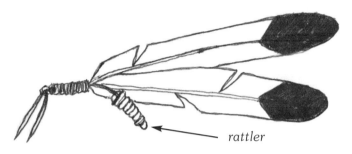

rattler

The feather ornament above was worn by a ball player in 1889 on the day of the ball game. The rattler tied to the feathers was hoped to strike fear in the opposing team. The eagle feathers gave the player speed and flight while playing the game. Such an ornament could be used as part of the ball player's dance costume as well.

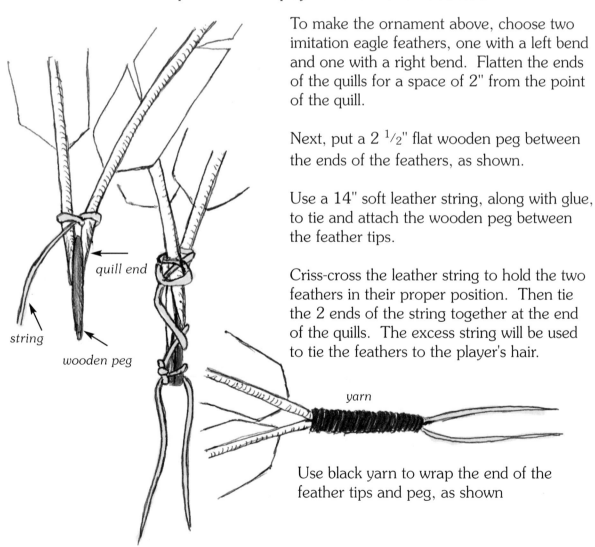

quill end

string

wooden peg

yarn

To make the ornament above, choose two imitation eagle feathers, one with a left bend and one with a right bend. Flatten the ends of the quills for a space of 2" from the point of the quill.

Next, put a 2 $\frac{1}{2}$" flat wooden peg between the ends of the feathers, as shown.

Use a 14" soft leather string, along with glue, to tie and attach the wooden peg between the feather tips.

Criss-cross the leather string to hold the two feathers in their proper position. Then tie the 2 ends of the string together at the end of the quills. The excess string will be used to tie the feathers to the player's hair.

Use black yarn to wrap the end of the feather tips and peg, as shown

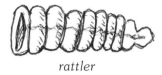

rattler

Now you will need a rattler from a rattlesnake. Fortunately, I had rattles given to me by other people. Try to use one that has seven buttons - this was the sacred number of the Cherokee.

← *use a little glue*

← *button*

tie strings

The rattler is attached to the feathers with a black yarn string. Tie the string around the first button, tying the string in a knot, as shown.

Be careful while pulling the thread tight around the button, or the button may come off.

Tie the other end of the string to the feathers.

Tie strings are used to attach the feather to the ball player or dancer's hair.

Eagle feathers were worn as hair ornaments by ball players for speed and flight. The rattler attached, was to strike fear in the other team. These feathers were also worn in the Ball Dance.

This type of feather could also be worn by a ball player or male dancer.

268

HOW TO MAKE A BALL PLAYER'S FEATHER WITH RED DEER HAIR STRING

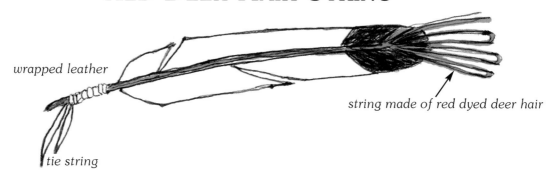

wrapped leather

string made of red dyed deer hair

tie string

The feather ornament shown above is similar to one collected by James Mooney in 1889. It was worn by a Cherokee ball player. String made of red or scarlet dyed deer hair is sewn or glued along the quill of the feather.

To make the above feather ornament, an imitation feather is needed. It should be 12" - 14" long. This type of feather can be purchased from a Tandy Leather Craft Store. (see "source page" in back of book)

Select a splinter of wood or whittle one from a pine board. taper the splinter, $^{1}/_{4}$" wide and 2 $^{1}/_{2}$" - 3" long. Cut a series of "V" shaped notches along the sides of the splinter for tying.

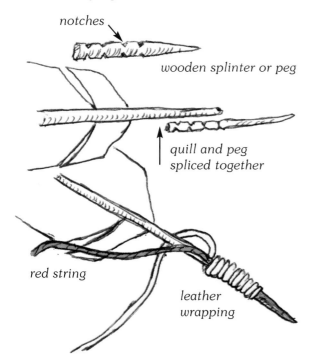

notches

wooden splinter or peg

quill and peg spliced together

red string

leather wrapping

Flatten the end of the quill to splice onto the wooden splinter or peg.

Next, put glue along both sides of the wooden peg and press the peg to the quill end, wrapping them in place with a soft leather string. Deerskin or Chamois skin can be cut into string, $^{1}/_{8}$" wide and 16" long. Before finishing this process, work in a red or scarlet string. Yarn or embroidery thread will work as well.

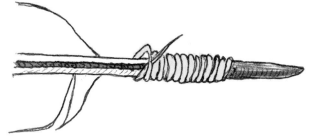

The red string should be positioned on the quill, so it will run up the middle of the front side of the feather, as shown.

Tie off the leather string and use a small amount of glue when clipping and concealing the end of the string.

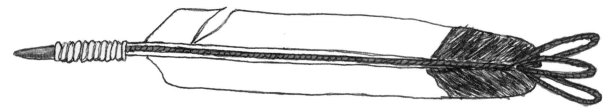

Either glue or use a needle and thread to sew the red string onto the feather quill. When the red thread reaches the end of the black portion of the feather, form a few loops. These loops should be 2 - 3" long and are also glued or sewn in place.

A tie string can be added to the wrapped end of the feather to attach to the hair. Otherwise, it can be placed in the hair and held in place with a headband. This feather was considered a very powerful charm for the ball player.

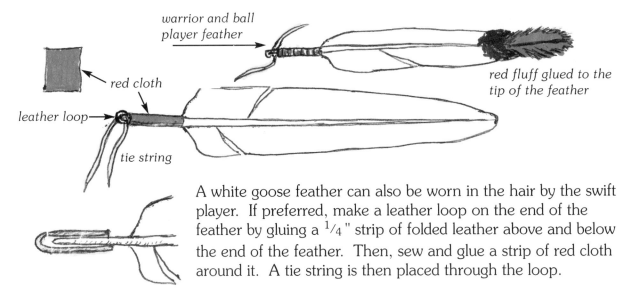

warrior and ball player feather

red cloth

red fluff glued to the tip of the feather

leather loop

tie string

A white goose feather can also be worn in the hair by the swift player. If preferred, make a leather loop on the end of the feather by gluing a $^1/_4$" strip of folded leather above and below the end of the feather. Then, sew and glue a strip of red cloth around it. A tie string is then placed through the loop.

Other feather types are as suitable for the Ball Dance costume and the ball player.

THE FEATHERED TAILS FOR BALL PLAYERS

Above, is a feathered tail attached to a beaded belt. At one time, ball players sometimes wore such an item during the game to help them in being quick and swift

Before the 1840 period, Cherokee ball players wore tails made of feathers, usually eagle, hawk or goose feathers. Sometimes, players would attach a deer's tail.

The belt with a feathered tail was worn during the game but not the dance. However, due to the aesthetics of the tail, it would be appropriate in modern ball play.

A good example of how the ball players dressed can be found in George Catlin's paintings of ball players and games in 1834. One such champion player is wearing a black beaded belt with an extended horsetail attached.

Players usually wore a tail that indicated they had been qualified for a certain skill as a player. For instance, if a player wore the white goose tail, he was considered the fastest member of the team.

The player that wore a tail made of eagle or hawk feathers was considered one of the teams strongest players. If a belt with a deer tail attached was worn, that player was considered extremely quick and hard to keep up with.

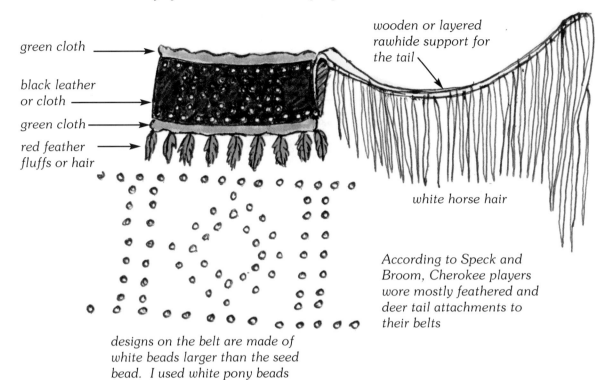

green cloth

black leather or cloth

green cloth

red feather fluffs or hair

wooden or layered rawhide support for the tail

white horse hair

According to Speck and Broom, Cherokee players wore mostly feathered and deer tail attachments to their belts

designs on the belt are made of white beads larger than the seed bead. I used white pony beads

The sketch above depicts the horse tail belt worn by a Choctaw stickball player in one of the George Catlin paintings. Cherokee belts would have been made similar.

woven sash

In the sketch at left, a sash is used as a belt and has eagle feathers attached to form a tail. The quills of the eagle feathers are painted red and red fluffs or hair decorate the tips of the feathers.

The feathers can be sewn or laced onto a base made of soft leather, cloth or netting.

The tail feathers reached down to the bend of the knee or lower.

NOTE: *Many birds are protected by law and the use of their feathers forbidden. Check the laws, both federal and state, before using bird feathers in your projects.*

A ball player's outfit. His team wears red breechclouts.
(model is Frankie Mafnas)

The opposing team's outfit.
(model is Jimmy Gwinner)

HOW TO MAKE A FEATHERED TAIL

The instructions below are of my own design. I substituted brown turkey feathers for hawk feathers.

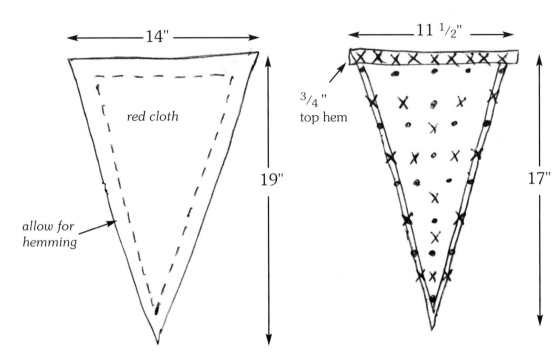

Cut a piece of red cloth to dimensions as shown

Hem around the edges of the cloth, as shown. Make the top hem $^3/_4$" wide. Then, when the base is finished, put pencil markings on the base for the feather positions. The "Dots" are for the wing feather positions. The "X's" are for long fluffy feather positions.

20 turkey wing feathers, 1" to 14" long are needed here. There should be 10 left bent feathers, and 10 bent to the right. More feathers can make the tail appear fuller. Prepare as follows to attach the feathers to the cloth base:

razor blade

cut with a razor blade from the tip of the quill

cut the quill in the opposite direction

$^3/_4$" gap

$^1/_2$"

flatten gap when cut

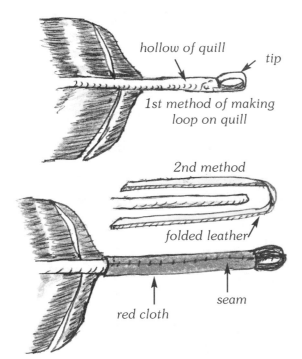

hollow of quill

tip

1st method of making loop on quill

2nd method

folded leather

seam

red cloth

After the $3/4$" gap has been cut out $1/2$" back from the tip of the feather quill, bend the tip back toward the opening in the hollow part of the quill, as shown. Put a little glue inside the hollow of the quill, then insert the tip of the quill back into the opening of the quill. This is a basic way of attaching feathers.

If the tip of the quill is blunt or damaged, and the above method cannot be used, cut a 2" long by $1/4$" wide strip of soft leather. Next, fold the piece of leather, gluing it to the quill. If the quill tips are damaged, cut a 1" by $2 1/2$" long piece of red cloth. Sew the cloth together on the backside of the quill, placing the seam as shown.

Each wing feather must be prepared in one of these two ways before they can be attached to the triangular cloth base.

Use a large needle and strong twine to fasten the wing feathers on the red triangular cloth base at the positions marked by the dots in earlier sketch. Put the left bend feathers on the left side of the cloth base and the right bend feathers on the right side of the triangular base. Refer to the photo.

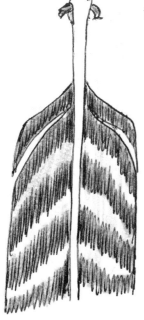

After all the large feathers are sewn on, use a smaller needle and strong thread to sew on long large fluffs. The fluffs are sewn in the positions marked "x" on the triangular base. The purpose of the fluffs is to fill in the empty spots on the base, between the large feathers. Fluffs should be 6-7" long.

Depicted above is a stickball game in progress.
Note the belt and feathered tails worn by the two ball players.

this photo shows details of the belt

the other team might wear belts trimmed in yellow

HOW TO MAKE A BALL PLAYER'S BEADED BELT

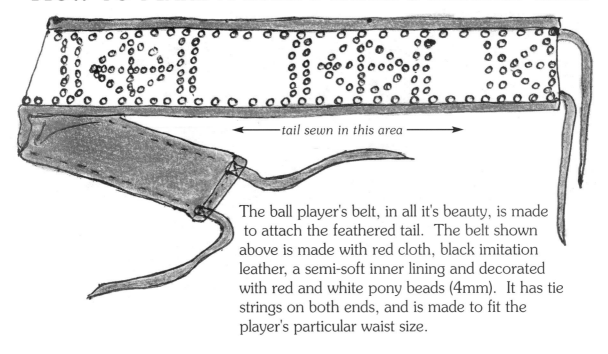

tail sewn in this area

The ball player's belt, in all it's beauty, is made to attach the feathered tail. The belt shown above is made with red cloth, black imitation leather, a semi-soft inner lining and decorated with red and white pony beads (4mm). It has tie strings on both ends, and is made to fit the player's particular waist size.

After cutting a strip of red cloth to the proper dimensions, hem all of the edges, reducing the width of the belt down to 5". Adjust measurements for individual waist size.

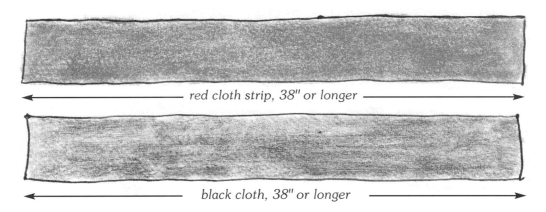

red cloth strip, 38" or longer

black cloth, 38" or longer

Next, hem all edges of the black strip of cloth, reducing it down to a 4" width. Center the black strip of cloth on the red strip and sew the black strip onto the red. Before sewing the bottom edge of black cloth, insert a $3^1/_2$" wide strip of semi-soft leather as a liner underneath. Once the liner is n place between the black and red strips, sew the bottom edge of the black strip to conceal the liner. The liner should be almost as long as the black strip, and will help to hold it's shape

liner ——————

note: *the liner can be
made of a strip of
vinyl rug, cut to size*

Once the belt is sewn together, make and sew two $^1/_2$" by 12" long tie strings for each end of the belt. Sew tie strings onto the back side of the belt, as shown below. This particular belt ties on one's waist at the right side.

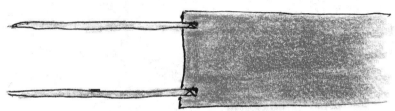

The beadwork on this belt seems to be an old style of spot beading with wampum beads or small shell beads. Pony beads or 4mm beads can be used. This type of beading is done also on sashes and other types of clothing. Tiny seed beads became common as traders came into the area.

First, mark the design on the black part of the belt, using a yellow leaded pencil. Then sew down a bead by anchoring the thread to the cloth, stringing a bead and back through the cloth outside the bead. Then come back through the cloth with the needle and thread and attach another bead. Then repeat the process until the pattern is complete.

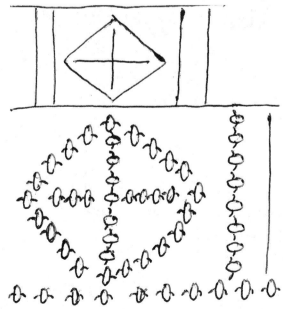

Red and white beads like the ones used here may be obtained from a craft store. See "source list" in the back of this book.

When the bead work is finished, position the feathered tail in place at the bottom edge of the belt. Align the tail properly and stitch the top $^3/_4$" seam of the tail to the belt. Refer to prior sketches and photographs.

279

HOW TO MAKE A DEER TAIL BELT FOR BALL PLAYER

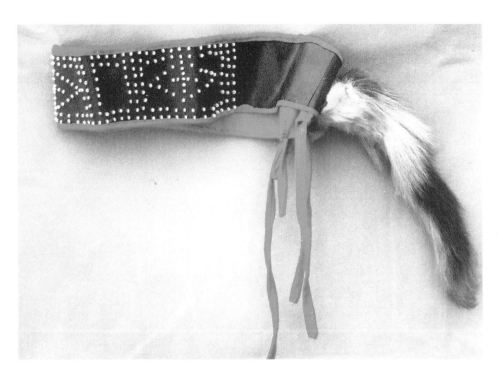

A deer tail belt made by the author

The purpose of the deer tail belt is to empower the ball player with a swift running ability during the ball game.

The basic belt is made in the same way as the preceding belts. An authentic design can be found in a 1767 painting by Joshua Reynolds of Syacust Ukah This painting is found in the Thomas Gilgrease Institute in Tulsa, Oklahoma. Below is a sketch of these designs.

Mark the outline of the diamond design in a repeated pattern

The spot beading method, used with white 4mm, or pony beads

The easiest way to make a tail attachment for the deer tail belt, is to create an imitation tail. This is done by simply cutting out a brown piece of fur for the upper side, and a white piece of fur for the underside of the tail. The hair on these fur pieces should be long and shaggy. The dimensions are shown below.

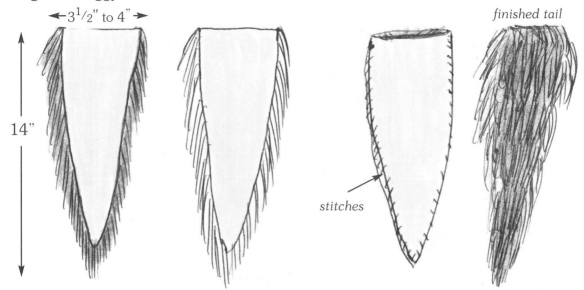

finished tail

stitches

The skin side of the two fur pieces

Place the two pieces of fur together, with the fur on the inside. Then stitch up the sides and turn the fur inside out. The tail is then ready to attach to the belt.

If you prefer the tail to extend out from the belt to look the way it does as a deer is in flight, it is necessary to whittle a wooden support. Use a pocket knife and refer to the sketch below.

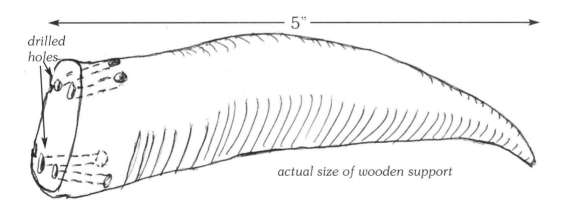

drilled holes

actual size of wooden support

This support can be carved from pine wood. Drill holes and use strong twine to fasten to the belt. The area shown, where the holes are drilled, should be $1^1/4$" wide x 1 $^3/4$" high.

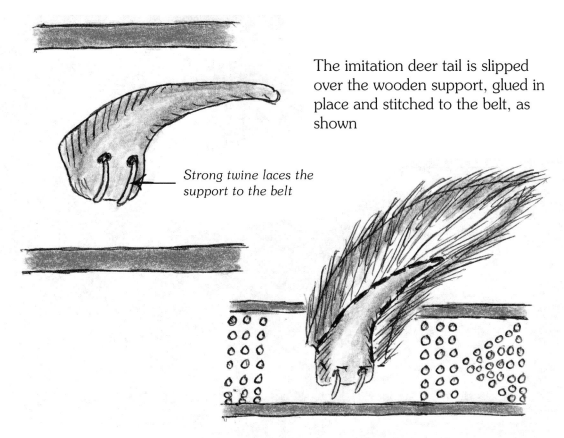

The imitation deer tail is slipped over the wooden support, glued in place and stitched to the belt, as shown

Strong twine laces the support to the belt

Most players wearing the belt prefer to let the tail dangle loosely.

If an actual deer tail is used, it should be tanned and the bone removed.

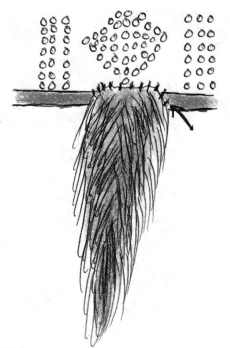

The deer tail is easily attached to the belt, as shown. This is the most common method.

Let me restate that the deer tail was worn, in the old days, in the ball game only. However, in modern times, it can be a very attractive addition to the Ball Dance. Though not authentic, it can add flavor and color to the dance. This is left to the dancer's discretion

BALL STICKS FOR THE BALL DANCE

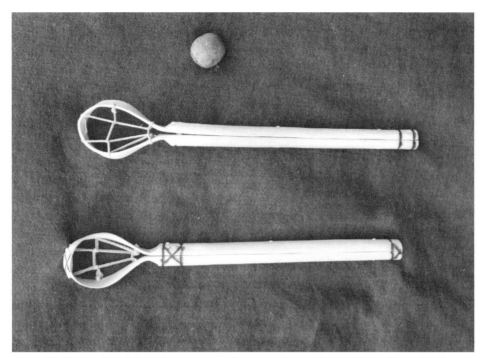

Ball sticks, like these, can be purchased in Cherokee, NC.
Note the small deerskin ball

In the old days, when the Ball Dance was done, the players carried their ball sticks. Refer to the previous sketch of the Ball Dance.

Two sticks are needed for a set. To make a set of ball sticks, straight hickory limbs or young hickory trees are needed. Use a section that is 1 $1/4$" wide and about 45" long. Recent sticks have handles approximately 16" long, while older ones had longer handles.

Remove the bark from the hickory sticks. This can be done with a pocket knife or a drawknife tool. Split the hickory stick down the center, lengthwise. A butcher knife can be used to split the stick by hammering it through. Two ball sticks can be made from one stick, if the section is large enough when split. When making my own stick, I used a small tree, removing the bark and then using a drawknife to flatten one side of it, lengthwise. It may be preferable to use a power saw to make a smooth straight cut, but use caution.

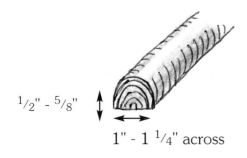

$1/2$" - $5/8$"

1" - 1 $1/4$" across

This illustration shows how the hickory stick should look after it has been flattened on one side.

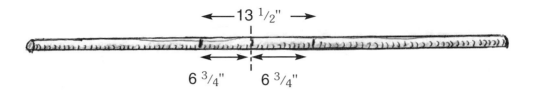

The hickory stick is marked in the center, and marked again 6 $\frac{3}{4}$" to each side of the center. The split side of the stick should be smoothed with a drawknife or sander. Next, use a pocket knife to cut out a tapered $\frac{1}{2}$" notch from the left and right markings, as shown below. Allow $\frac{1}{8}$" of the wood to remain at the bottom of the notches.

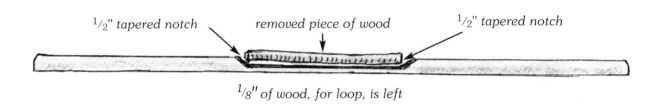

$\frac{1}{2}$" tapered notch   removed piece of wood $\frac{1}{2}$" tapered notch

$\frac{1}{8}$" of wood, for loop, is left

The center portion of the wood is removed down to $\frac{1}{8}$". A pocket knife, or draw knife works well for this. The sketch below gives greater detail of the process used in forming the loop on a ball stick.

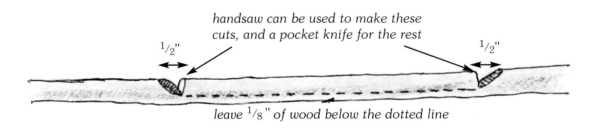

handsaw can be used to make these cuts, and a pocket knife for the rest

$\frac{1}{2}$" $\frac{1}{2}$"

leave $\frac{1}{8}$" of wood below the dotted line

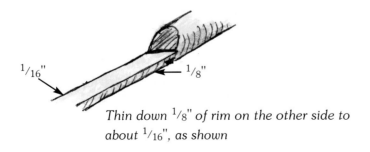

$\frac{1}{16}$" $\frac{1}{8}$"

Thin down $\frac{1}{8}$" of rim on the other side to about $\frac{1}{16}$", as shown

284

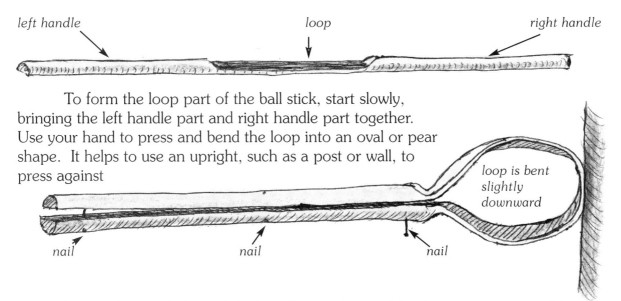

left handle   *loop*   *right handle*

*loop is bent
slightly
downward*

nail   *nail*   *nail*

To form the loop part of the ball stick, start slowly, bringing the left handle part and right handle part together. Use your hand to press and bend the loop into an oval or pear shape. It helps to use an upright, such as a post or wall, to press against

Fasten the two halves of the handle together with leather strings, or small finishing nails. Some craftsmen drill holes through the handle halves, and then drive small wooden pegs through. Note: If seasoned hickory is used, soak the loop part in water overnight before trying to form the loop.

Before the netting is put on the rackets or sticks, they should be sanded all over.

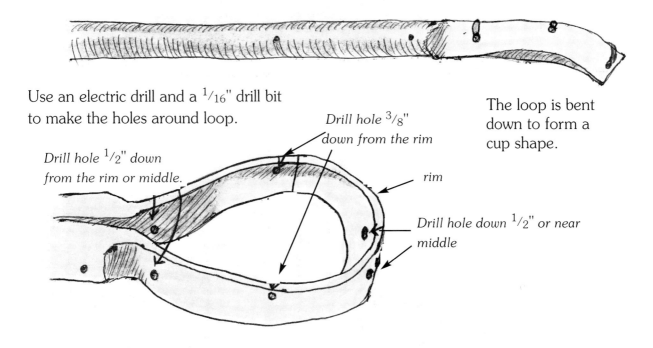

Use an electric drill and a $1/16$" drill bit to make the holes around loop.

*Drill hole $3/8$"
down from the rim*

*Drill hole $1/2$" down
from the rim or middle.*

The loop is bent down to form a cup shape.

rim

*Drill hole down $1/2$" or near
middle*

Use these numbered steps to lace the deerskin string to the loop of the ball stick. Cut the lacing string $1/4$" wide and about 18" long.

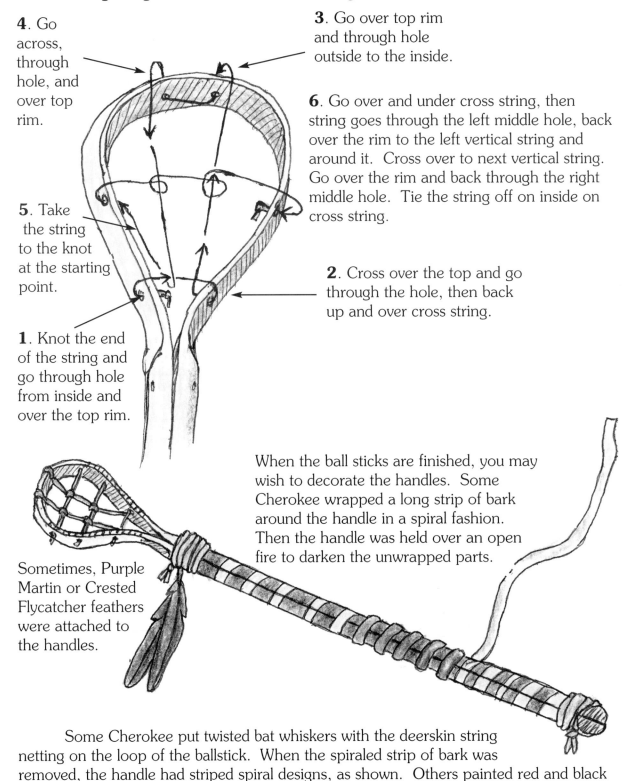

4. Go across, through hole, and over top rim.

3. Go over top rim and through hole outside to the inside.

6. Go over and under cross string, then string goes through the left middle hole, back over the rim to the left vertical string and around it. Cross over to next vertical string. Go over the rim and back through the right middle hole. Tie the string off on inside on cross string.

5. Take the string to the knot at the starting point.

1. Knot the end of the string and go through hole from inside and over the top rim.

2. Cross over the top and go through the hole, then back up and over cross string.

When the ball sticks are finished, you may wish to decorate the handles. Some Cherokee wrapped a long strip of bark around the handle in a spiral fashion. Then the handle was held over an open fire to darken the unwrapped parts.

Sometimes, Purple Martin or Crested Flycatcher feathers were attached to the handles.

Some Cherokee put twisted bat whiskers with the deerskin string netting on the loop of the ballstick. When the spiraled strip of bark was removed, the handle had striped spiral designs, as shown. Others painted red and black stripes on the handles. Sometimes the handles had leather string wrappings for decoration and to hold it together.

HOW TO DO THE BALL DANCE

The ball dance, in the old days, was held before the stickball game and gave the players strength and spiritual power. It boosted the ego of the players, in the same manner as the modern pep rally. The dance served the same purpose as our cheerleaders do today. It was believed to make the other team less likely to win.

The Ball Dance and the game of stickball had traits very similar to rituals and movements of warfare. Many times, the Ball Dance and the game were held to solve an argument between villages, instead of going to war with each other. The winner of the game was considered the one in the right.

A place for the Ball Dance was chosen near a creek or river. Between dances, and after the last night-time dance, when the male dancers rested, they went to the river where they immersed themselves in water for purification.

William Bartram, an early traveler, visited the village of Cowe and witnessed a rehearsal of the Ball Dance performed in the town council house. Most of the dance was held outside around a fire. Near the fire, to one side, was a hanger composed of two upright poles with a cross pole. On the hanger, the ball sticks were attached until they were needed for the dance and game. Usually, the Ball Dance and game took place several times from summer until the beginning of cold weather.

A medicine man or priest, as he was called, was chosen to lead the dance for the male dancers. He used a gourd rattle and did the chanting, as the male dancers entered the dance ground shouting out war whoops. These men formed a circle around the fire, dancing counter-clockwise. Using a shuffle step, the men would motion with their ballsticks in each hand, as if they were playing a game. As they danced, a man called the "woodpecker", who is the "whooper", gives out a war whoop - the male dancers respond by saying "Wah".

The priest or medicine man walks around the circle of dancers. He shakes his gourd rattle and chants, "Ha hi u", over and over. Each time he says this, the male dancers respond by saying, "Hah Hah Hah".

Occasionally the dancers will sound a war whoop. After circling four times, they go into the second phase of the dance.

In the second part, two single file rows, side by side, are formed by the male dancers. They go a short distance in the direction of the enemy ball team camp. This part of the dance symbolizes warriors going out on a war party. As they go, their ball sticks are waved or shook as a war club is done. The man called the "woodpecker" or "whooper" runs between the two single file rows of dancers, just ahead of them. He then stops and says seven times, "Ga", giving out a war whoop by putting his hand to his mouth and yelling, "Hu-u, Hu-u, Hu-u, H-u-u". The dancers respond by shouting "Wah", and giving out war whoops.

Then the "whooper" runs back through the two lines of dancers again, jumping and yelling, "De du ni ai la", meaning the other team is weak and won't be successful. He brags about how the other team is beaten before the game even starts. They then go back to the dance ground and dance again as in the first part of the dance. They sing, "we yu 'ha ha". Another song sung by the chanter during the Ball Dance, is hai lo hi sa", meaning "to look". It ends with "Hi Ya". The ballsticks are then returned to the hanger.

The Ball Dance is usually done at least seven times during the night before the game. At the last dance, pine tree limbs are thrown into the dance fire producing a lot of smoke. The smoke is thick as they dance around the fire. As the smoke passes over the dancers' bodies, it was thought to make them strong for the game. They go to a stream of water and dip themselves seven times to purify their bodies.

A man called the "Driver" is the one who gives the ball sticks to the dancers, and collects them when the dance is finished. The ball sticks are returned back to the hanger by him. At the end of each dance, the priest or medicine man says, "Ho kwa", meaning "stop". That's when the men pause and go for the water purification rituals.

Each time the men leave the dance ground, the women dancers come to dance. There are, traditionally, seven women, one from each clan. One of the women wears turtle-shell leg rattles. A priest or medicine man stands on the left side of the women. He uses a gourd rattle and chats during their dance. Sometimes a drum is used for the music. Their area for dancing is between the ball stick hanger and the dance fire.

To do their dance, the women form a straight line standing side by side with the chanter in front of the ball stick hanger. As they stand, the chanter sings, "Ya ho wi, yo ka ne". They respond by singing the same. They then take a few steps forward, turning around and dancing back to where they started. On the ground near the stick ball hanger is a flat rock. Underneath the rock are black beads placed by the medicine man to work a spell against the other team. Once in a while, when the women dance forward in their line, they take turns putting their feet on the rock. This action makes the other team weak and slow.

The dance steps of the women were described by William Bartram. Following is my interpretation of his description. While one dancer is up on tip-toes, the next is on her heels, alternating in this way to the end of the line. The steps were done in rhythm with the musician. The women dance in line, going forward, turning and dancing back, repeating several times.

Then the dance changes, as the women begin dancing in a counter-clockwise moving circle, side by side.

As the male dancers return, the women leave the dance ground. They are then led to the water by their priest, who sings the flycatcher song. At the river, the women wash their face and hands.

When the men finish their dance, the women can then go back and resume their dance. This interchange of men and women dancing is repeated several times before the actual game. During the women's final dance, they switch to a quick dance step.

To get a better idea of a Ball Dance, one may study a painting by George Catlin of a Choctaw Ball Dance. In his painting, the male dance group and the women's' group are next to each other, with the men and women from the other team on the other side, dancing at the same time. The dancing of men and women simultaneously, seems to be unique among the Cherokee.

The Ball Dance can be a very colorful dance, given the costumes previously described.

The Ball Dance Song

"Wah"
(either the "whooper" or male dancers can shout the sound of "wah" at the beginning and end of the song)

Chanter: "Ha hi u, Ha hi u
Dancers: Hah, hah, hah
Chanter: Ha hi u, Ha hi u
Dancers: Hah, hah, hah"

"Wah"

The song phases above can be said over and over during the dance by those who know no other songs for the dance. A dance is more effective when a song is sung.

THE UKAH DANCE COSTUME
THE YELLOW OUTFIT OF THE UKAH DANCE

The yellow hat of swan or heron feathers was made the same way as the white headdress of the Uku, previously described. Other methods can be found in my other book, *How to Make Cherokee Clothing.*

A white stripe is painted from center of forehead, nose, chin and neck

mantle

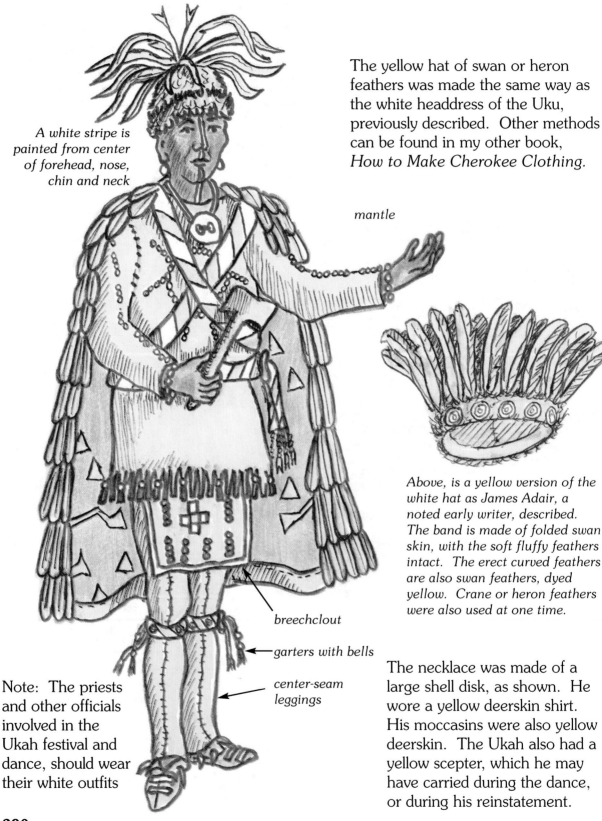

breechclout

garters with bells

center-seam leggings

Above, is a yellow version of the white hat as James Adair, a noted early writer, described. The band is made of folded swan skin, with the soft fluffy feathers intact. The erect curved feathers are also swan feathers, dyed yellow. Crane or heron feathers were also used at one time.

Note: The priests and other officials involved in the Ukah festival and dance, should wear their white outfits

The necklace was made of a large shell disk, as shown. He wore a yellow deerskin shirt. His moccasins were also yellow deerskin. The Ukah also had a yellow scepter, which he may have carried during the dance, or during his reinstatement.

290

The Ukah wore a yellow deerskin shirt during the festival and dance. At other times he wore a sleeveless waist-coat made of white deerskin. This type of shirt can be adapted for the Ukah Dance, but it must be dyed yellow. This shirt is especially suitable in warm weather.

Since the festival and Ukah Dance took place in September during the change of seasons from summer to fall, as Gilbert states in *The Eastern Cherokees*, the weather may be cool, and a long sleeve shirt necessary

sleeveless shirt

The long sleeved shirt below is made of yellow cloth. It is similar to the shirts described in *How To Make Cherokee Clothing* by the author

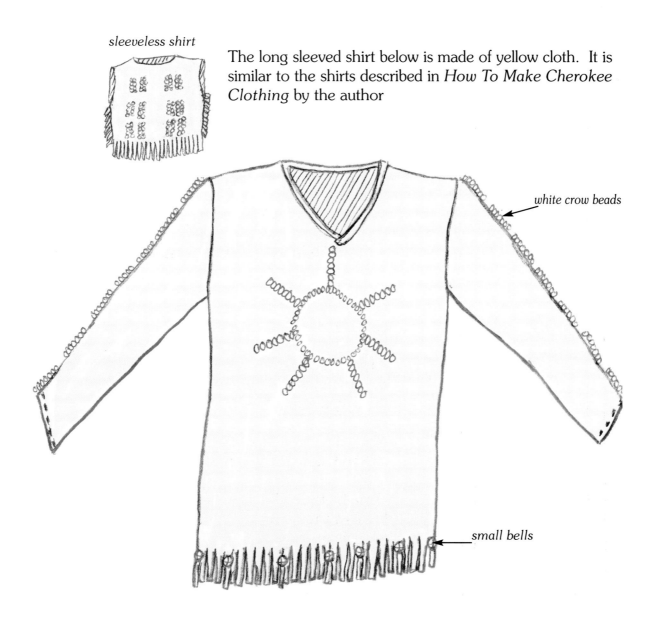

white crow beads

small bells

The sun symbol on the shirt has seven rays, representing the seven clans. The design is beaded in white crow and pony beads. I surmise that the Ukah shirt was an elaborate and highly decorated shirt.

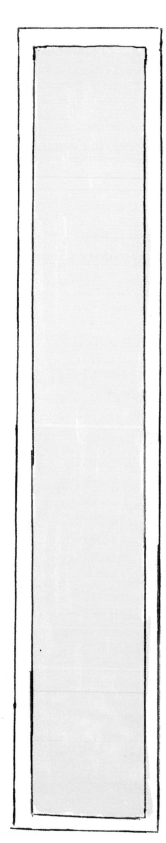

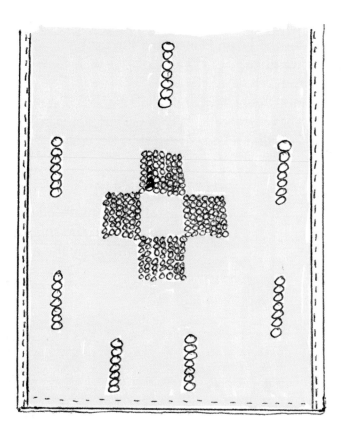

Another item of the Ukah Dance costume was the yellow breechclout. The breechclout shown above can be made of yellow dyed deerskin or yellow cloth.

If using yellow cloth, cut a strip 5' 8" by 13" and hem the bottom of the front and back flap. This will reduce the length to 5' 6".

Next, cut a strip of thin white blanket cloth to 5' 8" by 17" and place the yellow strip on top of it, as shown.

Turn the left and right edges over the yellow cloth and hem, as shown above. Also sew the bottom of each flap again.

The beadwork will give the cloth it's beauty. The symbol of the cross design represents the sacred fire. It can be made using pony beads. The seven stripes represent the clans, and can be made using white crow beads

Above, is a strip of yellow cloth on top of a white blanket cloth

The yellow breechclout will need a belt. A simple belt can be made as shown below.

Cut a strip of yellow cloth 4'8" long by 6" wide. Fold it in half and sew along the bottom

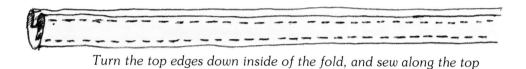

Turn the top edges down inside of the fold, and sew along the top

If you want the belt more narrow, fold it in half again and resew. Each end of the belt should be tapered. Simply fold the ends down to a point and sew in place, as shown.

The belt above is worn with the breechclout to hold it in place. The shirt is worn out over the belt. A finger woven sash is worn on the outside of the shirt at the waist. If a mantle is worn with the yellow costume, the straps of the mantle can be criss-crossed and wrapped at the waist, tying on the side, as in the prior sketch of the Ukah Costume. This serves the same purpose as a belt, worn on the outside of the shirt. Remember, we're talking about two belts, one for the breechclout and a decorated belt for the outside of the shirt.

Pictured below are two yellow dyed deerskin leggings, of the old center-seam style. The Ukah also wore these for his dance.

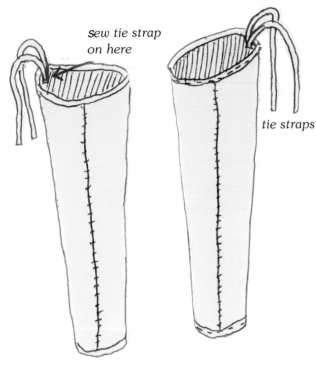

sew tie strap on here

tie straps

Yellow center-seam leggings

Yellow cotton cloth can be used in making the leggings.

Cut two pieces of yellow material to the dimensions shown, or to the measurements that will fit your own size. The legs from a pair of your own pants can serve as a pattern to customize the measurements.

Once the two pieces of material have been cut, hem the top an bottom of each piece.

Next, fold each piece in the middle and seam each legging up the middle from the top to the bottom, bringing point A to point B, as shown.

22"

33"

A

B

16"

folded strap

Turn the leggings inside out and make 2 hemmed cloth straps, about 28" long - one for each legging. A strap is made from a 2-3" wide cloth folded in layers, in the same way that the breechclout belt is made. These straps, when finished, should be narrowed down to about $1/2$" wide. Fold each strap in the middle, sewing a strap to the left legging and to the right legging. Refer to the upper sketch.

Leggings can also be beaded or decorated in a beautiful manner.

The Ukah Dance costume also included a pair of yellow-dyed deerskin moccasins. These could have been made using the *early Cherokee center-seam style.*

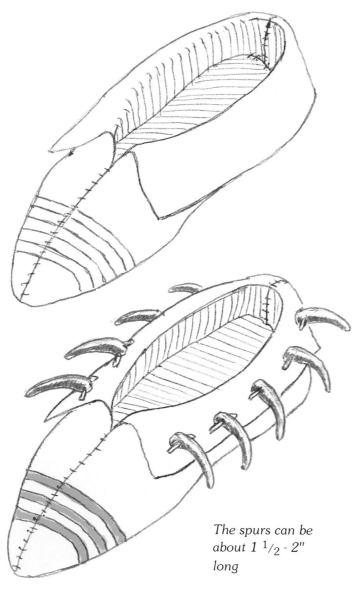

The spurs can be about 1 1/2 - 2" long

White deerskin can be dyed yellow to make the Ukah moccasins. I like to think that they were highly decorated with paint, beads, etc. Plain moccasins may be used however. The choice is yours.

The moccasins can be left plain, or decorated with stripes and turkey gobbler spurs.

According to the *John Howard Payne Papers*, Vol. 4, pg. 22, and the *History of the American Indians*, by James Adair, pgs. 87-89, the yellow outfit of the Ukah was much like his white outfit that he wore on other occasions.

The white moccasins, Adair described, may have been Creek in origin, but may have held true with the Cherokee as well. the moccasins had red stripes painted over the toe section for a span of 3".

Vermillion was not used on sacred clothes, because it is the war color. Rather, bloodroot was used for the red dye on sacred clothing. Also, white may be used instead of red.

Adair also described the white moccasins as having turkey spurs fastened to the upper portion. These blunted spurs can be carved of wood with a bored hole to lace them on the shoe. Small jingle bells might be substituted for spurs.

More instructions on making center-seam moccasins are found in *How to Make Cherokee Clothing* by the author.

NOTE: Ready-made center-seam moccasins are available from James Townsend and Son, Inc. See source page in the back of this book.

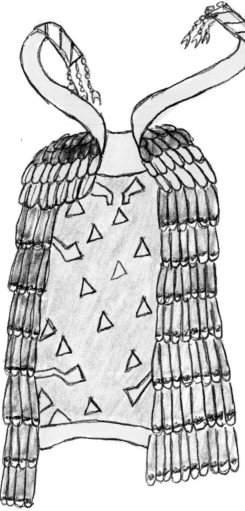

The Ukah costume can have a mantle as an optional item. The mantle makes for a very stylish costume on the day of the dance.

One version of this mantle is shown here. It has the brown turkey feathers and yellow dyed feathers mixed. The long straps can be criss-crossed in the form of a figure eight around the chest and waist. It is tied on the side of the waist.

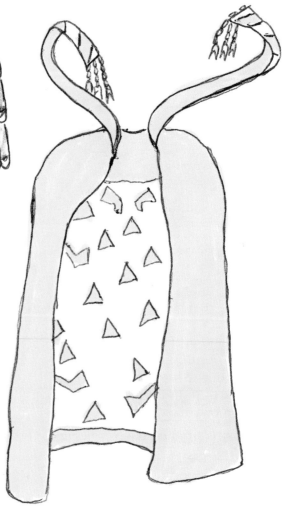

A reference for making the mantle is found on pgs. 41-47 in *How to Make Cherokee Clothing*. This mantle is made of yellow dyed deerskin or cloth. It can be left plain or embellished with designs.

Since the Uku at the National capitol wore a white outfit on other occasions, and had a white feathered mantle, it stands to reason that another one could be dyed yellow for the Ukah dance.

The mantle should be suited to the particular costume for this dance.

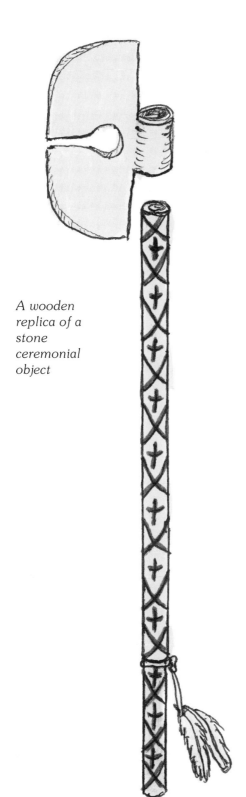

A wooden replica of a stone ceremonial object

wooden staff

At times, the Ukah carried his yellow painted scepter or staff as a symbol of his office. He held it in his right hand at certain occasions, while wearing his yellow outfit.

It is reasonable to believe that he carried his scepter while doing the dance, or sitting on his throne at the square grounds.

There are several symbols of the office of leaders or priests in the Museum of the Cherokee Indian, in Cherokee, North Carolina. These stone objects can give one an idea of how a Ukah staff may have looked.

Although it isn't certain what it looked like, it is known that he carried the staff during the dance.

The Great War Chief's main messenger sometimes carried a 3' staff, wrapped or wound with a string of red beads, from one end to the other. It was probably made of wood.

Given this, we can make our own Ukah staff of wood, which will be our own version. The staff may have carved or burned designs, similar to one found in *Tribes that Slumber*, by Lewis and Kneberg.

The stone-like object in this illustration is similar to one found in the Museum of the Cherokee Indian. It is made to fit over the end of a wooden staff. It can be carved from wood and painted yellow.

HOW TO DO THE UKU DANCE

The Uku Dance was performed every seven years by the Great Peace Chief of the National Cherokee Capitol When this dance and festival occurred, it replaced the Great New Moon Ceremony for that year. The next year, the Great New Moon Ceremony resumed for the next six years. The Uku festival and dance was held during the last part of summer, or at the latest start of fall.

The festival and dance was over a period of four days, and was known as the "Ukan or Ookay", meaning "Thanks Giver"

The Uku Dance and rites was a thanksgiving ceremony, and such a sacred event, that the Cherokee leader would rededicate and sanctify himself before the Great Man Above and the people. His standing as Uku was renewed so that he could lead his people with wisdom and knowledge from the Great Man Above.

Before the dance started, there were preliminary events that took place. Early, messengers were sent out by the Ukah and his seven counselors to all the villages. The village priests were informed of the coming dance and the date, so that they could pass the word on to the people. The news then spread rapidly.

During the seven days before the festival and Ukah Dance, a lot of preparations were done. A hunter from each of the clans was sent out to hunt deer. They brought the slain deer, at the latest, the day before the festival was to start. Seven men, one from each clan, were chosen to supervise and to see that duties were carried out for the feast day of the festival. The deer was given to a chosen group of women, to prepare and cook for the festival. A lot of food had to be prepared for the many crowds of people from all the villages. By the last day of the preparation, the national capitol was a very active place.

Two thrones were built and made ready for the Ukah, during the seven day pre-festival. One tall white throne with a canopy and footstool was placed halfway between the Ukah's house and the square ground. The second throne was put in the center of the square grounds. This area, called the square grounds, or dance grounds, was located to the east side of the council house front. The footstools mentioned were made of cane or other types of wood. It was also white, and it's purpose was to keep the Ukah's feet off of the ground as he sat on his throne. The canopies attached to the throne seats were made of white deerskin, along with the the coverings for the throne.

The square grounds had to be swept clean, and a circle was drawn on the ground around the throne in the center on the grounds. This circle was made for the Ukah to dance within on the day of his dance. The circle was also guarded by priests to keep people from entering the sacred ground. It was considered a desecration for a common person to touch the sacred throne or ground.

298

The yellow garments and headdress of the Uku were prepared during the pre-festival. During this period, the Uku's national flag was probably on the white flag pole in front of the council house. The flag was made of white deerskin or white cloth, and had red star-like designs.

The people probably wore their finest clothes and white deerskin for the event.

The festival began on the morning after the seven day preparation, and lasted for four days. On this first morning, the Uku's priests and seven counselors went toward the Ukah's house in a procession, chanting sacred songs as they walked. One such song was called the "Yowa Song". It had seven verses, each sung to a different tune and repeated four times.

The Yowa Song

Verse 1. Hi Yo wa ya ka ni
Verse 2. Hi te hu yu ya ka ni
Verse 3. Hi wa ta ki ya ka ni
Verse 4. Hi hi wa sa si ya ka ni
Verse 5. Hi a ni tsu si ya ka ni
Verse 6. Hi yo wa hi ye yo ya ka ni
Verse 7. Hi ani he hgo ya ka ni

A beloved woman was chosen to warm the bath water in a large pot for the ritual cleansing of the Ukah. At the Ukah's house, a chosen priest from the procession undressed the Ukah. Two other priests from the same group of priests bathed the Ukah. After the ritual bath, a priest dressed the Ukah in his yellow costume and headdress.

After the outfit was on, the Ukah climbed on the back of another priest who carried the Ukah out of the house. Part of the priests went ahead in the procession. Behind them was the Uku riding piggy-back style on the priest's back. A priest titled "U lo tee" was on the right side of the Uku in the procession. This priest used an eagle tail fan to fan the Uku. To the left of the Uku was a priest who led the chanting and music, called "Kv nv wi sti ski". He may have used a drum in this situation, as the other priests followed behind.

As they proceeded toward the first throne, all the priests in the procession chanted with their lead singer. The priest carrying the Ukah did not sing, however. This was a procession of joy and happiness. The observers of the parade followed along too. When the procession reached the first throne, the priest who carried the Ukah helped him onto his throne, for the Uku's feet were not allowed to touch the ground.

After the Ukah and the priest who had carried him rested a while, the Ukah climbed back on the same priest's back again. The procession proceeded as before, with the next stop being the second throne. This was the throne in the center of the grounds with the large circle drawn on the ground.

On this throne, the Ukah sat all night. His right hand man, his speaker and his counselors watched over him, along with the carrier priest, from outside the circle. During this night, the people danced in the council house, and out in the streets if the crowds were large. Thus concluded the first day.

The second day was very important. In the morning, the carrier priest, who had been consecrated and purified, went to the throne and allowed the Ukah to get on his back again. Then the priest carried the Ukah to the inside boundary of the large circle drawn on the ground. There, for the first time since the bath, the Ukah's feet touched the ground.

After the Ukah was on his feet, he began to dance slowly to the beat of the drum and chanting. He slowly went around the boundary of the circle, moving counter clockwise, moving his head right and left, viewing the people sitting. He would bow his head slightly to each person as he viewed them, and they bowed to him in turn. His fan person and the chanter stood nearby, just outside the circle.

As the Ukah danced with his yellow scepter, his assistants went around the outside of the circle in single file. They did the same dance steps as the Ukah. The principal assistant went first, followed by the speaker, seven counselors and the other priests.

After the Ukah and the others went one complete round, the Ukah was carried back to his throne in the square grounds as the guards resumed their positions. No woman was allowed to come near the Ukah or the sacred area at this time.

In the afternoon, as people were in their perspective clan seats, the Ukah told the people when it was time to eat. The people then had a great feast, however, the Ukah and his assistants fasted until the sun went down. When the Ukah and his men finally finished their meal, the procession was carried out again in reverse, stopping at the midway throne to rest, and then moving back to his house where he changed clothes and rested for the night.

On the morning of the third day, the same ritual and procession was carried out except for the bath.

On the forth and final day of the festival, the Ukah proceeded again like the day before. After his dance, he was carried back to the throne where the right hand man consecrated and invested the Ukah, thus renewing his office and authority.

After returning home on the forth day, the Ukah could remove his yellow outfits and wear the white clothes of his every day duties, and return to his white seat in the council house.

Below is my rendition of how the tall white canopy throne of the Ukah may have looked. The top was covered with white deer skin. The seat and footstool also had white deer skin spread over them.

A priest or selected person was given the job of making the two thrones during the seven days prior to the festival and dance.

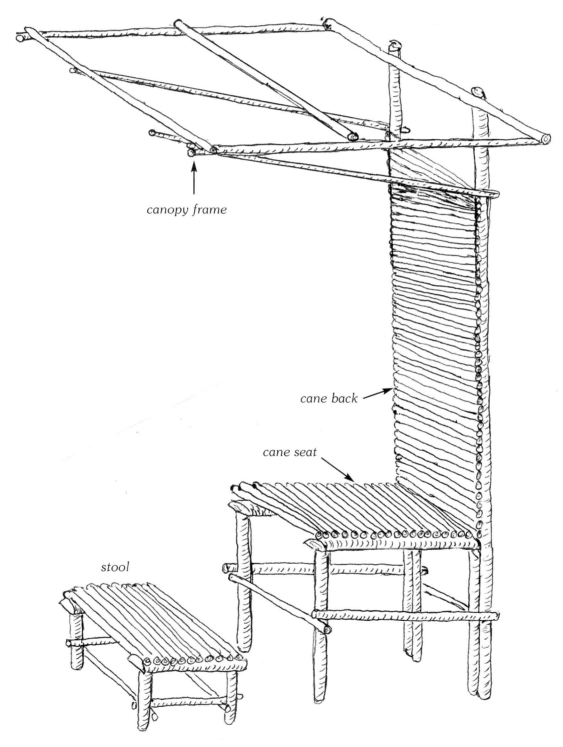

canopy frame

cane back

cane seat

stool

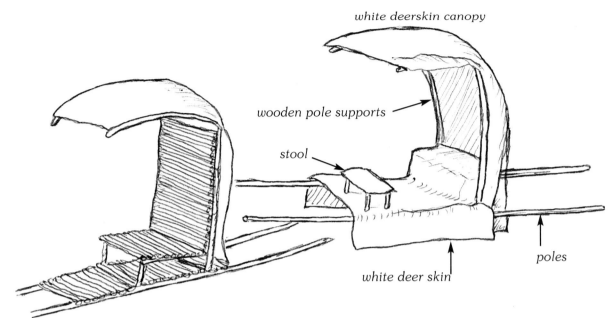

white deerskin canopy

wooden pole supports

stool

white deer skin

poles

Here, the wooden framework can be see. Cane was sometimes used for making seat bottoms, etc.

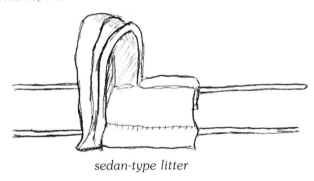

sedan-type litter

The sedan chair type litter shown is covered with white leather. It has a seat, stool and canopy. The wood pole extensions are for the men to hold to when carrying their Great Leader.

Such a platform was used among the Timucuas in Northern Florida. Jacques le Moyne drew a picture of a similar type litter back in 1564. See the book "Americas Fascinating Indian Heritage" by Reader's Digest, pg84-85.

You may also wish to refer to the *John Howard Payne Papers*, Vol. 1, pgs. 84-88

These illustrations should give a better understanding of how a litter or throne seat was made. The Ukah's throne didn't have handles, but was used only as a stationary chair for a particular time of the festival and dance.

SUGGESTIONS FOR FURTHER STUDY

ADAIR, JAMES
    1930 *History of the American Indians.*
Edited by Samuel Cole Williams, Johnson
City, Tennessee.

BARTRAM, WILLIAM
    1791 *Travels Through North and South
Carolina, Georgia, East and West Florida,
the Cherokee Country, Etc.,* Philadelphia.
    New Edition Facsimile Library, Barnes
and Noble, Inc. 1940

BIRD, TRAVELLER
    1971 *Tell Them They Lie,* Los Angeles,
Westernlore Publishers.

CATLIN, GEORGE
    1973 *Letters and Notes on the Manners,
Customs and Conditions of the North
American Indians.* New York, New York:
Dover   Publications, Inc.

EVANS, J.P.
    N.D. "Sketches of Cherokee Character,
Customs and Manners". John Howard
Papers, Vol.   6, No. 202,
Newberry Library, Chicago, Illinois.

FRENCH, LAURENCE, and HORNBUCKLE, JIM
    1981, eds. *The Cherokee Perspective,*
Boone, N.C.,
Appalachian Consortium Press.

FUNDERBURK, EMMA LILLA and FOREMAN,
MARY D., EDS.
    1957 *SunCircles and Human Hands.*
Luverne, Alabama: The Southeastern
  Indians Art and Industry.

GILBERT, WILLIAM HARLEN
    1943 *The Eastern Cherokees*: reprinted by
AMS Press, New York, 1978.

HORAN, JAMES
    1975 *North American Indian Portraits.*
New York, New York:
Crown Publishing, Inc.

HUDSON, CHARLES
    1976 *The Southeastern Indians,* Knoxville,
University of Tennessee Press

LEFTWICH, RODNEY
    1970 *Arts and Crafts of the Cherokee.*
Cherokee, N. C., Cherokee Publications

LEWIS, T.M.N. and KNEBERG, MADELINE
    1958 *Tribes That Slumber.* Knoxville,
Tennessee: University of Tennessee Press.

MAILS, THOMAS E.
    1995 *The Cherokee People.* Council Oak
Books, Tulsa, Oklahoma.

MAUER, EVAN
    1977 *The Native American Heritage.*
Chicago, Illinois: Institute of Chicago.

MOONEY, JAMES
    1900 *History, Myths and Sacred Formulas
of the Cherokees.* Cherokee, North Carolina:
reprinted by Cherokee Publications, 1992

PAYNE, JOHN HOWARD
    N.D. "Papers, Fourteen Volumes of
Manuscripts." Newberry Library, Chicago,
Ayer Ms 689. (Vols. 1, 3, 4 and 6).

PHILIPPE, LOUIS
    1977 *Diary of My Travels In America,* Louis
Philippe, King of France 1830-1848.
New York, New York: Delacorte Press.

RIGHTS, DOUGLAS L.
    1988 *The American Indian in North
Carolina.* Winston Salem, North Carolina:
John F. Blair, Publisher.

SPECK, FRANK G. and BROOM, LEONARD
    1983 *Cherokee Dance and Drama.*
Norman, Oklahoma:
University of Oklahoma Press.

STEELE, WILLIAM O.
    1917 *The Cherokee Crown of Tannassy.*
Reproduced in 1977, Charlotte, North
Carolina: Heritage Printers.

TAYLOR, COLIN F. and STURTEVANT, WILLIAM C.
    1991 *The Native Americans,* The Indigenous
People of North America. Smithmark
Publishers, Inc. New York, New York.

TIMBERLAKE, LIEUTENANT HENRY
    1927 *Memoirs, 1756-1765,* edited by Samuel
Cole Williams, L.L.D., Johnson City,
Tennessee, Watauga Press.

WOODWARD, GRACE STEELE
    1963 *The Cherokees,* Norman Oklahoma:
University of Oklahoma Press.

ABOUT THE AUTHOR - DONALD SIZEMORE

Donald Sizemore was born March 17, 1950, in the small mountain community of Poff Hill, near Pineville, Kentucky. His parents, Camie and Nora Baker Sizemore, had moved their belongings by wagon to this isolated area in the 1930's. Before 1949, there was no electricity or water in their home, and Donald's older sisters washed their clothing by the banks of the Cumberland River. By the time Donald and his twin sister Carol were born, things were a little easier on the homeplace. They now had electricity, a telephone, and a jeep for transportation. The once huge fields of crops his siblings had helped raise had shrunken to a small garden.

Donald started school at the old Moss Chapel Grade School at the age of seven. At that time, children walked off the mountain, down the railroad, and across the Wasiota swinging bridge to catch the bus for school.

As the twelfth child in the family and with most of his brothers and sisters gone from home, Donald had plenty of time to listen to the stories his father (and other relatives) told about their Cherokee ancestry. Reading, drawing, and making American Indian crafts became a part of his life as he tried to recapture some of his Indian heritage. He says, "I made my first war bonnet from cardboard and chicken feathers, which I thought was really something!" Using scraps and various items he had found, he continued to construct objects relating to the Indian culture, and, as he learned more and more, his work took on a more authentic look.

Donald graduated from the Bell County High School in 1968 and was called to the Army in 1970. In the service, he served as a medic in Germany. While abroad, he was able to visit eleven countries in Europe and the Middle East. Upon his return to Pineville, he worked at Pineville Community Hospital as a Physical Therapist Assistant and later was employed in a local nursing home. It was there he met Mabel Ramey, the woman who would become his wife and who would encourage him to continue with his research of Native American culture.

The Sizemores moved in 1983 to a one-room log cabin located near the old family homestead. There they lived the "old-fashioned way" with kerosene lamps, cooking over a fireplace, growing their own foodstuffs, and having "a very happy way of life." Visitors who admired the Indian crafts hanging on the walls of the cabin were taken to see a crude council house Donald had built several years earlier. There he had the opportunity to explain the uses and history behind the items they found there. "Many were the times I went to the council house to think and to talk to the Great Man Above," Sizemore says, "and believe me, I felt His presence just the same as I had often felt it in the white man's church."

After losing his father, moving into his aging mother's home to care for her, and undergoing the loss of his left hand in a tragic accident, Donald fought off bouts of depression and came to realize he could share his knowledge of the crafts of the Cherokee. Because of the loyal support of his wife, and the overwhelming interest in his work by Ed Sharpe (of Cherokee Publications), Donald was inspired to collect his notes and drawings, his creations and re-creations, for his books. He had found the purpose of his life.

SOURCES FOR PROJECT MATERIALS & SUPPLIES

Tandy Leather Company
1400 Everman Parkway
Fort Worth TX 76140
(Tandy has stores in major cities
- check yellow pages or write for
location in your area.)

Winona Trading Post
PO Box 324
SANTA Fe, NM 87501

Northeast Bead Trading Co.
12 Depot Street
Kennebunk, ME 04043

James Townsend & Son, Inc
133 N. First Street
P. O. Box 415
Pierceton IN 46562
(800) 338-1665

Walmart & Kmart Stores
(in most areas - check your
yellow pages)

Grey Owl Indian Craft
150-02 Beaver Road
Jamaica, Queens, NY 11433

Navajo Gallery
577 Main Street
Hamilton, OH 45013

Walco Products, Inc.
1200 Zerega Avenue
Bronx, NY 10462

Progress Feather Company
657 W. Lake Street
Chicago, IL 60606

Albert Constantine & Son, Inc.
(woodcarving tools)
2050 Eastchester Road
Bronx, NY 10461

Medicine Man Craft Shop
(beads, feathers, leather, masks, etc.)
PO Box 124
Cherokee, NC 28719
(828) 497-2202

NOC Bay Trading Co.
PO Box 295
Escanaba, MI 49829

Wandering Bull
(grease paint, crooked knife, etc.)
P.O. Box 175
Attleboro MA 02703
(800) 430-2885

NOTE: These are sources used by the author. Check for craft shops in your area carrying appropriate materials and supplies for your clothing projects